Staging Mobilities

In recent years, the social sciences have taken a 'mobilities turn'. There has been a developing realisation that mobilities do not 'just happen'. Mobilities are carefully and meticulously designed, planned and staged (from above). However, they are equally importantly acted out, performed and lived as people are 'staging themselves' (from below). Staging mobilities is a dynamic process between 'being staged' (for example, being stopped at traffic lights) and the 'mobile staging' of interacting individuals (negotiating a passage on the pavement).

Staging Mobilities is about the fact that mobility is more than movement between points A and B. It explores how the movement of people, goods, information, and signs influences human understandings of self, other and the built environment. Moving towards a new understanding of the relationship between movement, interaction and environments, the book asks: *what are the physical, social, technical, and cultural conditions to the staging of contemporary urban mobilities?*

Jensen argues that we need to understand the contemporary city as an assemblage of circulating people, goods, information and signs in relational networks creating the 'meaning of movement'. The book will be of interest to students and scholars of sociology, urban studies, mobility studies, architecture and cultural studies.

Ole B. Jensen is Professor of Urban Theory at Aalborg University, Denmark. His main research interests are mobilities and urban studies. He is the co-author of *Making European Space* (with Tim Richardson, Routledge) and has published extensively on mobility research in the journals *Mobilities, Culture and Space*, and *Urban Studies*.

International library of sociology
Founded by
Karl Mannheim
Editor: John Urry
Lancaster University

Recent publications in this series include:

Risk and Technological Culture
Towards a sociology of virulence
Joost Van Loon

Reconnecting Culture, Technology and Nature
Mike Michael

Advertising Myths
The strange half lives of images and commodities
Anne M. Cronin

Adorno on Popular Culture
Robert R. Witkin

Consuming the Caribbean
From arkwarks to zombies
Mimi Sheller

Between Sex and Power
Family in the world, 1900–2000
Goran Therborn

States of Knowledge
The co-production of social science and social order
Sheila Jasanoff

After Method
Mess in social science research
John Law

Brands
Logos of the global economy
Celia Lury

The Culture of Exception
Sociology facing the camp
*Bülent Diken and
Carsten Bagge Laustsen*

Visual Worlds
*John Hall, Blake Stimson and
Lisa Tamiris Becker*

Time, Innovation and Mobilities
Travel in technological cultures
Peter Frank Peters

Complexity and Social Movements
Multitudes acting at the edge of chaos
Ian Welsh and Graeme Chesters

Qualitative Complexity
Ecology, cognitive processes and the re-emergence of structures in post-humanist social theory
Chris Jenks and John Smith

Theories of the Information Society, 3rd Edition
Frank Webster

Crime and Punishment in Contemporary Culture
Claire Grant

Mediating Nature
Nils Lindahl Elliot

Haunting the Knowledge Economy
Jane Kenway, Elizabeth Bullen, Johannah Fahey and Simon Robb

Global Nomads
Techno and new age as transnational countercultures in Ibiza and Goa
Anthony D'Andrea

The Cinematic Tourist
Explorations in globalization, culture and resistance
Rodanthi Tzanelli

Non-Representational Theory
Space, politics, affect
Nigel Thrift

Urban Fears and Global Terrors
Citizenship, multicultures and belongings after 7/7
Victor J. Seidler

Sociology through the Projector
Bülent Diken and Carsten Bagge Laustsen

Multicultural Horizons
Diversity and the limits of the civil nation
Anne-Marie Fortier

Sound Moves
iPod culture and urban experience
Michael Bull

Jean Baudrillard
Fatal theories
David B. Clarke, Marcus A. Doel, William Merrin and Richard G. Smith

Aeromobilities
Theory and method
Saulo Cwerner, Sven Kesselring and John Urry

Social Transnationalism
Steffen Mau

Towards Relational Sociology
Nick Crossley

Mobile Lives
Anthony Elliott and John Urry

Stillness in a Mobile World
David Bissell and Gillian Fuller

Unintended Outcomes of Social Movements
The 1989 Chinese student movement
Fang Deng

Revolt, Revolution, Critique
The paradox of society
Bulent Diken

Travel Connections
Tourism, technology and togetherness in a mobile world
Jennie Germann-Molz

Mobility, Space and Culture
Peter Merriman

Transforming Images
Screens, affect, futures
Rebecca Coleman

Staging Mobilities
Ole B. Jensen

Forthcoming in the series:

China Constructing Capitalism
Economic life and urban change
Lash Scott, Keith Michael, Arnoldi Jakob and Rooker Tyler

Staging Mobilities

Ole B. Jensen

Routledge
Taylor & Francis Group
LONDON AND NEW YORK

First published 2013
by Routledge
2 Park Square, Milton Park, Abingdon, Oxon OX14 4RN

Simultaneously published in the USA and Canada
by Routledge
711 Third Avenue, New York, NY 10017

Routledge is an imprint of the Taylor & Francis Group, an informa business

© 2013 Ole B. Jensen

The right of Ole B. Jensen to be identified as author of this work has been asserted by him in accordance with sections 77 and 78 of the Copyright, Designs and Patents Act 1988.

All rights reserved. No part of this book may be reprinted or reproduced or utilised in any form or by any electronic, mechanical, or other means, now known or hereafter invented, including photocopying and recording, or in any information storage or retrieval system, without permission in writing from the publishers.

Trademark notice: Product or corporate names may be trademarks or registered trademarks, and are used only for identification and explanation without intent to infringe.

British Library Cataloguing in Publication Data
A catalogue record for this book is available from the British Library

Library of Congress Cataloging in Publication Data
Jensen, Ole B.
Staging mobilities/Ole B. Jensen.
   p. cm. – (International library of sociology)
Includes bibliographical references and index.
1. Sociology, Urban. 2. Social mobility. 3. Communication. 4. Transportation. I. Title.
HT111.J463 2013
305.5′13–dc23   2012036630

ISBN: 978-0-415-69373-8 (hbk)
ISBN: 978-0-203-07006-2 (ebk)

Typeset in Times New Roman
by Wearset Ltd, Boldon, Tyne and Wear

Printed and bound in Great Britain by
TJ International Ltd, Padstow, Cornwall

Contents

List of figures ix
Preface and acknowledgements x

PART I
Staging mobilities: review and positioning 1

1 *Staging Mobilities*: introduction 3
2 The mobile city: reviewing and positioning 19

PART II
Framing mobilities 43

3 Physical settings, material spaces and design 45
4 Facework, flow and the city 65
5 Mobile embodied performances 92

PART III
Practices of mobilities 121

6 Networked technologies and the will to connection 123
7 Negotiation in motion: unpacking a geography of mobility 138
8 Metro mobilities: the production of lived mobility in urban metro systems 154

PART IV
Towards a sociology of staging mobilities 173

9 Materialities of mobilities: learning from the design fields 175

10 *Staging Mobilities*: conclusion 194

Bibliography 206
Index 222

Figures

1.1	The staging mobilities model	6
1.2	Mobile situations	11
2.1	City of armatures	36
2.2	City of enclaves	36
3.1	Things might be different than their appearance	49
3.2	Sign whose interpretation relies on its physical placement	58
4.1	A mobile with	80
4.2	The networked self	85
5.1	Cycling as an embodied mobility practice	107
5.2	Mobile body semiotics	118
6.1	Hertz car rental 'never lost' GPS	124
7.1	Setting the scene – Nytorv, Aalborg	139
7.2	Techniques for 'negotiation in motion'	148
8.1	Generic circulation machine	158
8.2	Bangkok Sky Train	163
9.1	Designing materialities of mobilities	178
9.2	Post-car system	190
10.1	The staging of mobilities in codified systems	196
10.2	Mobilities design	204

Preface and acknowledgements

This work has been in progress for a long time – in fact, possibly long before I even realised I was embarking on this journey! As always when one looks back and realises that 'ten years or more have got behind you' (to borrow a phrase from Waters and Gilmour) one also realises the many, many social interactions, events, talks, discussions and friendships that have made such work possible. Due respect must be paid to all those who inspired, helped along and shaped this book. Let me start with institutions: in particular the Department of Architecture, Design and Media Technology that has hosted me as Professor of Urban Theory since 2004 and has proven to be a most inspiring and creative environment. Thanks to the Head of Department, Michael Mullins, who knew when to lend extra support to me during the peak phases of my work. Thanks are also due to the Urban Design Group, where good colleagues have provided the perfect environment for exploring not just theories of mobilities but, equally importantly, designs for mobilities. Also to the many students I have had the privilege to supervise in the Urban Design master's programme (and in particular our many study trips and redesigns of the Copenhagen Metro), which has proven invaluable for my understanding of urban mobilities. Thanks also to the members of the research cluster for Mobility and Tracking Technology (MoTT). The Faculty of Engineering and Science at Aalborg University has been a perfect venue for exploring not just social theory, but equally importantly the technical and design-oriented dimensions to mobilities. In particular the PhD course Critical Mobility Studies (the course has had various titles over the years), held at times with colleagues at Roskilde University and at other times in Aalborg, has proven to be of great importance. In this regard I wish to thank my co-organisers and fellow lecturers on that particular course in all its various forms over the years: John Urry, Lise Drewes Nielsen, Anne Jensen, Tim Richardson, Sven Kesselring, Mimi Sheller and Claus Lassen (and, of course, all the enthusiastic course participants) for inspiring me to articulate these thoughts.

Moreover, Aalborg University with its cross-disciplinary underpinnings inspired the establishment of the Centre for Mobilities and Urban Studies (C-MUS), of which I am a co-founder and a board member. The creation of this centre (with generous support from departments and faculties across social science, humanities and engineering) provided the home ground for these thoughts and a place where ideas could always be explored. I thank all the participants in C-MUS events over the years as well as my colleagues on the board, in particular Antje Gimmler, Paul McIlvenny, Tim Richardson, Petter Næss and Claus Lassen. Here, special gratitude is due to Claus Lassen whom I supervised during his MSc and PhD studies and who has since become an always-reliable source of support, regardless of whether the issue is research strategies or critical-review comments on manuscripts and papers. In relation to C-MUS I wish also to thank the Obel Family Foundation for supporting the centre financially. During my years of work in the Department of Architecture, Design and Media Technology I have supervised a number of PhD students whose work has also had a positive influence on this book. I want to thank Bo Stjerne Thomsen, Esben Skouboe Poulsen, Anne-Marie Sandvig Knudsen, Ditte Bendix Lanng, Simon Wind, Christian Fisker and Salmiah Hamid (thanks Sal for being patient with all my changes to the *Staging Mobilities* diagram!) for their inspirational collaboration. Also, my research assistants over the last couple of years, Anne Sofie Hartelius, Simon Wind and Jacob Bjerre Mikkelsen, did most valuable work on many of the empirical cases presented in this book. Department Librarian Jacob Hansen and Research Assistant Cecilie Breinholm Christensen are to be thanked for providing the most obscure references in the shortest span of time.

Over the years strong international links have shaped the global context for this book. In the United Kingdom the connections with Sheffield University have been valuable, as has the collaboration with Malcolm Tait in particular. At Lancaster University, John Urry must be thanked for his hospitality and inspiration in the United Kingdom, and just as importantly for great company when we meet abroad in all sorts of places (as well as for encouraging me to submit this book for the ILS series at Routledge). Also special thanks to Mimi Sheller of Drexel University whose collaborative attitude and welcoming environment at the mCenter were a great stimulus to my work. The joint work in the Cosmobilities Network has also been a great influence and here I want thank Sven Kesselring and Malene Freudendal-Pedersen for their great insight and good spirits. This also goes for the fine people in the Pan-American Mobilities Network, and here I must mention Phillip Vannini and Jim Conley in particular – I value our transnational dialogues very highly. Furthermore, a number of good colleagues have over the years helped my thoughts along with stimulating conversations. Amongst these are Bent Flyvbjerg, Grahame Shane, Jim Throgmorton and the late Ron Scollon – I thank you all.

Special thanks are owed to my 'critical friends' who took time to read part or all of the manuscript and comment on it: Claus Lassen, Christian Fisker, Simon Wind, Jacob Bjerre Mikkelsen and Malene Freudendal-Pedersen – IOU.

Much of the research in this book is either a direct spin-off from field studies or a reflection of the many visiting scholarships I have enjoyed over the years. In this respect I thank Ole Fryd for provision of documents, insightful guidance, many useful contacts and fun rides across town in Bangkok. Thanks to Simon Landy, Chairman of the RICS Bangkok for reflecting upon the relationship between the BTS and the property market by email. Thanks to Mark Tewdwr-Jones for sharing his knowledge on a theme that proves to be a major passion of his: the London 'Tube', and to Dominique Laousse of the RATP in Paris and Chief Architect Lise Lind of the Metro Company in Copenhagen. Also thanks to the students in the Urban Design studio on the Copenhagen Metro who gave me permission to reproduce their photos from our field trips: Stine K. Jakobsen, Kirk Hovenkotter, Bergitte Hatteland, Louise Nørgaard and Pierrick Aubert.

Over the years several institutions have hosted me as a visiting scholar. Thanks to the mCenter, Drexel University, Philadelphia; the Department of Sociology and Anthropology, Swarthmore College, Philadelphia; the Graduate Program in Urban and Regional Planning, Iowa University; the Department of Town and Regional Planning, University of Sheffield; the Graduate School of Architecture, Planning and Preservation (GSAPP), Columbia University, New York; and the Faculty of Architecture, Chulalongkorn University, Bangkok.

The book is based on more than a decade of research into mobilities covering a wide array of empirical and ethnographic studies as well as a number of theoretical papers and books. The following works have been revised and reused for this book: O.B. Jensen (2010) 'Erving Goffman and Everyday Life Mobility', in M. Hviid Jacobsen (ed.) *The Contemporary Goffman*, New York: Routledge, pp. 333–351; O.B. Jensen (2009) 'Flows of meaning, cultures of movements: urban mobility as meaningful everyday life practice', *Mobilities*, 4(1): 139–158; O.B. Jensen (2007) 'City of layers: Bangkok's Sky Train and how it works in socially segregating mobility patterns', *Swiss Journal of Sociology*, 33(3): 387–405; O.B. Jensen (2006) 'Facework, flow and the city: Simmel, Goffman and mobility in the contemporary city', *Mobilities*, 2(2): 143–165; O.B. Jensen (2012) 'Metroens Arkitektur og Bevægelser', in J. Andersen, M. Freudendal-Pedersen, L. Koefoed and J. Larsen (eds) *Byen i Bevægelse: Mobilitet – Politik – Performativitet*, Frederiksberg: Roskilde Universitetsforlag, pp. 40–60; O.B. Jensen (forthcoming) 'Mobile semiotics: signs and mobilities', in P. Adey, D. Bissell, K. Hannam, P. Merriman and M. Sheller (eds) *Handbook of Mobilities*, Abingdon: Routledge. The copyright holders have all kindly granted permission for the work to be used in this context. Polity Press has kindly granted permission to reproduce Figure 9.2.

At Routledge I want to thank Gerhard Boomgaarden, Jennifer Dodd and in particular Emily Briggs, who have all been very supportive and helpful indeed.

Thanks to Leo F. for making every day a thrill!

The final word of gratitude goes to my family. Thank you Lone, Christine and Julie: to explore the world in your company or simply to hang out at home are my favourite experiences, and learning from your vivid interpretations of the world is the strongest motivator. Through our joint experiences and love my work on these matters has taken shape, and I am most grateful for your presence in my life.

As always, even though many were called upon, no one else is to blame for shortcomings, errors or omissions but yours truly.

Ole B. Jensen
Aalborg

Part I
Staging mobilities
Review and positioning

1 *Staging Mobilities*
Introduction

> Cities are an everyday invention. They are formed and imagined by many people at a time. A city's physical form is expressed in a vortex of temporal relations, mirrored in the activities of a collective body of individuals interacting with each other. Cities are an open stage for complementary and conflicting encounters, and allow for multiple identities to emerge and evaporate. They are backdrops for dreams and desires, a platform for departures and arrivals. As individuals pass through, new connections arise while others fade away. By wearing various masks and playing different roles, people change the urban landscape through their encounters
>
> Petra Kempf, *You Are the City*, 2009, p. 2

Introduction

Imagine travelling (by car, bus, train or bike) to work and walking from the car park or station to your office. During your trip you must certainly have been involved in multiple interactions with fellow drivers and pedestrians. You are likely to have drawn on routines as well as having to improvise to make your way. Regardless of whether you can recall what was on your mind, the trip is sure to be a reflection of who you are and how you relate to the built environment and your consociates. The morning trip to work is thus an embodied practice, often influenced by other human subjects and always within a material and physical setting. Your situational mobility from the morning trip, moreover, has elements of your own choice, such as selected route, mode of transport, relaxed or aggressive driving, choice of seat etc. These elements are all expressions of a 'staging' with a relatively high degree of self-determination. But along the way your practices were modified by traffic lights, timetables, road design, traffic regulations, information systems etc., reminding you that there is a 'staging' going on from above as well. If you think about the actual situations of getting to work in this way, you are very close to the key theme of this book: situational mobilities.

Put differently, this book is about the fact that mobility is more than movement between points A and B. It concerns how the movement of people, goods, information and signs influences human understandings of self, other and the built environment. The book takes its point of departure from the so-called 'mobilities turn' (see Cresswell 2010b; Sheller 2011; and Vannini 2010 for review articles, and Adey 2010 and Urry 2007 for review books on this topic) but takes the analysis further towards a new understanding of the relationship between movement and interaction and their environments. Mobilities do not 'just happen' or simply 'take place'. Mobilities are carefully and meticulously designed, planned and 'staged' (from above). However, they are equally importantly acted out, performed and lived as people are 'staging themselves' (from below). *Staging Mobilities* explores the dynamic process between 'being staged' (as, for example, when traffic lights command us to stop or when timetables organise your route and itineraries) and the 'mobile staging' of interacting individuals (as, for example, when we negotiate a passage on the pavement, or when we choose a particular mode of transport in accordance with our self-perception). The rationale for the book is therefore to address the following overall research question: What are the physical, social, technical and cultural conditions for the staging of contemporary urban mobilities?

As a particular contribution to the field of mobilities research, the book offers a number of theoretically derived and empirically enriched concepts that contribute a new lexicon of mobilities. An example is the notion of the 'mobile with', which may be exemplified as the dynamic and ephemeral flowing in and out of groupings as one moves in the city, or the 'team' on the move such as friends, family or couples. Another example is the notion of 'temporary congregations', which may be experienced when we walk towards a road crossing and, by stopping for a red light, become a group waiting to cross, or the elevator ride with people with whom, until we embark on the ride, we have no common interests. The notion of 'negotiation in motion' is equally derived from the *Staging Mobilities* perspective to describe the dynamic interaction that takes place when we perform mobilities in a busy transit space or when the 'mobile with' is engaged on more or less explicit decision-making concerning routes or modes of transportation. A number of other concepts derived from the *Staging Mobilities* framework are developed and will form the backbone of this book's contribution to mobilities research. The key insight is that we need to understand the contemporary city as an assemblage of circulating people, goods, information and signs in relational networks creating the 'meaning of movement'. The lifescapes of such mobile and networked conditions create individual experiences as well as collective processes of inclusion and exclusion. Sites, areas and people may be 'switched on' or 'switched off', thereby becoming subject to complex relations of mobilities capital and capacity to move (motility). As the book takes its point of departure from the 'mobilities turn' (e.g. Adey 2010; Cresswell 2006; Cwerner *et al.* 2009; Freudendal-Pedersen 2009; Larsen *et al.* 2006; Sheller and Urry 2006; Urry 2000a, 2007) it brings the analysis closer to the material and design-oriented realm by stressing that 'how it materialises' is essential to 'how it works and feels' (and this will be followed up in even more detail in an accompanying book entitled *Designing Mobilities*). Somewhat parallel to Urry's argument for a 'resource sociology' connecting the material resource base of societies to their sociality (Urry 2011), I argue here for a shift to include material and technological dimensions much more directly in relation to the social dimensions of mobilities research. In particular the design dimension seems less theorised and analysed. This book is thus the first of two aiming to remedy and bridge this gap. The book foregrounds the meaning of movement to social and cultural practices by paying particular attention to the way infrastructures, technologies and networks are designed, laid out and built. The main objective of the book is to contribute theoretically to the mobilities literature by adding the dimension of design and architecture of the built environment to a sociological framing. The book is organised so that it theoretically illustrates the state of the art of the 'mobilities turn' in which it positions itself. Empirically the book is rich with illustrations of how mobility is practised in the everyday life of the contemporary city.

Staging Mobilities

As mentioned above, mobilities do not 'just happen' or simply 'take place'. According to the *Staging Mobilities* framework we should think of mobilities as being carefully and meticulously designed and planned 'from above', as one might say. However, they are equally importantly acted out, performed and lived 'from below'. Mobilities are staged and people performing mobilities are engaged in social interactions of staging mobilities. *Staging Mobilities* is therefore a process of creating lived mobility practices and the material preconditions to these. In this research, contemporary urbanism is understood as highly influenced by the staged mobilities of planning, design, architecture, governance systems and technological networks as well as by the social interactions, cultural meanings and the production of social order. *Staging Mobilities* is a socio-spatio-temporal process designing mobile lifescapes 'from above' and performed mobile engagements and interactions 'from below'. There may be seen a certain affinity with the notion of DeCerteau wherein he speaks of 'strategies' and 'tactics' as the top-down regimes versus the bottom-up resistances of everyday life (DeCerteau 1984). However, this resemblance only goes so far since DeCerteau argues that 'strategies' are dominant and 'tactics' are emancipative. Such a pre-coding of the staging from above and from below does not apply. The creation of infrastructures as scenes for our everyday-life mobilities in planning, architecture and design cannot a priori be seen as dominating. And equally the multiple mobile interactions taking place between social consociates cannot always be seen as emancipating. Until now the mobilities literature has not sufficiently grasped the dynamic and complex interactions of people in motion mediated by material sites and networked technologies. *Staging Mobilities* therefore brings a new perspective to mobilities research by documenting how the urban situation at the brink of the twenty-first century must be understood from a perspective that sees 'staging' as a dominant feature of mobilities. It must be said that this work is predominantly focused on cities and the urban context for mobilities and is, as such, an example of the 'urban bias' Vannini find in much

6 *Review and positioning*

contemporary mobilities research (Vannini 2011). However, given the fact that this work comes out of a Department of Architecture, Design and Media Technology in general, a research group for Urban Design in particular and from the hands of a professor of urban theory, a certain urban focus might be expected. Moreover, the world is becoming more and more urbanized, thus increasing the reliance on urban infrastructures as sites of mobilities (Graham 2010:2). This does not, however, mean that I do not sympathize with Vannini's criticism on a more general note (and surely many of the insights provided by this book may apply to non-urban settings). Likewise, does the foregrounding of mobilities not mean that everything is in flux, that there is no social stability or that 'everything solid melts into air', to borrow a phrase from Marx? Rather it means that places, sites, buildings, terminals, cities and regions must be understood in their complex relationship to the fluid and fixed, flow and stasis, friction and movement. *Staging Mobilities* moves beyond the dichotomy of sedentary and nomad ontologies and epistemologies and points at dynamic lived mobilities as they manifest themselves in relation to three key themes: the physical settings, material spaces and design; the social interactions; and the embodied performances (see Figure 1.1). Each of these three areas are discussed in Chapters 3, 4 and 5, respectively. This division is obviously made for operational reasons rather than as a claim to be the only and all-embracing model. Moreover, within the physical and material dimension I shall include the infrastructures and networked

Figure 1.1 The staging mobilities model.

technologies mediating and affording contemporary mobilities. As I speak of staging from above I want to propose the metaphor of 'scenography', as in the sense of creating 'scenes' within a manuscript or a play. To capture the staging from below I propose, in a similar vein, the metaphor of 'choreography'. Obviously choreography may also be created from the vantage point of a disengaged director. But here the immediate embodied and sense-oriented dimension is what makes me prefer this metaphor for the bottom-up and embodied acts of self-choreography that individuals perform as they create 'mobilities *in situ*'.

The perspective of seeing 'staging' and 'the staged' as the key metaphors for framing mobilities is inspired by the work of the Canadian sociologist Erving Goffman. Goffman was the student of the 'ordinary' and the everyday social order par excellence. In earlier works I have developed an emerging understanding of the fruitfulness of Goffman for mobilities research (e.g. Jensen 2006, 2010a). However, with this work a more fully developed analytical framework is constructed that takes key insights from Goffman's perspective of role play and 'dramaturgic' analysis of social interactions. One of Goffman's best-known concepts might serve to briefly illustrate this point. In his notion of 'front stage/back stage' many urban scholars have seen the distinction between public and private spaces (e.g. Madanipour 2003). In the light of *Staging Mobilities*, however, I want to bring this concept into a much more dynamic and complex framing. What takes place accordingly is a 'mobile front staging/back staging' process within which mobile subjects undertake performative work in a process of negotiating 'staged' demarcations of front and back stage as well as 'staging' their own mobile lines of demarcation. For example, when we appropriate space in the train compartment by means of mobile objects (newspapers, books, mobile phones etc.) or whatever takes place within the car as a mobile domestic site (back stage), these actions are often utterly publicly transparent (front stage). By applying the front/back stage metaphor to the *Staging Mobilities* frame we see a process of 'mobile territorialisation' illustrating the dynamic character of contemporary urban life. The key idea behind the *Staging Mobilities* perspective is thus to capture the fact that mobilities are being staged, as well as the fact that the social interaction taking place must be understood in the light of a 'staging' process. The analytical perspective of *Staging Mobilities* explores who stages mobilities, and how, why, where and by which technologies, artefacts and design principles does 'staging' takes place? Equally, the perspective engages with who are staged, how they perceive staging, how they enact or react in accommodating or subversive ways, how they feel about being staged and moved in particular ways and using particular modes of mobilities? *Staging Mobilities* is, as explained, an investigation of concrete and ordinary mobile situations. However, it also grows out of a research agenda I term 'critical mobilities thinking' (Jensen 2009a). By this is partly meant that there is a focus on the social repercussions that different mobility arrangements and designs may have in terms of social inclusion/exclusion. This applies both as mobilities may be staged 'from above' in controlled systems as well as the power plays 'from below' between moving people. Importantly, moreover, is the fact that 'critical' thinking means to question the taken-for-granted assumptions about mobilities. This goes both for the way we think about mobilities in academic and theoretical understanding and, equally importantly, for the way we comprehend it in our daily lives, in ordinary practices and in policy-making and planning of mobilities. The position points at seeing mobile situations as much more than instrumental acts of movement from A to B. The importance of relating mobilities research to the physical layout of the city may sound trivial at first but it contains a number of significant social and cultural processes that reveal it to be not so trivial after all. Any location, building, city or site derives its symbolic meaning as well as its physical functionality by means of its accessibility or its inaccessibility. Or, in the words of Lynch and Hack:

> Access is the prerequisite to using any space. Without the ability to enter or to move within it, to receive and transmit information or goods, space is of no value, however vast or rich in resources. A city is a communication net, made of roads, paths, rails, pipes, and wires.
>
> (Lynch and Hack 1984:193)

Moreover, what takes place as people negotiate the material environment and engage in social interactions as they move is crucial to the functionality of cities and the wellbeing of its inhabitants. In the words of Goffman:

> when the individual is in a public place, he [sic] is not merely moving from point to point silently and mechanically managing traffic problems; he is also involved in taking constant care to sustain a viable position relative to what has come to happen around him, and he will initiate gestural interchanges with acquainted and unacquainted others in order to establish what this position is!
>
> (Goffman 1972:154)

Many other classic and contemporary mobilities researchers and thinkers are brought into this book. But if one key thinker should be emphasised it is Goffman. This work sets 'Goffman on the move', so to speak, in order to develop a new and innovative perspective on the mundane and ordinary practices of situational mobilities.

From the very simple model (Figure 1.1) we may envision a situation where we move in a built environment amongst other people and in some sort of mediated condition as when travel information is accessible via a mobile phone or directions are given by a GPS. Such a situation contains all three dimensions of the model. Needless to say there are mobile situations where this is not the case in such a straightforward manner. The solitary walker in the woods may meet no one and may also not be related to any networked technologies (even though the paving of paths and the erecting of signs and markers for wayfinding may also be present as traces of staging from above and involving some elements of technology). Still, this obviously qualifies as a 'mobile situation'. However, seen from the analytical perspective of *Staging Mobilities* such cases of non-social and non-mediated mobilities are less interesting. Not in the sense of being less important to human existence but in relation to this particular theoretical framing. Surely no frame may include everything and this is one of the deliberate delimitations to the *Staging Mobilities* perspective. This should come as no surprise since the intellectual background for this is the social sciences and thus there is an imminent interest in situations where 'the social' becomes the pivotal issue. To borrow an expression from Cedric Price: 'it is interaction, not place, that is the essence of the city and city life' (Price, quoted in Sadler 2005:128). Another reservation concerning the model is that it deals with mobile situations where the human–human or the human–technology/object relations are primary. Increasingly, mobilities are being staged and afforded by non-human to non-human communication such as when systems communicate to technological artefacts (e.g. flight-control systems and aeroplanes or driverless metro systems). Such non-human mobility staging is equally on the edge of what this theoretical framing may include. However, as soon as the human subject becomes embedded and assembled into networks of M2M (machine-to-machine) communication the situation becomes of relevance to the theoretical model, in other words when there are 'humans in the loop'. Another important element of self-reflection in relation to the model is that this is a heuristic tool and thereby a shorthand for the actual complexity of real-life interaction and mobile situations. One dimension of this is that the model may seem like a dualistic understanding of staging from 'above' and 'below', which is certainly not the case. Coming out of a relational and mobility-oriented understanding of place and theorising from the vantage point of a post-positivist and 'more than representational' (Andersson and Harrison 2010:19) epistemology, this work aims at moving beyond dichotomies of agency/structure, nomad/sedentary, global/local. What I am interested in is the actual mobility practices '*in situ*' in all their complexity and thus any conceptual divides that may signal dualistic thinking are not meant to work this way. Having said that, it is useful to organise one's understandings of staged mobilities so that they may be thought of as afforded by systems, infrastructures and designs made elsewhere in planning departments or by developing agencies as well as the situational mobilities acted out and 'performed' by humans on the ground, so to speak. The division between staging mobilities 'from above' and 'from below' is thus not an ontological claim but rather an analytical framing of material practices in such a way that we may increase our understanding herein. As always a model is a reduction of the realities studied. A final remark on the underpinning conditions to the frame/model is that by no means should it be thought to be an all-embracing and fully comprehensive analysis of mobilities. I think such 'holistic' ambitions are appreciative intellectually but often less useful when it comes to understanding a complex reality. For analysis we need theories, concepts and models of some reductive nature. Or, as the saying goes, 'the map is not the territory'. Rather the *Staging Mobilities* framing puts forward a selected number of perspectives from which I examine situational mobility practices. This means that I will be looking at how situations of everyday-life mobility are seen from the point of view of the body, the material site and the social interactions as mobile practices are acted out in the situation, as well as planned, designed and orchestrated from elsewhere.

Towards a 'mobile situationism'

This work may be understood as 'mobile situationism' if by this is meant an endeavour to set the actual and situational practices at the centre of the analysis (Figure 1.2). Thus the 'mobile situation' is the focal point of our discussion and analysis. Goffman spoke of 'situations' with his characteristic focus on the dynamic and communicative interactions taking place:

> Social situations were defined as arenas of mutual monitoring. It is possible for the student to take social situations very seriously as one natural vantage point from which to view all of social life. After all, it is in social situations that individuals can communicate in the fullest sense of the term, and it is only in them that individuals can physically coerce one another, assault one another, interact sexually, importune one another gesturally, give physical comfort, and so forth. Moreover, it is in social situations that most of the world's work gets done ... it is mainly in such contexts [social situations] that individuals can use their faces and bodies, as well as small materials at hand to engage in social portraiture. It is here in these small, local places that they can arrange themselves microecologically to depict what is taken as their place in the wider social frame.
>
> (Goffman 1979:5–6)

A 'mobile situationism' is thus engaging with the situational microecologies of mobile practices. However, a few remarks of clarification are needed. First of all, the 'mobile situation' may be acted out by a single individual, for example, if I am alone in the train compartment riding the driverless (albeit remote-monitored and staged) metro train of Copenhagen, or walking in the woods not meeting anyone but performing mobilities in relation to paths, signs, GPS apps etc. The mobile situation is an assemblage of human subjects, physical design and material infrastructures of the built environment in which we may find complex mobile situations with multiple social interactions taking place (as well as finding them enacted by the sole individual, provided we then focus on the relationship to, for example, 'systems' affording or preventing that person's mobility). *Staging Mobilities* thereby focuses on the situation as it is framed and 'created' in three analytically distinct dimensions: in physical settings and material spaces, in embodied performances and in social interactions.

In the *Staging Mobilities* perspective I understand the 'mobile situation' as a dynamic and process-oriented event in time–space and thus not as a 'fixed point' (for a critique of 'pointilist' understandings, see Bissell 2012). Moreover, as the technologies and networks of mobile communication (GPS, mobile phones, laptops etc.) are defining an increasing part of everyday-life mobile situations in

Figure 1.2 Mobile situations.

contemporary society, I may also have to insert another reservation. This is of importance particularly since I do rely on Goffman's work substantially. Face-to-face interactions are obviously a key feature of the 'mobile situation'. However, increasingly 'non-proxemic mobile interactions' such as two or more people moving in separate infrastructures but in contact by digital media actually qualify as a mobile situation. Since the days of Goffman the interrelations of multiple networks and non-proxemic dependencies have grown dramatically, resulting in what Gordon and Silva term 'remote co-presence' (2011:43). So when Goffman in his book *Interaction Ritual* (1967/82) defines a 'sociology of occasions' I concur with his argument that a study of interaction should not be focused on the individual and his/her psychology but instead on the relations between acts of different persons. However, the next part is more problematic as he then argues that these persons must be mutually present to one another. By this Goffman meant physically co-present, and this does only apply to some mobile situations. Likewise, he argues in his book *Behaviour in Public Places* that the 'situation' is defined by its physical boundaries (1963:21). However, this was not fully consistent as he elsewhere in the same book opened up to include the communication dimension in an expanded notion of the situation. He spoke of a possibility of communication that would 'transform a mere physical region into the locus of a sociologically relevant entity, the situation' (Goffman

1963:154). Though he made this opening to a more 'stretched' definition, it never became much more precise in the book. In *Frame Analysis* published a decade later, Goffman again noticed that a situation may 'stretch out' when he presented his approach as: 'situational, meaning here a concern for what one individual can be alive to at a particular moment, this often involving a few other particular individuals and not necessarily restricted to the mutually monitored area of a face-to-face gathering' (Goffman 1974/86:8). Meyrowitz also points to the problem that Goffman gave exclusive priority to physical co-presence and thus ignored the role of communication technologies in social interaction. Meyrowitz thus argues for thinking of situations as 'information systems' rather than bounded localities (1990:89). This resonates very well with the *Staging Mobilities* framework. In recontextualising Goffman's analysis the situation may thus be seen as 'stretching' beyond the immediate face-to-face engagement, and given the contemporary complexity of networked communication systems Goffman would in all likelihood have explored this dimension in much more detail had he lived to do so. The networked technologies embedded into the systems of contemporary mobilities are indeed stretched and mobile situations are thereby not solely a case of physical co-presence.

The many systems of ITS (Intelligent Traffic Systems) that give information on traffic jams, roadworks or accidents ahead via messages to mobile phones, or the location-based services facilitating the choice of where to shop, eat or drink are but a few examples of 'systems' interfering in the situation. Moreover, a large number of trips are now undertaken whilst people are communicating online or texting, pointing even more in the direction of including 'non-proxemic interactions' and communications into the theoretical framing of the 'mobile situation'. Technologies are increasingly loosening interactions from spatial constraints, so to speak (Sommer 2007:95). In consequence this perspective runs in parallel with claims that the 'virtual' or 'digital' realm cannot be separated from the 'real' or 'material' (Gordon and Silva 2011; M. Jensen 2011; McCullough 2004). Of course, there are still mobile situations of 'clean simplicity' like one person walking on a remote beach or two people negotiating a passing on the pavement. However, in all sorts of ways the situation 'reaches out'. In material terms this may be in dependencies on hardware and physical connecting infrastructures or as in the case of networked technologies like our mobile phones and how they may enact the situation in all sorts of ways. So a 'mobile situation' may be when someone is on the move in the most traditional sense and it may include complex communications across time and space that influences the mobile situation. Such practices take place through what Fisker (2011) terms 'mobility action chains' working to script mobilities in everyday life. The mobile situations studied in this book include both the 'focused' and the 'unfocused' interactions that Goffman (1961) distinguishes between. Being mobile together on a particular journey is focused, whereas interacting with strangers on the street is unfocused. Both are of equal relevance to the study of mobilities. In summary I might say that a 'mobile situationism' is an analytical focus that moves across 'scales' reaching from the body to the global (e.g. GPS afforded bodily mobilities). The situational focus explores mobile practices of both instrumental and affective and emotional motivation and en route explores the creative and skilful dimensions to mobilities. 'Mobilities *in situ*' uncovers the relational and associational character of practices within networks and environments both affording and restricting practices. *Staging Mobilities* is not denying the over-individual and systemic properties impacting what is doable, and neither is the 'human agent' an omnipotent and isolated 'field of force' but rather a constantly mediated and negotiated emerging element of a situation made possible by networks, infrastructures, environments and material ecologies.

Bringing in space

As the material and physical situations are at the centre, let us briefly look at one influential attempt to 'bring in space' to the sociological understanding of the world. Although Anthony Giddens has been criticised for his attempt to include time and space in his seminal work *The Constitution of Society* (1984; for the criticism see Bryant and Jary 1991 and Held and Thompson 1989) I shall use his work as a pointer to a sympathetic and revisionary approach to Goffman and in particular to the key ideas about the situation. At the time of writing *Constitution* Giddens targeted an important agenda of getting social theory and sociology to pay more attention to the 'spatiality of social life'. This interesting debate and its close relationship with human geography (e.g. by attaching to the 'time-geography' of Hägerstrand) cannot be addressed here. Suffice it to say that Giddens argued his case in a way that seems rather self-evident to present-day mobilities research when he stated that: 'Interactions of individuals moving in time–space compose "bundles" (encounters or social occasions in Goffman's terminology) meeting at "stations" or definite time–space locations within bounded regions' (1984:112). Giddens relied, as mentioned, very much on the then progressive idea of 'time-geography' coined by Hägerstrand. Accordingly he spoke of 'stations' as fixed localities where meeting and interaction would take place. In a complex web of terminologies he thus argued for a hierarchy of concepts: 'Locales refer to the use of space to provide the settings of interaction, the *settings* of interaction in turn being essential to specifying its *contextuality*' (Giddens 1984:118; italics original). To Giddens, 'gatherings' are informal and ephemeral whereas 'social occasions' are formal and more permanent (1984:71). What is more interesting in this context are his attempts to overcome the challenge of conceptualising the fact that interaction may take place across time–space and not only within situations defined by proximity and face-to-face encounters. He coins the notion of 'time–space distanciation', which is defined as 'the stretching of social systems across time–space, on the basis of mechanisms of social and systems integration' (Giddens 1984:377). Without having to go deeply into the underpinning ideas of Giddens' work we may pay attention to the idea that 'social integration' concerns the reciprocity between actors in contexts of co-presence whereas 'system integration' is understood to relate to reciprocity between collectives across extended time–space (Giddens 1984:28).

In the practical mobile situation of my concern this means that I will be studying complex inter-weavings of both system and social integration as social actors move in time–space interacting with co-present consociates as well as possibly interacting with others at a distance and being 'staged' by systems reaching across time and space. To put matters differently, we are in relation with those who are not present and this needs to be accounted for as an 'extra layer' of the situation compared to the society described by Goffman. The key here is the 'stretching' of interactions and relations across time and space that needs to be accounted for if contemporary mobilities are to be understood more clearly. Importantly, though, we should underline that the 'stretched mobile interactions' may be the ones facilitated and afforded by networked technologies of all sorts. But in line with Goffman's basic insights they may actually also include the simple and non-technologically mediated situation, such as, for example, walking in the wide open or across an almost empty city square and from afar seeing another person or group walking or moving. Noticing these may affect our own mobility practices in terms of 'preparing' for a meeting by adjusting the 'front stage' impression during passing or perhaps undertaking a complete re-routing in order to avoid such a situation. In even more detail, the potential approach of mobile others may affect the way our bodies perform, for example by adjusting the way we walk or what we are doing due to the potential or near-presence of mobile others. This would then also be an example of how the presence of mobile others may modify our actions and behaviour. In fact, this was a key observation Goffman made during his ethnographic field study on a Shetland Island where he noticed, amongst other things, how people being spotted from afar due to the wide-open spaces was influencing how people 'prepared' themselves for an upcoming encounter or visit (Goffman 1953). That the 'stretched mobile interactions' need not be technologically mediated to exist can also be seen in, for example, the family moving (a 'mobile with') along a public park, beach or street where a child is 'allowed' to move away from the parents until an invisible boundary or threshold is crossed and the parents start 'calling in' the child in an attempt to bring the child back within the range of the 'stretched' zone of interaction and 'situational control'.

The performative and embodied dimension of the 'mobile situation' is equally vital to comprehend. I shall lean on Goffman's notions of performativity, but not exclusively as I shall rely on other perspectives of performance theory (e.g. Massumi 2002; Schechner 1988; Schusterman 2000; Turner 1982). I shall also expand into the contemporary notions of embodiment as they are to be found within the so-called 'non-representational' geographies (e.g. Cresswell and Merriman 2011; Thrift 2008) as well to more philosophical perspectives (e.g. Heidegger 1927/62; Ihde 1990, 1993; Merleau-Ponty 1945/94). In Chapter 5 on embodied mobilities I return to this in more depth, but for now I may highlight that the 'mobile situation' is enacted by embodied practices where reflexive and rationally calculated practices meet and mingle with embodied and affective tacit acts of mobile performativity. Thus the social interaction dimension of the analytical frame carries not only social interaction but equally importantly an awareness to the body and the performances related to 'doing mobilities' in its material and physical sense. The material and geographical location for the 'mobile situation' is furthermore understood as an expanded version of Goffman's 'setting'. According to Goffman:

> there is the 'setting', involving furniture, décor, physical layout, and other background items which supply the scenery and stage props for the space of human action played out before, within, or upon it. A setting tends to stay put, geographically speaking, so that those who would use a particular setting as part of their performance cannot begin their act until they have brought themselves to the appropriate place and must terminate their performance when they leave it.
> (Goffman 1959:32–33)

What I generally find lacking in Goffman's work, however, is a deeper sensitivity to the material, physical and even architectural dimensions of the setting (as well as the fact that with networked technologies we may be said to 'bring along' elements of the setting as we move). Goffman does offer some additional help in this if we look to his discussion in *Behaviour in Public Places* (1963), in which he opens the notion of situational interactions up towards the material:

> I shall use the term *gathering* to refer to any set of two or more individuals whose members include all and only those who are at the moment in one another's presence. By the term *situation* I shall refer to the full spatial environment anywhere within which an entering person becomes a member of the gathering that is (or does then become) present ... Along with 'gathering' and 'situation', another basic concept must be tentatively defined. When persons come into each other's immediate presence they tend to do so as participants of what I shall call a *social occasion*. This is a wider social affair, undertaking, or event, bounded in regard to place and time and typically facilitated by fixed equipment.
> (Goffman 1963:18; italics original)

As mentioned, Goffman primarily argued that 'the term situated may be used to refer to any event occurring within the physical boundaries of a situation' (1963:21). This understanding, however, did not show sufficient depth in understanding the socio-spatial dimension of the situation. I also noted that the 'stretching' and non-proxemic dimensions were not addressed (but were acknowledged) by Goffman. The direction towards a more material or 'spatial turn' is indicated, but we may add significantly to this by including the perspectives coming out of architecture (Lawson 2001), urban theory (Lefebvre 1974/91) and, needless to say, the spatially sensitive scholars within the 'mobilities turn' (Cresswell 2006; Sheller and Urry 2006; Vannini 2009; Urry 2000a, 2007). Furthermore, in order to bridge the material, social and technological dimensions of the mobile situation the notion of 'assemblage' is helpful (Ek

2012; Farias and Bender 2010; DeLanda 2006; Latour 2005; Vannini 2012; Vannini et al. 2012). The mobile situation takes place within a setting that we may see as an assemblage of material spaces, artefacts and objects, infrastructures and social subjects.

The research questions

As mentioned at the beginning of this chapter, the rationale for this book is to address the following overall research question: *What are the physical, social, technical and cultural conditions for the staging of contemporary urban mobilities?* This overall question hosts a number of sub-questions that the book explores both theoretically and empirically en route:

1   What are the implications of the physical form and material design of sites and spaces hosting mobilities to the sociality of contemporary urban life?
2   How are social interactions and their dynamic interrelations produced by reproducing mobilities and cultures of contemporary urban life?
3   How does it feel to be a social agent on the move within the contemporary network city, and what normative and social ties are created between social agents, places and objects in the network?
4   How are mobilities being shaped and given meaning by semiotic systems of communication, circulation and mobilities processing?
5   How are networked technologies facilitating and underpinning mobilities of contemporary urban life?
6   How are infrastructures of the network city creating new cultural practices and ways of using the city, and how are they creating mechanisms of social exclusion and power?

The work is anchored in a cross-disciplinary institutional context of an urban design research environment hosted within an architecture, design and media technology department. This means that a number of the discussions and examples are drawn from the urban design field and thus carry the particular sensitivity to the way things appear and configure in a physical and material sense. To be a sociologist within a context of what I may term the 'interventionist disciplines' (e.g. urban design, planning and architecture) studying mobilities has truly been a privilege and does have a profound effect on this book and its new perspective on *Staging Mobilities* (as well as on the accompanying book titled *Designing Mobilities*).

The ontology and epistemology of this work cannot be spelled out in a simple sentence, nor should it be. Such are expressions of constant acts of reflection upon one's perspectives and research rather than a fixed and permanent position within a predefined 'school of thought'. Thus I shall remain faithful to the old proverb I present to the PhD students I supervise, namely 'seek the truth, but keep firm distance from those who have found it!' In this work the notions of thinking beyond the nomad versus the sedentary, the local versus the global and structure versus agency will be crucial effects of the philosophical underpinnings. Being informed by phenomenological and interpretive thinking this work, however, also insists on a materialist and relational perspective on both social interactions and their environments. Furthermore, the situational and concrete focus on the body in real-life situations of this work points towards pragmatism as another intellectual heritage. Attempting to be anti-dualistic and not naively 'representational' of the phenomena studied, this work seek a constant focus on the relations and distinctions between areas of concern. *Staging Mobilities* works on the contextual, situational, embodied practices of contemporary mobilities and has therefore an underpinning of various streams of thought. In this way it seems to fall within the (rather wide) description of Sheller's when she argues that

> Mobilities research combines social and spatial theory in new ways, and in so doing has provided a transformative nexus for bridging micro-interactional research on the phenomenology of embodiment, to cultural turn and hermeneutics, postcolonial and critical theory, macro-structural approaches to the state and political-economy, and elements of science and technology studies (STS) and new media studies.
>
> (Sheller 2011:1)

Not all of these approaches are covered within the *Staging Mobilities* frame, but quite a few are indeed. The perspective on contemporary mobility studies is therefore at one and the same time multi-disciplinary and focused on a situational and material form of sociology.

The content and organisation of the book

The book is organised into four main parts. The first contains a review of the field and positioning of this work. The second part is the theoretical framing specific to the *Staging Mobilities* framework. In the third part cases and empirical examples of material practices are explored. In the fourth and final part the more general discussion pointing towards a sociology of *Staging Mobilities* is on the agenda.

Part I is titled 'Staging Mobilities: Review and Positioning'. Chapter 1 presents the overall research question and the issues of the book. In Chapter 2 I move towards a more thorough discussion of the 'mobilities turn' and its repercussions for understanding the contemporary city. Part I is the foundation and positioning of the work in relation to the 'mobilities turn' as well as engaging with the critical reception thereof.

Part II is titled 'Framing Mobilities'. In this part three chapters present the core ideas behind the *Staging Mobilities* perspective. This part of the book mirrors the three themes of the *Staging Mobilities* model (see Figure 1.1) and aims to frame situational mobilities. In Chapter 3 the theme of physical settings, material spaces and design will be explored and articulated. In particular I put

18 *Review and positioning*

emphasis on issues less explored within the mobilities literature such as the more architectural and design-oriented insights into the material organisation of mobilities. Also, key issues such as how the mobilities perspective is affecting the understanding of place will be addressed here. In Chapter 4 I present the framing for understanding the social interactions amongst mobile consociates. The chapter presents thoughts and ideas reaching back to Georg Simmel but will put particular focus on the theories of Goffman. The part ends with Chapter 5 on mobile embodied performances. The sensing and moving human body is the pivotal theme of that chapter, which explores the 'way it moves' in quite some detail.

Part III has the focus of 'Practices of Mobilities'. This part opens with Chapter 6 on networked technologies and discusses the mobile practices afforded by new digital media and technologies. Chapter 6 explores the way that these new technologies afford new types of mobile interaction and at times become embraced as cultural artefacts that resemble 'second nature'. In Chapter 7 I move on to explore a mobile ethnographic account of 'negotiation in motion' based on a detailed urban field study. Chapter 8 sheds light on the altogether different theme of urban subways and metros as sites for mobile interaction. In the chapter I discuss how urban metro systems mediate lived mobilities in the contemporary city.

Part IV has the title 'Towards a Sociology of Staging Mobilities'. In Chapter 9 the issue of the material and physical design dimension to mobilities is readdressed; this time, however, with more direct discussions of the potential for adding this as a much more elaborate dimension to the mobilities research agenda. Chapter 10 is the concluding chapter and in it I return to the outset question of what it takes to stage mobilities as part of the contemporary urban experience. Moreover, I end the chapter and the book by offering 'ten pointers' for the future of mobilities research.

2 The mobile city
Reviewing and positioning

> Our cities are made up at the same time of flows and places, and of their relationships.
> Manuel Castells, 'Urban Sociology in the Twenty-First Century', 2002, p. 397

> Our geographies have radically shifted: from sidewalks into traffic; from car to screen; from arcade to inside your head; from stasis to speed.
> Michael J. Dear, *The Postmodern Urban Condition*, 2000, p. 210

> The expanded and mobile city implies a new agenda for the design of public space, not only in relation to the urban centres or in the new residential districts, but especially in the ambiguous in-between areas ... Furthermore, we seem to think too much about public space in the sense of fixed and permanent physical spaces, and we give insufficient consideration to the way in which public domain comes into being in flux, often extremely temporarily.
> Marten Hajer and Arnold Reijndorp, *In Search of New Public Domain*, 2001, pp. 14, 16

Introduction

This chapter identifies the 'mobilities turn' and the state-of-the-art research as well as being a positioning chapter laying out the theoretical background particular to *Staging Mobilities*. The chapter discusses the fundamental building blocks of the theoretical framework including notions of sedentary and nomadic ontologies, mobilities and the socio-spatial relation, and the understanding of places and cities.

Cities and urban spaces have long been described and understood in terms of their form, structure and morphology. However, contemporary change in the socio-spatial relation has made it clear that urban analysts are in need of a new vocabulary and new concepts. Thus an increasing number of urban theorists are turning towards flows and mobilities as something that can no longer merely be seen as a 'side effect'. Contemporary cities and urban spaces are defined by their connectivity and their relationships to other nodes in a global network. There is a need to conceptualise and theorise the multiple and complex flows of images, signs, meanings, goods, vehicles and people that not only move within urban and inter-urban infrastructures but that constitute the contemporary city. In the words of Castells:

> The analysis of networked spatial mobility is another frontier for the new theory of urbanism. To explore it in terms that would not be solely descriptive we need new concepts. The connection between networks and places has to be understood in a variable geometry of these connections ... we can build on an ethnographic tradition ... But here again speed, complexity, and planetary reach of the transportation system have changed the scale and meaning of these issues. Furthermore, the key reminder is that we move physically while staying put in our electronic connections. We carry flows and move across places.
>
> (Castells 2005:54)

Looking at mobilities '*in situ*' and understanding how these are configured between flow and stasis in structures and practices suggests that the relations between humans and between humans and material objects and infrastructure systems and spaces are what matters. *Staging Mobilities* is therefore a theoretical understanding foregrounding the connectivity or disconnectivity between relevant empirical entities (human as well as non-human) in order to focus on relations. The meaning of mobilities lies in the relations and embodied practice of mobile situations. *Staging Mobilities* represents a new sensitivity to the interrelatedness of people, objects, spaces and their interactions as mobility/immobility is in the foreground. En route to such new understanding we need to pause and reflect upon the underpinning ideas of mobilities and flow.

The study of mobilities within the 'turn' is an 'authentically interdisciplinary field' (Vannini 2010:112), suggesting that there has to be work across disciplines to engage with mobilities research in an innovative way. In a reissued version of his 1999 paper 'Mobile Sociology', John Urry points to the need for opening up the research agenda within sociology, breaking away from notions of 'society' as something fixed, static and bounded (Urry 2010). The paper is a short version of the key arguments presented in the book that in many ways must be said to be the opening of the 'mobility turn', namely Urry's influential *Sociology beyond Societies: Mobilities for the Twenty-first Century* (2000). Since then he has followed up in papers and books on the refinement and articulation of this research agenda (e.g. Adey and Bissell 2010; Urry 2007) but the opening of the 'mobilities turn' with *Sociology beyond Societies* was a pathbreaking statement indeed.

Positioning the 'mobilities turn'

Contemporary mobilities thinking needs grounding in a cross-disciplinary understanding of the flow in cities and between cities. Therefore reworking issues of mobility, scale and network becomes fundamental. Shields identifies 'flow' as the core of a new paradigm:

Flow as a paradigm: the notion of 'flow', most widely known from the work of Deleuze and Irigaray occur repeatedly in social theory. Associated with a paradigm shift within cultural studies and sociology from the analysis of objects to processes, it is also linked by geographers to the notion of 'nomadism' and the breakdown of the fixity of boundaries and barriers. More poignantly, it is the lived experience of the global mass migrations and movements of refugees. In effect, the dominant metaphors for discussions of sociality have swung from models of affinity to those of viscosity ... Flows, are spatial, temporal – but above all, material. In this issue [volume 1, issue 1 of *Space and Culture*], we advocate an analysis of flows, which examines their qualities, but avoids their analytical reduction to causes, origins and destinations.

(Shields 1997:2; bold in original)

For Shields the research focus thus moves from objects to processes, from affinity to viscosity in an attempt to avoid simple causal explanations. What is at stake is a way of thinking about the social and the spatial that is characterised by a changing set of concepts: the city as 'moments of encounter' (Amin and Thrift 2002), lines of flight and smooth/striate spaces (Deleuze and Guattari 1997), the network city (Borja and Castells 1997), spaces of flows/spaces of place (Castells 1996, 2005), fluidity and mixity in an uneven relational geography (Massey 1999; Harvey 1996) and the multiplex dialectics of mobility/moorings (Urry 2003). So the professional and academic preoccupation with objects and stasis has led to a situation of not just decreased understanding of what the city may mean today, but also more profoundly what contemporary culture means. A basic proposition is therefore that we should recognise the need for a new vocabulary and a new frame for understanding the urban. Thus the way we think about space, place and flows needs to be dwelt upon. Or, in the words of Shields:

conceptions of space – which are central to any ontology – are part and parcel of notions of reality. Much more than simply a world view, this sense of space, one's 'spatiality', is a fundamental component of one's relationship to the world.

(Shields 1991:31)

However, articulating a mobilities understanding does not imply that cities and urban places are 'melting into the air'. Rather it means foregrounding a neglected dimension to cities and urban space. Thus within a mobilities understanding cities still have physical form and material morphologies. What is contested though is that the static and 'solid' character of urban form is the key characteristic. Such a way of thinking should be seen as part of a larger effort of 'restructuring the "social as society" into the "social as mobility"' (Urry 2000a:2). Such an agenda is about 'mobile theorising', which according to Urry concerns, amongst other things, the development of appropriate metaphors focusing on movement, mobility and contingent ordering (Urry 2000a:18–19). A mobile theorising put flows at the centre: 'Rather than an empiricism of isolated and static objects, setting flows at the centre of social investigation, forces one to confront a world in motion and to acknowledge oneself, always moving position and perspective' (Shields 1997:3). This 'setting flows at the centre' of our exploration of the socio-spatial relation in general and urban space in particular is thus not an act of reduction or substitution of one one-eyed perspective with another. Rather it is a question of 'foregrounding' flows:

> We must ask, what are the characteristics of flow? They have a tempo and rhythm as well as a direction. The significance of the material quality of flows is that they have content, beyond mere being processes. They have the advantage of recasting the idealist notion of processual change into the changing material itself. Processes generally indicate the transformative 'gap' between states or dispositions. Process thus is strongly defined on the basis of origin and terminus as a definite line or path between two points or waystations in a further process.
>
> (Shields 1997:3)

Amin and Thrift articulate poignantly what such 'flow-thinking' may mean ontologically:

> We have begun to see how urban life is placed by lines of mobilities and travel and by namings and imaginaries ... The city thus needs to be seen as an institutionalised practice, a systematized network, in an expanded everyday urbanism ... an ontology of encounter or togetherness based in the principles of connection, extension and continuous novelty ... In such a conception, the city is made up of potential and actual entities/associations/togetherness which there is no going beyond to find anything 'more real' ... In other words, it belongs to the nature of a 'being' that it is a potential for every 'becoming'.
>
> (Amin and Thrift 2002:26, 27)

Accordingly, places are therefore better thought of as 'moments of encounters' rather than enduring sites (Amin and Thrift 2002:301), a point that Merrifield takes even further in a critique of the 'Cartesian' ontology and perception of space that threatens to 'separate out and "thingify" different aspects of social reality' (1993:518). Resisting such a 'Cartesian atomized ontology' means to think in terms of dialectics and processes. Accordingly a place must be understood as a site of relations to other sites since no entity exists in isolation (Harvey 1996:261). This resonates with the way Massey thinks about cities and their relational interdependence based upon a process of flow. It is a way of thinking about cities that

> lays a stress in movement, fluidity and 'mixity' in such a way that it becomes apparent that any approach to urban governance and urban planning, say,

cannot proceed on the basis of some final, formal plan, nor work with an assumption of a reachable permanent harmony and peace. The order of cities is a dynamic order. What is necessary is a way of approaching this fluidity, openness and density of interaction: a thinking about process.

(Massey 1999:161)

The relational theory of contemporary cities means a rejection of space, place and time as having fixed meanings (Graham and Marvin 2001:203). Thus cities are seen as social processes rather than as things. As Graham and Marvin argue: 'the city is a gearbox full of speeds' (2001:204). Relational and process-oriented thinking (Healey 2000; Urry 2000a) therefore requires an ontological break with the notion of space as a 'container' (Guy *et al.* 2001:204). The implication of a relational and dialectical understanding of a global geography criss-crossed by flows in networks has been eminently articulated by French urban theorist Henri Lefebvre. For Lefebvre, understanding the relational features of places also means understanding the transgression of fixed spatial scales into a multi-scalar optics (Lefebvre 1974/91:88). Such an understanding of the 'politics of scale' has since been taken on by analysts like Brenner (2004) and more explicitly in the theory of Urry. Furthermore, the dialectical relationship between flow and stasis has made Urry articulate a very important relationship between the fluid and the fixed: 'it is the dialectics of mobility/moorings that produces social complexity. If all relationality were mobile or "liquid", then there would be no complexity. Complexity, I suggest, stems from this dialectics of mobility and moorings' (2003:126). In other words, 'flow needs fixity' (McCullough 2004), as social and urban life is constantly flickering between movement and immobility. Cities are indeed marked by the physical 'traces of dead' and passive layered morphologies. But they are equally constituted by the multiple flows, interactions and linkages from the local to the global. Humans are moving animals, or 'homo movens' in Vannini's terminology (2010:118). Thus the experiences of either being still or moving are pivotal modes of experiencing the world both in terms of the senses as well as cognitively. We make sense of the world and our consociates as we move and thus also produce meaning, culture and norms as we interact in motion.

Critics of the 'mobilities turn'

No academic field can be articulated and created without opposition and critique. This lies in the nature of the scientific venture and in the ethos of research. The 'mobilities turn' is no exception to this, and here I shall engage some of this criticism. One of the key points of critique from Knowles concerns the usage of the notion of 'flow'. Accordingly the notion reifies and homogenises mobilities as unhindered and effortless movements of similar entities (Knowles 2010:374). Put polemically, Knowles states that 'people don't flow: they have plans and they travel. Travel for me, is a way of thinking about people engaged in the long and short-haul mobilities of routine life' (2010:374). However, there does not seem to be any contradiction to the way the 'mobilities turn' articulates mobilities as real-life events. There is, though, a point in saying that seeing mobilities as 'flows' means that we bring entities studied (whether cars, people, good, signs or something entirely different) onto the same ontological level. However, I fail to see that working with the notion of flow as a central dimension to the mobilities concept should mean an a priori bias towards the frictionless and unhindered. Flows are indeed opposed, differential, redirected, challenged, stopped, etc., in an infinite number of ways. A different proposal altogether would be to argue for mobilities seen as homogeneous flows at certain times and as differential mobile practices at others. This shift of foreground and background to the analysis has been captured in the twin metaphors of the 'river' and the 'ballet' (Jensen 2010b). In a study of a public space working both as transit space and public plaza I used the river/ballet metaphors to capture mobilities seen 'from above' (river) where we deliberately homogenise the 'entities' as if it were flows of identical entities, and 'from below' (ballet) where we engage with individuals and subjective differences (the study will be presented in detail in Chapter 7). So the claim here is that mobilities may be thought of both as something akin to Knowles' notion of flows (as homogeneous) but equally importantly as something personalised, individual and highly differentiated. To claim that the one is more 'true' than the other (and thus in closer contact with the ontological status of mobilities) seems to me to be a dead end. In epistemological terms I argue that we should be able to shift between the gestalts of mobility as homogenous flows and differentiated practices. According to Kaufmann one of the key benefits from Urry's tireless work on the 'mobilities turn' was to bring the notion of space into sociology (Kaufmann 2010:369). This has to be understood in its historical context since there has been a number of attempts and debates on 'bringing in space' in social theory (Casey 1997; Tonboe 1993). However, Kaufmann is correctly observing that the material and spatial dimension to mobilities research has now also become evident in sociology (the disciplines of geography, planning and architecture have been much closer to this recognition for a while). Kaufman seems to suggest that notions of networks and flows are ideologically biased towards neo-liberal systems of thought (Kaufmann 2010:371). This is an interesting viewpoint that may hold true for some CEOs' perception of globalisation and the world economy, but it fails to be substantiated as something inherent to the 'mobilities turn'. The proof of the pudding is in the eating, however, and if one looks into the actual research done within the 'turn' nothing seems to support the thesis that the thinking about mobilities and networks automatically takes one towards the realm of neo-liberal sympathies. In fact, a critical understanding is much more prevalent amongst mobilities scholars.

Another vocal critic is Simonsen, who argues that the mobilities turn ignores 'ordinary life', develops a homogenising discourse anchored in a male, middle-class perception of the world, subscribes to a one-dimensional and mono-directional notion of abstract space and time and, finally, that the mobility notion is over-generalising and simplifying at its core (Simonsen 2004:44, 2005:33–39). Also not quite satisfied (understandably, I think) with traditional 'community research' as an alternative, Simonsen argues for what she terms a more 'humble' theorisation developed around Lefebvre's notion of 'rhythm analysis' (and thus actually subscribing to seeing mobilities as a key issue to contemporary urban studies!). The relatively large number of ethnographic accounts for everyday-life mobilities and their differentiated character, however, do invalidate this rather hard critique (see, e.g., Freudendal-Pedersen 2009; Vannini 2009, 2011, 2012). During the course of this book I shall hopefully be able to refute the idea that mobilities studies are reifying, homogenising and overlooking the everyday-life perspective. In an analysis of Hurricane Katrina in New Orleans in 2005 Thiessen raises another critique of the 'mobilities turn'. In short the critique argues that mobilities is not a new field of study, that it objectifies, homogenises, banalises and is being overused, and that the 'turn' lacks sensibility towards immobility (Thiessen 2008). Furthermore, Thiessen targets Urry's 'modest' theories rather aggressively whilst leaving the more far-fetched ideas of Paul Virilio to pass as unquestionable and valid analysis (Virilio 1991, 1977/2001). Thiessen also speaks of the importance of the capacity to move (without applying notions of 'motility', though) and the differences in mobility and capacity. These issues are, however, not exotic to the mobilities-turn literature and Thiessen's critique seems unnecessarily aggressive, straw-man-like and rather hard to sustain. Interestingly, he ends the heated critique by stating that 'mobilities are means, not ends' (Thiessen 2008:123). This may, of course, be so in certain instances, but as a general statement Thiessen actually becomes guilty of reducing mobilities to instrumental acts of moving mindlessly from A to B. Rather, and this is the pivotal theme of this book, I shall argue that mobilities and acts of moving may be meaningful practices on their own that generate emotional, affective and cultural relations between people on the move or at a standstill. Seen this way, mobilities are (also) ends indeed. Coming from a position more sympathetic to the 'mobilities turn', Adey (2006) has a sobering and logical point stating that if mobility is everything, then maybe it is nothing! An even more constructive corrective to the 'turn' is to be found in Bissell and Fuller's notion of 'stillness'. In their book *Stillness in a Mobile World*, they convincingly argue that an understanding of stillness in all its valences opens up new appreciations of mobile relations (Bissell and Fuller 2011:4). By reflecting upon the notion of stillness they are moving beyond the dichotomy of flow or stasis in a novel and insightful way. Latham *et al.* identify the 'paradigm' as well and make a rather interesting and balancing statement in their introduction to key concepts in urban geography. Thus they argue that

> Exactly where the mobility paradigm's conceptual propositions will take urban research is unclear. The turn towards mobility within the social sciences in general – and urban geography in particular – is still relatively recent, and the mobility paradigm remains a diffuse and rapidly evolving intellectual movement. Nonetheless ... the mobility paradigm has helped to re-energise and reanimate urban geography.
>
> (Latham *et al.* 2009:34)

My interest is to link the 'turn' to empirical research focusing on mobilities as social interaction on the one hand, and the design of sites, places and venues for mobile practices on the other. So this work must be understood as localised within the 'turn' but with a new and different focus. Also, I recognise a eurocentric tendency within the turn (Jensen 2009b) but I am sure that it is on the retreat. Vannini also identified the European centrality of research within the 'turn' (Vannini 2010:112) but this is changing with the establishment of new research infrastructures. Thus to supplement the European-anchored Cosmobilities Network and the research centres in Lancaster (CeMore), Munich (mobil.TUM) and Aalborg (C-MUS), the Pan-American Mobilities Network established in 2009 and the launch of the first North American mobilities research centre – the 'mCenter' at Drexel University, Philadelphia – in 2010 may be promise of a new shift within mobilities research.

Sedentary and nomad thought

According to Cresswell (2006) and Kaufmann (2002), there is a fundamental dividing line between, on the one hand, side theories seeing mobilities through the lens of place, roots, spatial order and belonging. Such thinking is termed 'sedentary' and understood as based upon a distinct 'sedentary metaphysics' (or ontology). On the other hand, we have the nomad conception. In this line of thinking the optics is related to a 'nomad metaphysics' focused on flow, flux and dynamism. As the space within this book cannot do justice to the complex sedentary–nomad dispute only a few short examples will be mentioned here. One of the earliest written accounts for the distinction between nomad and sedentary cultures is the Arab scholar Ibn Khaldûn's '*Muqaddimah*' from 1370 (Khaldûn 2005). The text is marked by racial and religious prejudice (e.g. 2005:59) but is one of the very early accounts for the nomad–sedentary ontology clash. Khaldûn separates 'Bedouin civilisation' from 'sedentary civilisation' (2005:91–98, 263–269). Accordingly, the former is marked by simplicity whereas the latter is marked by luxury. To Khaldûn the Bedouin civilisation is historically prior to the sedentary civilisation, but sedentary culture is the 'goal of civilisation' (2005:285). To Ibn Khaldûn the nomad was seen as an anti-urban, mobile other. This notion of the subversive nomad is in accordance with a number of other academic works pointing at the state-led interest in controllable mobile citizens and subjects. Thus there is a rich literature identifying mobility as deviant behaviour (Cresswell 2006; Morley 2000; Scott 1998). Another example of sedentary thinking is the analysis of urban mobility conducted by Richard Sennett in his insightful book *Flesh and Stone* (1994). Sennett argues that the modern preoccupation with 'circulating bodies' has led to a situation of alienation from the more authentic relations to the environment, as 'the modern mobile individual has suffered a kind of tactile crisis: motion has helped desensitize the body' (1994:255–256). Here we find articulated the idea that mobility leads to a de-sensing, a disembodiment from the real or authentic. According to Sennett, mobility destroys identity:

> As urban space becomes a mere function of motion, it thus becomes less stimulating in itself; the driver wants to go through the space, not to be aroused by it ... the body moves passively, desensitized in space, to destinations set in a fragmented and discontinuous urban geography.
>
> (Sennett 1994:18)

Sennett was theorising what he seems to understand as the socially disintegrating forces of mobilities from the perspective of sociology; similarly, Bauman claims that 'We are witnessing the revenge of nomadism over the principle of territoriality and settlement. In the fluid stage of modernity, the settled majority is ruled by the nomadic and extraterritorial elite' (2000:13). Such arguments are just as common within the realm of architecture where the phenomenology of Norberg-Schulz has for some time been synonymous with seeing mobility and movement as socially eroding mechanisms:

> Whereas the human environment so far has had a structure corresponding to the existential space described above, present-day development seems to favour a new mobility ... an increasing number of people have become physically mobile. Many seem to believe that this development offers possibilities for a richer social interaction ... the Dutch utopist Constant Niuwenhuis has given a particular illuminating image of a mobile world in his 'New Babylon' fantasy ... but such a mobile world, which is not based on the repetition of similarities, in connection with a stable system of places, would make human development impossible.
>
> (Nordberg-Schulz 1971:35)

To Nordberg-Schulz humans have become homeless in a world of movement in a very sedentary and Heidegger-inspired phenomenological frame of analysis (e.g. Heidegger 1927/62; Tuan 1977). Interestingly, much of the sedentary critique of mobilities thinking seems to come from precisely this phenomenological perspective. This needs to be challenged since the key insights of embodiment and 'being-in-the-world' has no logical relation to sedentary underpinnings more than to nomad perspectives. In Chapter 5 I return to this and see how more recent developments within 'post-phenomenological' thinking has developed the capacity to comprehend the human body and its sense making in both stasis and motion without sharing sedentary thought. Kolb counters the sedentary sense of place with a direct address to Nordberg-Schulz:

> I have argued that contemporary places do just what Nordberg-Schulz denied: they gather open relations of nets and links into new modes of non-centered, non hierarchical unity ... Place identity is not all or nothing; we do not have to choose between being rooted in the local soil or wandering in directionless space.
>
> (Kolb 2008:190, 192)

It is not only unnecessary to connect phenomenology with sedentary thought, it also means missing the opportunities for developing a culturally and subjectively sensitive understanding of mobilities – a new 'phenomenology of mobilities', so to speak. Moreover, I fail to see why it is assumed that interest in mobilities automatically makes one a fan of global capital, homogenising non-places and neo-liberal visions of more movement equivalent to 'the good life'. In much sedentary philosophy there is a 'moral geography' as an underpinning value base that rarely becomes articulated, let alone problematised. This is the case, for example, in the best-known of all sedentary theory positions: the 'Chicago School' of urban analysis (Park and Burgess 1925). The founding manifesto written by Park and Burgess exposes an ambivalent understanding of mobility, as, on the one hand, they saw mobility as the lifeblood of 'urban metabolism' (1925:59). On the other hand, they considered mobility as a key factor in moral decay: 'the mobility of city life, with its increase in the number of and intensity of stimulations, tends inevitably to confuse and to demoralise the person' (1925:59). They saw mobility flickering between the ambivalence of being a growth condition and a pathological condition. In the words of Cresswell: 'What is evident in both spatial science and humanistic geography is a very strong moral geography that marginalizes mobility ontologically, epistemologically, and normatively' (2006:32). When it comes to mobility thinking the moral geography of the Chicago School is perhaps best illustrated by the short essay titled 'The Mind of the Hobo' (Park and Burgess 1925:156–160). The sedentary and moral assessment of the nomad 'Hobo' is undisputable: 'All forms of association among human beings rest finally upon locality and local association ... he [the hobo] is not only a "homeless man", but a man without a cause and without a country' (Park and Burgess 1925:159). Putnam's (2000) analysis of the 'bowling alone' phenomenon is another example of contemporary sedentary thinking. In his analysis of American cultural transformation he sees sprawl and mobility as the main eroding forces of community.

However, the antidote to sedentary thinking as we find it in nomad thinking is equally problematic. Some speak of nomad ontology (Natter and Jones 1997) and others of fluid geography (Fuller 1963). According to Deleuze and Guattari (nomad theorists par excellence), the key feature of the nomad is exactly the importance of the 'in-between', the path and the intermezzo:

> The nomad has a territory; he follows customary paths; he goes from one point to another; he is not ignorant of points (water points, dwelling points, assembly points etc.). But the question is what in nomad life is a principle and what is only a consequence ... A path is always between two points, but the in-between has taken on all the consistency and enjoys both an autonomy and a direction of its own. The life of the nomad is the intermezzo.
> (Deleuze and Guattari 1987/2003:380)

In addition, a theorist such as Virilio tends to over-emphasise the fluid and stretches the argument well into the direction of technological determinism

(Virilio 1977/2001, 1991). The basic point of departure for nomad metaphysics is a reversal of the hierarchy between the fluid and the fixed:

> Nomad space is characterised by the dominance of the trajectory of movement (pathway or line) over the destination (node or fixed point). Points are secondary – in as much as one is arrived at only to be left behind. Therefore, the space between points is critical. This functions in contrast to sedentary space that privileges the fixed point over the line.
>
> (Simpson 2006:4)

Nomad metaphysics also underpins a number of binary understandings such as tourists versus vagabonds (Bauman 1998), or the sailor versus the landlubber (Fuller 1963:119), or roots versus wings (Zachary 2000:49). To Fuller, the sailor embeds a dynamic sensibility whereas the landsman is static-minded: 'to the landsman "the East" and "the West" are places, to the sailorman they are directions in which he may move' (1963:120). In a radical praising of the business potential in the new hybrid and global forms of identity constructions Zachary argues for a notion of a 'global Me' (2000:xv). There is a certain rim of methodological individualism to this perspective of Zachary when he claims that 'the freedom to choose one's identity is critical, since the sources of identity are shifting from "belonging" to "achievement"' (2000:49). In an equally individualised and free-floating fashion Poster argues that the individual is dissolved into the networked and electronically mediated virtual realm:

> In the electronically mediated communications, subjects now float, suspended between points of objectivity, being constituted and reconstituted in different configurations in relation to the discursive arrangement of the occasion ... In the mode of information the subject is no longer located in a point in absolute time/space, enjoying a physical, fixed vantage point from which rationally to calculate its options.
>
> (Poster 1990:11–15)

Such radicalised nomad metaphysics do seem a far cry from the everyday realities of most people living in contemporary cities. Poster argues for such radicalised disembedding of the social agent on the basis of Deleuze and Guattari's notion of the post-modern in which individuals are constituted through their place in the circuit of information flows, and where 'staying tuned is the chief political act' (Poster 1990:136). According to Casey, nomad works like that of Deleuze and Guattari overlook the potentials of settled dwellings as in the case of 'built places'. Nomadic circulation represents only a part of the human interaction with environment (Casey 1997:309). I believe we should attempt to get beyond sedentary and nomad thought in our efforts critically to think mobilities. Instead of moral condemnation or uncritical enthusiasm of contemporary mobile practices we need to 'think mobilities critically'. We may be inspired by the sedentary and nomad theories, but in order to capture the mobility practices of contemporary urbanism we need to go beyond these dichotomies. In the words of Casey: 'as between nomadic and sedentary space, we cannot simply choose; it is a matter of "not better, just different"' (1997:308), or as Morley claims, 'sedentarism is far from finished' (2000:14). Equally, to Cresswell the post-modern nomad is a remarkable unsocial being with an abstract, de-historicised and undifferentiated status (2006:55). So here shall be argued for a third position beyond the sedentary and nomad. This attempt to reflect mobilities beyond the sedentary–nomad dichotomy correlate with the insights of relational geographical theory (Massey 1994:154). This is the case, for example, when the 'trajectory' and the 'route' comes to foreground in Massey's conceptualisation of the way spatio-temporal practices constitute places in a complex web of flows: 'You are, on that train, travelling not across space-as-surface ... you are travelling *across trajectories*' (2005:118–119; emphasis original). There is hardly much to be gained from wanting to take sides with either the nomad or the sedentary positions. In the words of Dovey, 'The task is not to decide between an architecture of roots or wings but to understand that it is always both' (2010:24). The need to move beyond sedentary and nomad thoughts is important and should rather be based on ideas about relational geography, network cities and a mobility-oriented perspective on places.

Cities as networks: places as assemblages

One of the most widely used metaphors for the contemporary societal changes is perhaps the notion of the 'network society' (Castells 1996, 1997; Graham and Marvin 2001). Cities and urban spaces are criss-crossed by flows of information, people, goods and powers thereby invalidating an understanding of cities as fixed and static 'built environments'. Obviously cites are spatial entities with a morphology and structure of permanence. The thing is, however, that by shifting the focus to the way that mobility defines places we get a much more sensitive understanding of what is going on in and between cities (Borja and Castells 1997:23). A further vital dimension of the 'network city' is the decreased importance of nation-state boundaries coupled with increased transnational inter-urban connectivity and interaction (Brenner 2004; Jensen and Richardson 2004). For example, within the European Union this trend of transnational metropolitanisation is increasingly fuelled by the Union's support for particular mobility-oriented urban mega-regions like the Swedish–Danish Öresund region. Such mega-regions constructed across the nation-state boundary by the chief means of a fixed link – being part of the Transeuropean Transport Net – illustrate the new role of urban agglomeration within the (increasingly) seamless European 'space of flow'. Or what has been termed the 'Europe of monotopia', which is:

> an organising set of ideas that looks upon the European Union territory within a single overarching rationality of making a 'one space', made possible by seamless networks enabling frictionless mobility ... a space of monotopia. By this we mean an organised, ordered and totalised space of

zero-friction and seamless logistic flows ... The future of places and people across Europe seems closely linked to the possibility of monotopia.

(Jensen and Richardson 2004:3)

The urban nodes, within the transnational urban system in the European Union, are evidence of a new global networked condition for the cities and urban nodes. The cities emerge in a new transnational scalar dynamic. However, this is not the city as a bounded unit but the 'city as a node in a grid of cross-boundary processes' (Sassen 2000:146). As a further development within contemporary urban theory there is a debate on the application of the notion of 'assemblage' to the field. The idea of cities as assemblages may be said to express an elaboration of the notions of the network city laid down decades ago. Farias frames the general discussion in the following manner:

> The notion of urban assemblages in the plural form offers a powerful foundation to grasp the city anew, as an object which is relentlessly being assembled at concrete sites of urban practices or, to put it differently, as a multiplicity of processes of becoming, affixing sociotechnical networks, hybrid collectives and alternative topologies. From this perspective, the city becomes a difficult and decentered object, which cannot any more be taken for granted as a bounded object, specific context or delimited site. The city is rather an improbable ontological achievement that necessitates an elucidation.
>
> (Farias 2010:2)

The application of assemblage theory to mobilities studies fit with the more design-oriented perspectives coming from architectural scholars such as Varnelis and Easterling. To Varnelis, the network city assembled by multiple entities comes together in 'networked ecologies' which are defined as:

> A series of co-dependent systems of environmental mitigation, land-use organization, communication and service delivery ... [being] networked, hyper-complex systems produced by technology, laws, political pressures, disciplinary desires, environmental constraints and a myriad of other pressures, tied together with feedback mechanisms.
>
> (Varnelis 2008:15)

To Easterling such understanding of assembled mobilities leans on a particular understanding of infrastructure that underpins the material as well as the cultural dimension to contemporary mobilities:

> While infrastructure typically conjures associations with physical networks for transportation, communication, or utilities, it also includes the countless shared protocols that format everything from technical objects to management styles of the spaces of urbanism – defining the world as it is clasped

and engaged in the space of everyday life. Infrastructural space is, as the word suggests, customarily regarded as a hidden substrate – the binding medium or current between objects of positive consequence, shape, and law – yet it is also the point of contact and access, the spatial outcropping of underlying laws and logics.

(Easterling 2011:10)

McFarlane argues that the notion of assemblage is helpful to capture the indeterminate, turbulent and processuality of socio-material phenomena (McFarlane 2011:5). Moreover, the assemblage theories applied to urban studies make it evident that a sedentary and fixed notion of 'scale' is unhelpful to say the least (see also Ek 2012 for this position):

a sense of scale is not simply about reach: it is also about how resonant affects move and circulate between closely packed bodies moving together and differently. And the intensity of scale is also a matter of duration: not just a matter of how long an event lasts, but of how the temporality of an event registers differently in moving bodies.

(Latham and McCormack 2010:67)

From the vantage point of urban design and architectural theory, Dovey argues that: 'assemblage theory has the capacity to heal the breach in design thinking that separates question of expression from those of materiality, a particular problem in architectural theory' (2010:17). The assembled infrastructures modify and interact with the human body and sensations as the person moves and thus affords particular motions, directions, speeds, modes, temporalities and routes. This perspective relates to ideas about 'assemblages', large technical systems and actor-network theories in urban studies and mobilities research (e.g. DeLanda 2006; Deleuze and Guattari 2003; Farias and Bender 2010; Graham and Marvin 2001; Hård and Misa 2008; Jensen *et al.* 2007; Latour 1996, 2005; Thrift 2008; Valderrama and Jørgensen 2008; Valderrama 2010; Varnelis 2008). The key issue is how such 'systems and networks' assemble human and non-human agents in an attempt to create and 'stage' mobilities. Coming from a theoretical perspective of a 'relational and mobility oriented' understanding of places (Jensen 2009a) I argue that mobilities are being created and afforded in 'Critical Points of Contacts' (Jensen and Morelli 2011). A 'Critical Point of Contact' (CPC) is a feature of the 'network society' (Castells 1996) in which there are multiple points of interaction and meetings between all sorts of networks from technological communication systems like the Internet to the street corner where traffic is being mediated by electric traffic-light controls. A CPC concerns nodes that connect and work as meeting points between systems that makes a difference. That is to say that some points of contacts are more interesting than others and this is what makes them 'critical'. Seen this way, a CPC may work as gateways or switches that become 'critical' by referring to a particular value or yardstick as, for example, risk, volume, economic output, equal access,

The mobile city 33

technical efficiency, density, volume, friction or strategic importance. Again this may have repercussions for the CPC's ability to function as facilitating exclusion or inclusion, access or inaccess. CPCs become critical when the one system changes/influences the conditions of the other as where entities, flows and qualities are modified as a consequence of the CPC. For example (and as we shall see in more detail in Chapter 8), when I become a passenger by a function of the CPC made by the metro station and my economic resources and other capabilities to embark by navigating and using the information displayed at signs in the system. Or, in the words of Ron Scollon, 'some actions are more interesting than others. These are "rubber meets the road" actions where multiple geographies are coupled through the action' (2008:18). Seeing the urban and the networks affording mobilities through the lens of assemblages and CPCs opens up to new insights and a critical gaze at key concepts such as 'scale' and 'place'.

Mobilities: between places and networks

Mobilities in the sense of the physical movement of humans, goods, information, capital, symbols etc. can hardly be underestimated in relation to the contemporary city or, put differently, 'circulation is a paradigm of modern urban life' (Hård and Misa 2008:10). My point is that a city cannot be understood if its external connections (e.g. motorways, Internet connections, airport connections or waterways) and its internal connections and networks (e.g. ring roads, bike lanes, light rail or subways) are excluded from the analysis. The networked connectivity is a key feature not only of an urban agglomeration's functional transport system but, equally importantly, of its urban culture. Such a framing takes its point of departure in a 'relational and mobility-oriented sense of place' (Jensen 2009a) and would resonate with Urry's definition of place as:

> a set of spaces where ranges of relational networks and flows coalesce, interconnect and fragment. Any such place can be viewed as the particular nexus between, on the one hand, propinquity characterised by intensely thick co-present interaction, and on the other hand, fast flowing webs and networks stretched corporeally, virtually and imaginatively across distances.
> (Urry 2000a:140)

This means that a place (or a city) must be comprehended in its relative placement within a network of flows of goods, people, cars etc. However, this does not mean that 'everything flows', that places lose their importance or that technology determines the social (Simonsen 2005:38). Rather it means that one must understand the relational configuration of a place in a network which partly defines the place 'positively' by supplying flows of goods and people etc. and partly defines it 'negatively' by not being coupled to networks or by being by-passed due to topological, technical or political and economic reasons. Thereby the city is defined by its relational coupling or decoupling to a network without fixed scale. As Henri Lefebvre pointed out already, even a house in all its static majestic singularity is only truly comprehended if we include the manifold flows of light, electricity, water, sewer systems etc:

> Consider a house, and a street, for example. The house has six storeys and an air of stability about it. One might almost see it as the epitome of immovability, with its concrete and its stark, cold and rigid outlines. (Built around 1950: no metal or plate glass yet). Now, a critical analysis would doubtless destroy the appearance of solidity of this house, stripping it, as it were, of its concrete slabs and its thin non-load-bearing walls, which are really glorified screens, and uncovering a very different picture. In the light of this imaginary analysis, our house would emerge as permeated from every direction by streams of energy which run in and out of every imaginable route: water, gas, electricity, telephone lines, radio and television signals, and so on. Its image of immobility would then be replaced by an image of a complex of mobilities, a nexus of in and out conduits. By depicting this convergence of waves and currents, this new image, much more accurately than any drawing or photograph, would at the same time disclose the fact that this piece of 'immovable property' is actually a two-faceted machine analogous to an active body: at once a machine calling for massive energy supplies, and an information-based machine with low energy requirements. The occupants of the house perceive, receive and manipulate the energies which the house itself consumes on a massive scale (for the lift, kitchen, bathroom etc.).
>
> (Lefebvre 1974/91:92–93)

Such a point of departure is inherently related to a number of key positions within human geography and mobility studies. From the relational sense of place seen in Cresswell (2006) and Massey (2005) to the socio-technical systems highlighted by Latour (2005), Ek (2012) and Farias and Bender (2010) over the network-city analysis by Castells (1996) and Graham and Marvin (2001) to the explicit mobility theory in Adey (2010), Elliott and Urry (2010), Jensen (2009a), Sheller and Urry (2006) and Urry (2000a, 2007) – these all converge into a perspective of a 'relational and mobility-oriented sense of place'. The key thinker within geography, Nigel Thrift argues that the notion of 'place' is challenged as a consequence of the shift in focus to mobilities: 'What is place in this new "in-between-world"? The short answer is – compromised: permanently in a state of enunciation, between addresses, always deferred. Places are "stages of intensity", traces of movement, speed and circulation' (1996:289). Equally, the philosopher David Kolb questions the moral geographies of sedentary place understandings that have evolved from the automatic critique of undesired phenomena such as 'sprawl'. However, combating uncontrolled and unsustainable growth should not be based on a sedentary notion of place:

> places today should be evaluated according to criteria of linkage and complexity rather than classic authenticity and centered unity … there is no

doubt that many newer places have little to recommend them aesthetically. But they remain places shaped by social norm and expectations.

(Kolb 2008:vii, 8)

The places of today are perhaps less in accordance with moral and aesthetic codifications from the golden days of modernist planning and architecture. Nevertheless, they are sites of interaction and 'staged mobilities' in the everyday lives of billions of people.

Having said this, however, there seems to be less attention given to how urban everyday-life mobility is produced and re-produced as a 'staging' of events and how the concrete lived urban life is dependent on a long line of serial microscopic interaction orders to succeed. Dahl argues in his 2008 book *Den Usynlige Verden* ('The Invisible World') that the 'trivial' acts we perform, for example in what he terms 'Transport Denmark', are lacking meta-processing. By this is meant that we tend to overlook the ordinary and trivial experiences with transportation and mobility in everyday life. This is not least due to the fact that we lack concepts and language to describe mundane things like buying a ticket, standing in line, entering a train compartment, being stuck in traffic etc. Precisely this lack of meta-processing and concepts for these central but overlooked social practices is in line with the ambition of the *Staging Mobilities* framing.

The city of armatures and enclaves

One of the most distinct conceptual divisions in urban analysis is whether to put emphasis on the buildings or the 'spaces in-between', as it were. A way of opening this up towards mobilities is to look at Shane's distinction between 'armatures' and 'enclaves'. In his discussion of urban design Shane argues for the use of Lynch's concepts of the 'armature' and the 'enclave' as key categories (Shane 2005, 2011). Shane offers an interesting and wide-ranging description of the concepts on his way to diagnosing the contemporary urban situation as one that calls for a 'recombinant urbanism'. According to Shane, the main features of armatures are that they are 'linear systems for sorting sub-elements in the city and arranging them in sequence' (2005:199). Accordingly, armatures are channelling flows and linking nodes in complex networks of distribution (Figure 2.1).

They work as sorting and sequencing devices, and may come as linear, stretched and compressed or even as rhizomic armatures. The armature is the backbone of any network and is scalable from the pavement to the global flight corridors. On the other hand, we find the enclave, which, apart from functioning as the bounded territory, is also defined by its ability to add friction to mobility: 'All enclaves centre, slow down, and store urban flows and energies, forming temporary node structures. The emergence of enclave recognition is fundamental to the urbanization and settlement process' (Shane 2005:176). The enclave may therefore be understood as a relatively bounded entity and may come in the form of an isolated district or enclosed site and territory (Figure 2.2).

Figure 2.1 City of armatures.

Figure 2.2 City of enclaves.

However, enclaves may also differ in their relative openness to their context. They are found from hermetically sealed-off sites to permeable places criss-crossed by the flows of armatures. One particular important feature is the difference in speed that the enclave offers compared to the armature. Enclaves are sites of friction and relative slowness. Like armatures they may perform in various guises: as linear, stretched and compressed enclaves:

> The city works, despite its mythology of speed, to slow down people and to bring them together in spectacular assemblies, either as individuals face to face or as great masses. The city provides a multitude of slowing down functions in special enclaves attached to its clogged armatures of transportation and communication (where the pace is further slowed, even to a halt).
> (Shane 2002:234)

For a long time the enclave has been seen as the urban rationale. It was in the bounded and sealed-off centre of the concentric city that the enclave marked the functional and symbolic core. Cities (and more generally human habitats) have been understood as enclaves and from the early ages of nomadic civilisations movement between enclaves has been seen as a necessary evil. This is probably not the case in the 'true' nomadic societies (whatever that may be) where the movement is the actual life and not some stage that needs to be overcome. However, this way of thinking about mobilities has been left as the relative hierarchy of the concepts has clearly given predominance and hegemony to the enclave. The armatures of the nomadic tribes (e.g. paths between habitats for the livestock – which themselves are mobile creatures) have not been able to compete with the symbolic importance of the bounded place. This can be seen in, for instance, attempts to symbolically communicate the power-holder's hegemony by establishing bounded quarters or gated communities, or by having the church or the castle as the central enclave of power. Needless to say, the enclave in form of the city and the bounded place still makes sense. However, understanding flows in the 'City of Armatures' means that contemporary urban transformations challenge the established predominance of enclaves over armatures.

In accordance with the research strategy of *Staging Mobilities* we need not only theory, but also operational methods and approaches to empirical analysis. I shall therefore end this chapter by putting more emphasis on the ways we might explore mobilities and the contemporary city. In other words, how might we investigate the staging of mobilities?

Exploring the mobile: mobile methods

As we saw in Chapter 1, the *Staging Mobilities* framework puts emphasis on the staging dynamics by systems, regulatory frameworks, design etc. as well as the staging amongst mobile subjects. This tension was framed with a scoping of three analytically distinct dimensions: the physical settings, material spaces and design; the embodied performances; and the social interactions. The advocacy for studying mobilities '*in situ*' or a 'mobile situationism' links to some of the many manifestos for what to study and how. One of the first attempts to frame the 'mobilities turn' as a coherent research agenda was made by Urry in his aforementioned seminal work *Sociology beyond Societies* (2000), which has had a profound impact not only on this book but as a key framing text for the whole 'mobilities turn'. In his book Urry links to the discipline of sociology as both the intellectual background of the 'mobilities turn' as well as something that represents confinement and narrowing. In respect to the latter this is related to the lack of real understanding of space and material practices within sociology as well as the limited value of seeing societies in a national perspective in an age of global connectivity. However, in praise of the relationship to sociology Urry uses the paraphrastic reference that Giddens made to Durkheim in the book *New Rules of Sociological Method* (Giddens 1976). The title of the book was a comment on Durkheim's classic text on the 'rules' of sociological methods (Durkheim 1982). From Durkheim over Giddens, Urry ends up with a set of 'more new rules of sociological method'. Adapted from Urry (2000a:18–19), a new and mobility-oriented social science should:

- develop a sociology focusing upon movement, mobility and contingent ordering;
- examine effects of corporeal, imagined and virtual mobilities of people;
- consider things as 'social facts';
- embody the analysis through including the sensuous constitutions of humans and objects;
- investigate the uneven and diverse reach of networks and flows;
- examine temporal regimes and modes of dwelling and travelling;
- describe the bases of people's sense of dwelling and their dependencies upon various mobilities;
- comprehend the changing nature of citizenship, rights and duties;
- illuminate the increased mediatisation of social life and their 'imagined communities';
- investigate the changing powers and determinations of state powers;
- explain changes within states' regulating mobilities;
- interpret chaotic, unintended and non-linear social consequences of mobilities;
- explore if there is an emergent global and autopoietic system.

Furthermore, Urry argues that mobilities research should concern itself with five interdependent forms of mobilities: corporeal travel, movement of objects, imaginative travel, virtual travel and communicative travel (2007:47). Taken together, Elliott and Urry (2010:15–20) summarise the key concerns of the 'mobilities turn', which I list as follows:

- Social relationships should be seen as involving diverse 'connections' that are more or less 'at-a-distance'.

- Social relations stem from the five interdependent mobilities.
- Physical travel involves embodied, sensed and performed practices.
- People physically travel to connect face-to-face.
- The different social practices of contemporary mobility each involves specific sets of network capital.
- Distances generate massive problems for the sovereignty of modern states.
- The social and the natural, as well as the social and the technological, cannot be separated.
- Different surfaces and objects provide affordances for different mobilities.
- Carbon-based mobility systems are producing substantial inequalities between people and places.
- All societies are organised around a hegemonic system of circulation.
- The various mobility systems and route-ways linger over time.
- Mobility systems are based on increasingly expert forms of knowledge.
- Systems of mobilities create immobilities and multiple fixities.

What seems to be more and more evident following the work of Urry is partly an increased awareness of the bleak perspectives following carbon-based mobilities technologies (Dennis and Urry 2009; Urry 2011) and an increased focus on 'systems' and the ways these interlock and interact in complex and often unforeseen ways. Merriman and Cresswell (2011) rightly argue that not all the work coming out of the 'mobilities turn' can be seen as 'new' and groundbreaking. Thus they argue that human geography has been occupied with many of the issues relaunched as new by the 'mobilities turn'. There may be some truth to this. However, there are new ways of combining ideas and approaches on the agenda as well. There are, of course, a number of other important and influential thinkers in this field as well. One of these is Cresswell, who writes from the perspective of human geography rather than sociology. Already in his introduction to 'place' (Cresswell 2004), there are clear links to an understanding of mobility and relational thinking. In his book *On the Move* (2006) the most coherent perspective is presented, but what I shall refer to here is the shorter text published later. In this, Cresswell advocates that we should ask the following six key questions (2010a:22–26):

- Why does a person or thing move?
- How fast does a person or thing move?
- In what rhythm does a person or thing move?
- What route does it take?
- How does it feel to be moved/be moving?
- When and how does it stop?

In particular, the question 'how does it feel?' deserves intensified attention and will be given such in the *Staging Mobilities* perspective in order to uncover the ways mobilities are creating signification, culture and meaning to mobile subjects. In this context I should like to add another couple of key questions such as:

with whom does the entity move, and facilitated by what technology/infrastructure? Also, one may list a set of issues that to some degree cross and overlap with these, arguing that we should discriminate (inspired by Lynch 1980) between what we may term 'muscular powered mobility modes' (e.g. walking, biking, running, swimming, riding) versus 'machine powered mobility modes' (e.g. car, motorbike, plane, train, bus, ship). Equally, we may draw a distinction between 'mobility armatures/channels' (e.g. pavements, roads, paths, highways, networks) versus 'mobility nodes' (e.g. terminals, large buildings, crossings). From these themes the focus is both on sites and places hosting flows and mobility, as well as on 'how flow takes place'. Most of these questions and dimensions presented until now have been of an ontological nature or related to the epistemology of theorising mobilities. There are, however, also the very important questions related to the methods of mobilities research (see Fincham *et al.* 2010). Bücher *et al.* (2010) identify what they term a 'dozen mobile methods' (2010:7–12), which I summarise as follows:

- observing people's movements ('follow the people');
- participating in patterns of movement (e.g. 'walking with', 'travelling with');
- mobile video ethnography;
- time–space diaries;
- virtual mobility through texting, websites, blogging, emails etc.;
- art and design interventions and experiments;
- mobile positioning methods (e.g. GPS);
- capturing 'atmosphere';
- researching mobile memories (e.g. souvenirs, postcards, letters etc.);
- mapping 'real' places;
- examining conversations of the mobile situation;
- researching slowing-down, redirecting and friction places and routes.

In this book I shall explore some of these methods, though not all of them. Not because some are less relevant to mobilities analysis, but simply as a limitation to what I have been able to accomplish so far (as I write I am engaged in research projects using GPS, heat-sensitive cameras and other tracking technologies, but these results are yet too preliminary to reach the pages of this book). These lists are all dimensions of the *Staging Mobilities* framing that put situational practices at the centre of analysis and explore the many modes, routes, technologies, artefacts, speeds and practices in relation to physical settings, material spaces and design; embodied performances; and social interactions.

Staging Mobilities: towards 'critical mobilities thinking'

The research engaged with under the label of *Staging Mobilities* draws upon a number of distinct elements that will be explored in depth in chapters to come. However, we may start by acknowledging that the *Staging Mobilities* perspective grows out of what I have elsewhere termed 'critical mobilities thinking'. By this I mean that mobilities research should have:

> A focus on the critical issues related to social phenomena like power, social exclusion, and mobile justices. But it also means being critical about the taken-for-granted understanding of mobility, as for example a cost-full and rational minimization of travel distance from point A to point B. Critical mobilities thinking means that we have come to see that our lives are not just what happens in static enclaves, but also in all the interstices and the circulation in-between places.
>
> (Jensen 2009b:xvii)

To put matters overly simply, 'critical mobilities thinking' thus has two key dimensions. On the one hand it includes what I term the 'dark sides' of mobilities (see Flyvbjerg 1996 for an elaboration of the notion of 'dark side', which was initially coined as planning theory engaged with Nietzsche's notion of 'real rationality' and power). This is a normative concept for sure, and has to do with issues of power, social exclusion, marginalisation and segregation as well as systems breakdown, failure, disruption, shock and crisis (Graham 2010, 2011). The other dimension has to do with what I term mobilities 'potential thinking' and links to more innovative and novel ways of thinking about mobilities. The pretext for such thinking must grow out of a critique of seeing mobilities as simply instrumental movements or unnecessary evils. If mobilities are cultural and more than just A to B, there are unexploited potentials to be harvested (anything from new business opportunities to human flourishing and more meaningful forms of social interaction). To reflect upon mobilities from the point of view of 'critical mobilities thinking' is thus to include both the 'dark sides' of mobilities and 'potential thinking'. The ambivalences of mobilities are prevalent in multiple dimensions of contemporary society and in this work I want to point to the 'situated mobilities' as the field of enquiry that tie these dimensions together.

The analytical perspective of *Staging Mobilities* means paying specific attention to three areas of contemporary mobile practices. The underpinning and key logic is to always return to the specific situation. I am interested in understanding concrete and tangible mobilities '*in situ*', not abstract and imaginary concepts. Furthermore, this is undertaken from the perspective of social research, thus in one respect foregrounding 'the social' by paying particular attention to the situational relationship between mobilities and social interaction. However, much inspired by relational geography, theories of socio-technical systems and assemblage theory I shall include networked technologies in the analytical perspective, claiming that understanding the nature of mediated mobilities becomes an increasing challenge to contemporary mobilities research. Moreover, there is a distinct lack of putting the 'material' at the centre in the literature. Often the material and physical dimension is said to be important but when it comes to actual analysis the grip slackens. *Staging Mobilities* will as a consequence of the situational focus always put material space, physical settings and design centrally. In prolongation of such material and situational emphasis I shall argue that as important as the sites and material spaces are, so are the embodied performances of humans in motion. The *Staging Mobilities* perspective may omit certain themes and issues as no framing can meaningfully include everything. Starting and ending '*in situ*' is, however, a research strategic and epistemological choice as much as it is a signifier of the ontology at play.

I shall now move on to the section elaborating on the three dimensions of the framing. The first concerns the discussion of material spaces and design in Chapter 3.

Part II
Framing mobilities

3 Physical settings, material spaces and design

> Travelling is traditionally considered an unfortunate necessity, a 'waste of time' to be minimized. Yet recreational travel is widespread, and ordinary routes could easily be designed to make travelling a delight, and not just a necessity.
>
> Kevin Lynch, *City Sense and City Design*, 1990, p. 779

> In fact there is an art of relationship just as there is an art of architecture. Its purpose is to take all the elements that go to create the environment: buildings, trees, nature, water, traffic advertisements and so on, and to weave them together in such a way that drama is released. For a city is a dramatic event in the environment.... It is a tremendous human undertaking.
>
> Gordon Cullen, *The Concise Townscape*, 1996, pp. 7–8

Introduction

In this chapter I shall focus on the physical dimension and the material settings of the mobile situation. In particular I will use this opportunity to consult theories and concepts developed primarily within urban design and architecture, as this to a very high degree either has been a neglected dimension to social sciences or it has been done with less helpful results. The claim is therefore that by consulting the disciplines occupied with shaping the material form and design of the build environment, we shall enrich the mobilities perspective in general and the *Staging Mobilities* framework in particular (obviously human geography will be present as well, but even this 'spatial discipline' might benefit from interaction with more design-oriented perspectives). A word of caution is in order here, since I cannot possibly do justice to all the relevant literature. Some of this will be dealt with in the accompanying book to this work titled *Designing Mobilities*. Here I have chosen to use the work of one theorist as the basis for discussion, although many others will be chiming in. Just as the general *Staging Mobilities* framework relies heavily on Goffman (though many others are included as well), so this chapter shall have American urban designer and city planner Kevin Lynch as its centre of gravity. The works of Lynch are relevant in this context since he was very much oriented towards the practices and situations taking place in cities and the built environment. Furthermore, his view of mobilities (though not, however, using the term) recognised these as much more than instrumental movements from A to B, thereby tying in with the underpinning assumptions of the *Staging Mobilities* framework. Moreover, the sensitivity to sociological perspectives of urban life as being staged was not alien to Lynch's thinking. All in all, Lynch serves as a good guide for this discussion and as an operational point of departure.

The structure of the chapter is as follows. After this introduction, the next section discusses how material spaces and design influences mobilities as seen from the perspective of urban designers and city planners. The works of Lynch in particular, but also those of Lawson, Hall, Whyte, Gehl and Sommer and others, will inform this discussion. In the third section the notion of semiotics as the communicative and interpretative layer of the built environment in particular will be dealt with. The chapter ends with a general summary and conclusions on how all of this comes together in the *Staging Mobilities* framing.

Mobilities, urban design and city planning

As shown in Chapter 2 the advent of the 'mobilities turn' challenges key notions such as space and place. This is partly related to the new way of thinking within the 'turn' and partly also due to relational geographical perspectives (see more on this in Chapter 6). In this chapter I want to move more in the direction of urban designers, city planners and architects since they have a very tangible and material perspective on the city and its circulations. Here I shall consult Whyte (1988), Sommer (2007), Gehl (1971/96, 2010), Lawson (2001) and Lynch (1981), to mention the central thinkers. To Lawson, who is both an architect and a psychologist, space mediates social life and in ways that are crucial to mobilities: 'The space that surrounds us and the objects enclosing that space may determine how far we can move, how warm or cold we are, how much we can see and hear, and with whom we can interact' (2001:15).

As we think of 'stages' and 'settings' for the situation it is, however, very important not to reify and understand place and space as static backgrounds to dynamic actions. Rather the socio-spatial relation is dynamic and our material environment becomes part of the situations and actions in complex ways (Shields 1991). Places must be seen relationally and as shaped by mobilities and immobilities, just as actions by agents are highly dependent on the materiality of the situation, which, we learn from assemblage theories, means that settings are not just 'passive' and human agency not the only 'active' force shaping situations. In addition to this perspective of mobilities, we look at complex interactions across time and space that challenge the perception of place as solid and fixed and mobilities as fluid and detached. Humphry Osmond coined the notion of 'sociofugal' and 'sociopetal' spaces as one way of addressing this complexity (Hall 1966:108; Lawson 2001:140; Sommer 2007:173). Sociofugal places are those that distribute and 'push' people away. Conversely, sociopetal sites and places seem to 'draw' people and activities in. Some sites and settings perform and work by 'inviting' people to go there and offer effective, interesting, stimulating or rewarding facilities for their activities. Such settings may in the light of the *Staging Mobilities* framework be thought of as 'mobile sociopetals'. In other words they are sites and settings that are particularly well tuned in getting people to go there and unfold their activities. They could, for example, be a well-functioning public plaza or square where people will go both to transit from one area of the city to another and simply to enjoy the view of others. At times, Grand Central Station in New York, for instance, may perform in this manner. However, the same site and setting may perform as a 'mobile sociofugal' space if it 'pushes' people away or distributes them from its centre of gravity. In normative terms this need neither be good nor bad. Grand Central Station has to distribute people into the wider transport network of Manhattan and the New York region and will therefore have as its prime goal to perform in a sociofugal manner. However, sites and places may also perform sociofugally by their lack of security or aesthetic appeal. Grand Central Station manages to be both a mobile sociofugal and sociopetal at the same time, very much depending on the actual situation. The tourist looking to enjoy the transport spectacle and the mobile ballet is drawn into the concourse of the station at the same time as the everyday commuter is processed and distributed through the site. Or we may think of the urban shopping mall drawing in customers and goods, connecting these various objects and subjects only to recirculate them into the city again (if the economic transaction is successful). Seen this way, everyday-life mobilities are staged by mobile sociofugals and sociopetals offering complex mixtures of staged scenography and staging choreography.

Also, the way Goffman describes the notion of front stage/back stage may be seen as something much more sensitive towards mobilities than a simple static dichotomy between public and private (this distinction will be elaborated on in Chapter 4). In a passage taken from George Orwell, Goffman (1959) describes how the waiter, by moving between the restaurant and the kitchen, has to work in a mobile and highly dynamic fashion with the norms and codes appropriate for each setting. Furthermore, the complex negotiation of mobility cultures and norms in settings that are either sociofugal or sociopetal, front stages or back stages increasingly takes place in sites of human making:

> *both man [sic] and his environment participate in molding each other*. Man is now in the position of actually creating the total world in which he lives, what the ethologists refer to as his biotope. In creating this world he is actually determining *what kind of an organism* he will be.
>
> (Hall 1966:4; italics original)

Even though this is too voluntarist and abstract a notion, there is a point in noting the moment in history where humankind is living in almost totally self-created environments. In light of this, what we are exploring are 'mobile biotopes'. A mobile biotope is defined here as a fully human-created environment for mobilities and living where the mobile practices not only sustain the liveability of the sites and places but are also the outcomes of these environments:

> the city comes alive through movement and its rhythmic structure. The elements are no longer merely inanimate. They play a vital role, they become modulators of activity and are seen in juxtaposition with other moving objects. Within the spaces, movement flows, the paving and ramps become platforms for action, the street furniture is used, the sculpture in the street is seen and enjoyed. And the whole city landscape comes alive through movement as a total environment for the creative process of living.
>
> (Hall 1966:9)

The notion of 'platforms for action' precisely suggests that the 'mobile biotopes' are localities for situated and staged mobilities. Moreover, 'A City must be experienced through movement to come alive in its most unique sense. As an environment for choreography, many dimensions must be considered in the city. First is the dimension of speed' (Hall 1966:193). So the 'mobile biotopes' are sites of staged choreography as well as scenography, as I discussed this distinction in Chapter 1. In general the public spaces of the city must be analysed and understood in relationship to the movement systems, infrastructure and flows of people, symbols, vehicles and goods whose mobilities they mediate. The literature within urban planning and urban design is testimony to this (Carmona *et al.* 2010; Gehl 2010; Krieger and Saunders 2009). Even though urban mobilities take place in human-made 'systems' and spaces, the complex interweaving of multiple systems, networks and technologies together with human and non-human agents dismantles the idea that the isolated mobile subject is fully in control. The self-staged mobilities meet and mingle with systems and designs as well as with other mobile consociates complicating and at times even compromising the notion of the autonomous subject.

Pleasure, fun and flow: urban mobilities in the works of Kevin Lynch

Even though I shall use the work of other theorists in this chapter, there is particular focus on the work of American urban scholar Kevin Lynch. Through a lifelong commitment to urban design and urban planning, the legacy of Lynch is today influential. In particular this chapter will deal with the way he discussed, saw and analysed the role of urban mobilities. The issue had a very central place in his work, though it was not the only theme. The work of Lynch offers an opportunity to challenge mainstream ways of thinking about urban mobilities that often accesses mobilities on the basis of a 'moral geography' of negative judgement. The most illustrative example being the automatic manner in which the notion of 'non-place' (Augé 1995) is uncritically attached to any urban infrastructure space. Here the argument and analysis based upon the works of Lynch offer different and much more nuanced ground – and thus ultimately more insight and knowledge rather than just moral condemnation. Needless to say

Physical settings, material spaces and design 49

there are plenty of uninspiring and socially inactive sites for the contemporary mobile subject. However, the point about studying urban mobilities through the perspective of Lynch is that we may realise that there are (or perhaps could be) other potentials and options. In other words: that things may be different than they appear (Figure 3.1).

Urban morphology and mobilities

In the very definition of a settlement, flows and fluidity are central to Lynch. Although he claims to set aside social institutions in his analysis, it seems clear that his gaze is one of vivid awareness of the socio-spatial dialectics: 'social and spatial structure are only partially related to each other – loose coupled, as it were – since both affect the other only through an intervening variable (the human actor), and both are complex things of great inertia' (Lynch 1981:49). He focuses on what he terms 'patterns of internal circulation' and in relation to this he developed a vocabulary for dealing with the modal choice, circulation pattern, modal separation, management of travel distance and channel prototypes (Lynch 1981:419–436). The length of this chapter does not allow for a more in-depth exegesis of this urban mobilities vocabulary. However, a few central issues shall be drawn out here. First of all, Lynch makes a distinction between mobilities

Figure 3.1 Things might be different than their appearance.

technology and mobilities control. Accordingly, there was a technical continuum from simple and muscle-powered to complex and automated mobility forms (Lynch 1981:419). He focuses on the importance of 'paths' and in particular of the many different path systems, streets, rail lines, canals, promenades and airways (the 'armatures' in Shane's (2005) terminology). According to Lynch, 'paths, the network of habitual or potential lines of movement through the urban complex, are the most potent means by which the whole can be organised' (1960:96). He defines 'paths' as 'Channels along which the observer customarily, occasionally, or potentially moves. They may be streets, walkways, transit lines, canals, railroads. For many people, these are the predominant elements in their image. People observe the city while moving through it' (Lynch 1960:47). Here, however, a more radical stand shall be taken. People not only observe the city whilst moving through it, rather they create and recreate the city by moving through it. Furthermore, the infrastructure was seen as a hierarchical system transcending the urban:

> The major road system is a prime influence on environmental quality at the regional scale. As an instrument of access, a social link, and the viewpoint from which the urban area is actually seen and experienced, the road has a crucial functional, social, and aesthetic impact, and these impacts are interlinked.
>
> (Lynch 1990:212)

Thus the places of the city are constituted by flows and movement as much as by their morphological properties. Thus Lynch argues that the different types of paths are perhaps the most crucial elements of all (1990:69). There are a number of features that makes the urbanite navigate with particular emphasis and usage of the paths. First, there might be a concentration of specialised use or activity along the street (like shopping or amusement). Second, path layout in either of the extremes (width or narrowness) may serve as a pointer. Third, façade characteristics along the path are important to path identity. Furthermore pavement texture, details of planting and proximity to special features are amongst the important features determining the perception of the paths (Lynch 1960:50–51). Thus Lynch did put emphasis on the importance of understanding urban morphology and designing its mobilities layout as a basic feature for the city building discipline. As mentioned, Lynch did see beyond the 'hardware' and understood the city as a complex dialectic relationship between human and environment. Thus the way humans perceive and valorise the physical environment became a critical dimension to Lynch's urban theory. In particular the way urban landscapes were coded and de-coded in a complex process of 'mobile mapping' became a hallmark of Lynch's work.

Mental maps, mobilities and the urban imaginary

Perhaps the best-known work of Lynch, *The Image of the City* (1960), contains a study of the 'mental maps' urbanites carry and navigate by. Cities should be organised and planned according to a notion of 'legibility' meaning a structuring principle according to which the city could be recognised and organised into a coherent pattern. This is particularly important since 'structuring and identifying the environment is a vital ability among all mobile animals' (Lynch 1960:3). Lynch argued that there were five major formal types in which human agents divided the city through perception; path, landmark, edge, node and district (1960:8). Furthermore, any environmental image may be analysed according to its identity, structure and meaning. Thus the research of Lynch in this early work was aimed at understanding how subjects attach meaning to physical attributes and urban characteristics whilst being mobile: 'For most people interviewed, paths were the predominant city elements, although their importance varied according to the degree of familiarity with the city' (1960:49). However, here I shall not dwell on the empirical findings of the case studies as much as I shall explore how Lynch understood the importance of urban mobilities:

> Moving elements in a city, and in particular the people and their activities, are as important as the stationary physical parts. We are not simply observers of this spectacle, but are ourselves part of it, on the stage with the other participants.
>
> (Lynch 1960:2)

The most interesting thing about *The Image of the City* in this context is the main elements that Lynch identifies and their hierarchy. As mentioned, paths, edges, districts, nodes and landmarks make the basic visual vocabulary of the urbanite as she navigates in the city (Lynch 1960:47). Lynch thought of the paths as very important urban features. The path is the space from where people organise their notion and sense of the city. Lynch summarised his analysis of *The Image of the City* under ten form qualities: singularity (or figure-ground clarity), form simplicity, continuity, dominance, clarity of joint, directional differentiation, visual scope, motion awareness, time series and names and meanings (1960:105–108). Of these, 'motion awareness' is the most interesting in this context:

> Motion awareness: the qualities which make sensible to the observer, through both the visual and kinaesthetic senses, his [sic] own actual or potential motion. Such are the devices which improve the clarity of slopes, curves, and interpenetrations; give the experience of motion parallax and perspective; maintain the consistency of direction or direction change; or make visible the distance interval. Since a city is sensed in motion, these qualities are fundamental, and they are used to structure and even to identify, where ever they are coherent enough to make it possible ... with increasing speed, these techniques will need further development in the modern city.
>
> (Lynch 1960:107)

52 *Framing mobilities*

There is an important relationship between moving through the city and the mental maps generated. But even more interesting is the awareness of the bodily mediated and experienced mobile spaces. In his discussion of a language of city patterns, Lynch saw a neglect of time and time-based dynamics in urban theories (apart from traffic studies, which he found suffered from other deficits). In the Lynch's critical words, static urban theories took the wrong point of departure: 'People are located where they sleep. One gets no sense of the tidal rhythms of a city, which are so important to its function and quality' (1981:348).

Urban mobilities as fun and pleasure

Lynch claimed that 'place identity is closely linked to personal identity. "I am here" supports "I am"' (1981:132). However, if 'I am here' relates to 'I am', I would argue that 'I am on my way' (or, equally important, 'I wish I were on my way') seems to be as suggestive to the issue of understanding the relation between mobilities and identity production. To engage with mobilities as a key pointer of social and personal identity means to engage with elements of affect and emotion. One such dimension is pleasure and fun. Much has been written on mobility as a 'right' (Urry 2000a) but mobility as pleasure seems to be a less discussed dimension. But there is an affective pleasure principle at work when urban mobilities work at their best. This was noticed by Lynch as an important impetus to city planning and design:

> Travel can be a positive experience; we need not consider it pure cost. In potential, the access system is a prime piece of educational equipment. It enlarges the individual's reach, but in addition the act of moving through the city can in itself be an enlightenment. Taking advantage of that possibility, especially for children, means opening up the transport system, making is safer and easier to use, providing guidebooks, treating it seriously as an educational opportunity. Travel can be a pleasure, if we pay attention to the human experience: the visual sequences, the opportunities to learn or to meet other people.
>
> (Lynch 1981:274)

Sociologically speaking, the experiential dimension in the 'travel as fun' argument hinges on mobilities based upon other types of rationalities than the standard instrumental rationality (Jensen 2006:154). Lynch and Hack notice that social as well as aesthetic effects of mobilities must be understood and considered in city planning and design (a point just as relevant to the analytical disciplines):

> Wherever people are moving, there are social and aesthetic effects to be considered. The effects occur whenever people go, and not only when they happen to be on foot. In reaction to the horrors of American traffic, we think

Physical settings, material spaces and design 53

of persons as being unrelated to cars, which are mechanical monsters to be kept in tunnels and garages. But cars have drivers.

(Lynch and Hack 1984:202)

Lynch undertook a defence of seeing mobilities as much more than instrumental movement by opening up to the affective and sensed dimensions that he saw neglected in transport research. What Lynch opposed was an instrumental mobilities understanding or what may be termed a 'cost thinking':

> The common emphasis on the cost of travel reflects the underlying assumption that travel is a sheer waste time, an unproductive factor like leather trimmings or coffee breaks. Supposedly everybody hates it, unlike the coffee break. Yet driving for pleasure is the most common form of outdoor recreation in the United States. A pleasant trip in good company through a fine landscape is a positive experience. We might think of travel as a pleasure, rather than a brief and necessary evil. It is possible to provide fine roadscapes, pleasant vehicles, and opportunities for work, entertainment or companionship en route. Walking, cycling, or jogging can be encouraged for reasons of health and enjoyment. The arbitrary division that our culture makes between work and pleasure appears in transportation, just as it does elsewhere. Any comparative measurement of access must account for the benefits of moving, as well as just arriving.

(Lynch 1981:194)

Lynch regretted the tendency for public planning to relate too much to the statistics and the calculus of costs. Thus the notion of 'travel as cost' is embedded within the way transport planners and traffic engineers (and some urban planners) look upon the city (Lynch 1981:193). For urban theories with a particular focus on the city as a space for the production and distribution of material goods, space imposes costs due to the resources required for moving objects around (known within the discipline of geography as 'friction of distance'). To Lynch these theories of the city as an economic engine introduces space as a transportation cost. They work on an assumption of a state of equilibrium and are seen as immanently static (Lynch 1981:331). Amongst these theories were the classic ideas of Christaller and von Thünen. However, to Lynch they assumed the most interesting features of society and space away! They epitomised a way of thinking that was profoundly present in the minds of transportation and urban planners. It was a way of thinking in which 'reducing the transportation time is the ideal, since it is considered to be unproductive and unsatisfying idleness' (Lynch 1981:427). Within this 'cost perception' of urban transportation there was an inbuilt bias prohibiting the planners from seeing a positive potential in urban transport:

> We incline to think that roads and utilities are regretful but necessary – things that should be hidden. Yet the flow system is one of the two basic

attributes of a developed site and has much to do with its interest and meaning. Power lines and highways are components of the landscape; exposed pipes can be handsome.

(Lynch and Hack 1984:206)

Lynch even speaks of the 'educative significance' a properly designed expressway may provide the user, a feature that is rarely realised but which he saw as unexploited potential of urban infrastructure (Jensen 2007b). The issue of the journey having a value on its own in a sensory, aesthetic and perhaps even playful perspective is only one dimension to this understanding. Moreover, Lynch engages with a historic understanding of, for example, streets as more than infrastructures for moving objects: 'The traditional street served many functions beyond that of passage. It was market, workroom and meeting hall ... the public street can be a significant focus for site design. The street is a true community space' (Lynch and Hack 1984:202–203).

In other words, this is an understanding of city streets and armatures that may serve as a primer for rethinking infrastructural design in an age of global travel of high intensity. Here is a clear parallel to the now classic understanding of Jacobs (1961) who saw the street as much more than a traffic space. Furthermore, the notion of the street as a 'community space' resonates with the contemporary debate on the construction of 'new public domains' within urban mobility spaces (Hajer and Reijndorp 2001). There is a parallel to the interpretation of urban travel as 'fun' to the wild urban experiments suggested by people like Cedric Price (2003a, 2003b) and Archigram (1994). Accordingly, urbanism is about creating sites for the eventful, the unexpected and the playful. Even though the theme of this chapter is the (potential) enjoyment of urban mobility, there is no doubt that Lynch kept a critical understanding of the way urban mobilities had been planned for and the many less-successful examples of urban mobilities design:

> Pages could be devoted to terminals, the other essential element of the circulation system. I will do no more than lament the faded grandeur of the city rail road station, the crowded shabbiness of the contemporary bus station, the worldwide confusion and inhumanity of the modern airport, the barren discomfort of the parking lot, and the desolation, disorientation, and terror of any parking garage. Alas, we cannot even find a comfortable place to wait for the bus!
>
> (Lynch 1981:436)

At the end of the day the experiences with urban mobilities may be positive or they may be negative. However, in Lynch's vocabulary and analysis there is the insight that urban mobility is an important activity that produces cultural, social and emotional effects:

> city design can focus on the journeys by which people actually experience cities. City trips are enjoyed or suffered, but they are remembered. The

pleasures of motion, and its connotation of energy and life, are, perhaps, especially meaningful to us today [1984].

(Lynch 1990:503)

Lynch did rudimentarily discuss the potential for urban expressways, for example, to turn into 'public domains' (without using such nomenclature, though). Thus he was aware of the potential of billboards, signs and local radio stations as ways of adding a public sphere to urban infrastructure (Lynch 1990:575). However, the more fully fledged understanding of the potential of urban transportations paths to turn into public domains has only recently begun. As a 'legacy' of Lynch we find works appreciating the non-instrumental understanding of mobilities within the writings of Ingersoll (2006), Waldheim (2006a) and Houben and Calabrese (2003) that are all of interest, but lack of space prevents us from going deeper into them here (I shall refer to some of these in Chapter 9). Rather I will terminate the exploration of the huge topic of physical settings as urban planning and design and look into another dimension of this, namely the semiotic properties that any built environment is related to. 'Reading' sites and spaces as a clue to what sort of practices they are meant to afford as well as how they become embedded in people's everyday practices are as important to mobilities studies as to any other study of human activity in the material world. The semiotic dimension to mobilities studies ties in with both the 'staging from above' dimension (e.g. traffic lights and wayfinding systems) and the 'staging from below' (e.g. people's gestures and bodily postures signalling mobile intentions on the street or the mode of transport choice as a sign of status and social hierarchy). A vital part of *Staging Mobilities* is thus made of the mobile semiotics to which I now turn.

Mobile semiotics

An important dimension of the material spaces and physical settings related to mobilities is the signifying and interpretative dimension. The buildings, sites and infrastructure themselves are nested into socio-cultural practices with underpinning values and norms of the 'correct' mobility practices. Moreover, all material environments may be thought of as semiotic landscapes and sites, either simply because they are coded with signs and signage systems, or because we tend to 'read' them as signs. For example, we do not need to verify that we are in a motorway setting as soon as we observe key features such as separated lanes, large traffic signs and fast-moving vehicles. Or, in a similar vein, many of us know what to do and what to expect as we enter an international airport (although as I shall discuss in more detail in Chapter 4, there are of course people with no such 'mobility skills' and experiences). This section will consider the semiotic dimension of the physical settings, material space and design as an attempt to 'mobilise' semiotics by drawing on a central body of theory within and adjacent to the discipline. The founding works of C.S. Peirce will be related to the contemporary notions of 'geosemiotics' made by Scollon and

Scollon. The environment is 'read' as a semiotic system in order to make sense of the situation at hand as well as how it shapes and affords particular interpretations and action opportunities to the acting individual. In architecture and urban design theory the study of cities and buildings 'as signs' have been discussed for a long time as an option to explore the symbolic meanings of the material environment (see Venturi and Scott Brown 2004; Venturi *et al.* 1972; Ellin 1999; Jencks 1969; Nesbitt 1996). This is by no means an attempt to reduce the material and physical world to signs or texts but rather to claim that all our environs need some kind of interpretation to make sense of the key question: 'what is this situation?' These are rather general observations but they relate in an important manner to issues of mobilities since making sense of the world is dependent on movement in itself, and the organisation and orchestration of movement is crucial to the social interactions, cultural engagements and societal dynamics we encounter on a daily basis. In this daily practice there are sites where we see and understand the 'semiotics of mobilities' more clearly than in others (the readability of the great plains with a bush and a path is in principle as related to mobile semiotics as is the urban traffic system, but the semiotic complexity and explicitness of the latter is much higher).

Semiotics is the study of signs and signification in general. Moreover, it is the study of the conditions of potential meaning-production. So semiotics is concerned not so much with what a phenomenon means as how it may mean something (Jørgensen 1993:13). As such semiotics is part of understanding human communication (Fiske 1989), but also at a more profound level part of understanding human knowledge, meaning and culture. Charles Sanders Peirce is seen as one of the founders of semiotics. To him semiotics was a 'form of logic' (1994:93). The art of making sense of signs pre-dates the thinkers involved in this chapter. Most often, classical Greek medicine is mentioned as the birthplace of semiotics. In particular, Hippocrates in the fifth century BCE is cited for having founded medicine on a simple theory of signs connecting symptoms in the patient with an assumption of underlying causes for the illness (Jørgensen 1993:15). There are different trajectories and thinkers to follow within the broad discipline but here I shall take the work of Peirce as the point of departure since the pragmatic philosophy of this perspective lends itself with particular relevance to the study of the material world (Gottdeiner 1995:9; Scollon and Scollon 2003). To Peirce a sign is something that stands to somebody for something in some respect or capacity (Peirce 1994). The sign works according to Peirce as a triadic relation between a sign, an object and an interpretant. Peirce argued that signs may either be icons (defined by their resemblance to an object), indexes (defined by some direct and existential connection with the object) or symbols (where the relation to the object is a matter of social convention) (Peirce 1994:100). Furthermore, the Italian semiotic theorist and cultural analyst Umberto Eco makes a distinction between 'intentio auctoris' (the intention of the 'author'), 'intentio operis' (deciphering the image) and 'intentio lectoris' (the interpretation by the user) in his discussion of visual semiotics (Wagner 2006:313). Here I am interested in the nexus of the intentions derived from the 'sign maker' (staging from above) and the sense made of it from the 'sign reader' (staging from below) with a particular emphasis on the fact that all signs and meanings are materially situated in the world and that the moving human body creates particular challenges and complexities to this 'mobile sense making'. In particular the understanding of how signs and semiotics systems 'create mobile subjectivities' (Richardson and Jensen 2008) is interesting as 'signs turns individuals into crowds' (Fuller 2002:235). Airports are illustrative of the strict control and exercise of power utilising semiotic systems to orchestrate and order mobile bodies in space:

> Signs mean things. They also do things. For instance, a lot of signs at the airport not only 'make meaning' that can be interpreted, they also issue direct commands that must be obeyed. Often, signs work with matter and directly control movement and behaviour. These signs, line links and buttons on computer interfaces, conjoin semiotic and material flows in a world where the informational and the material increasingly stream through each other. The airport is full of signs that deliver 'messages' that we never interpret or question, because they don't deliver information. They deliver access, something we are granted or denied. Our airport semiology documents how airports deliver messages about the contemporary art of logistics.
>
> (Fuller and Harley 2004:126)

This 'performative capacity' of signs can be understood from the perspective of 'speech act theory'. Accordingly, some speech acts bring about change in the world by their ability to create what they name, as they are performative utterances (Austin 1962). In a slightly similar vein certain semiotic systems may 'create mobilities' by their ability to direct, organise and steer the flow of people, goods and vehicles.

Geosemiotics

For the purpose of understanding mobilities as well as in order to connect to the level of social interaction as I find it developed in the theories of Goffman, the 'geosemiotic' perspective is rather ideal. According to Scollon and Scollon, geosemiotics is 'the study of the social meaning of the material placement of signs and discourses and of our actions in the material world' (2003:211). Put very simply, there is a difference between the 'roadworks ahead' sign on the back of a municipal van being moved to the site of its placement and its final destination on a street corner (Figure 3.2). We all know not to pay attention to the sign if we are driving behind the van, but also to do so if we meet it on the street corner. The same sign may even be displayed in a local art gallery and then the relevant frame for making sense of the sign shifts again. Geosemiotics is thereby granting primacy to the 'index dimension' of the sign as we saw it in Peirce's semiotic theory. This is so because,

58 *Framing mobilities*

> Before we can think about *what* we are reading we have to have a principle to tell us *how* to read it ... the first principle in the interpretation of language is to solve the problem of indexability – to locate language in the physical world.
>
> (Scollon and Scollon 2003:6; italics original)

Or, in other words, 'Indexicality is the property of the context-dependency of signs' (Scollon and Scollon 2003:3). The physical and material location of the sign becomes the pivotal point of departure for the analysis since 'all signs must be located in the material world to exist' (Scollon and Scollon 2003:vii). In this respect the perspective also lends itself to mobilities studies as I am interested in how flows of goods and people are orchestrated and coordinated by using signs. A sign thus means 'any material object that indicates or refers to something other than itself' (Scollon and Scollon 2003:3). The signs and the

Figure 3.2 Sign whose interpretation relies on its physical placement.

sign systems not only afford and create circulation, however, they are also distributed across the urban landscape themselves (as when we follow a specific sign giving direction to a location). Geosemiotics connect the visual signs to their physical placement in order to comprehend which actions and interactions are afforded and encouraged as well as which are prevented or obstructed. Thereby the approach bridges different academic disciplines (from linguistics to geography and urban design). This makes it of particular relevance to mobilities studies. More importantly, these assemblages of infrastructure, sign systems, building complexes and commercial and leisure activities are understood from the perspective of the human interacting, situated and moving body (Scollon and Scollon 2003:15). Even beyond this existential level the perception and the ability to 'make sense' of the world (and its signs) meet challenges as we increase the speed of our bodily movement (which again is the explanation for why motorway signage needs large sizes and proportions in order to compensate for the human mind's ability to process data and turn it into information as we move at high speed).

Coming from a theoretical perspective of a 'relational and mobility-oriented' understanding of places, I argue that the signage and semiotics of network systems are important features of the contemporary mobilities landscape. In the words of Fuller: 'an arrow is a sign that has no referent; it assembles movement, it doesn't identify things' (2002:233). In a description of the semiotic systems, Fuller furthermore speaks of 'decision points' as the sites where sign systems mediate physical routes demanding crucial decisions to be made (e.g. 'something to declare?' at customs, or the off ramp on the freeway). At such points, finding one's way requires plotting predictable paths and 'decision' points within the signage systems (Fuller 2002:235). Understanding semiotic systems as collections of 'decision points' parallels the notion of 'Critical Point of Contact' (Jensen and Morelli 2011) that was presented in Chapter 2. The 'decision points' are semiotic CPCs where 'the rubber meets the road', to use Scollon's metaphor. Thus the semiotic system may be understood as a vital part of the urban assemblage facilitating and filtering mobilities (Fuller 2002:238). Or, in the words of Deleuze and Guattari:

> Semiotic systems depend on assemblages, and it is the assemblages that determine that a given people, period, or language, and even a given style, fashion, pathology, or minuscule event in a limited situation, can assure the predominance of one semiotic or another.
>
> (Deleuze and Guattari 1987:119)

The sign system as interface between the orchestration of mobilities 'from above' and lived mobile experiences seen 'from below' is the pivotal point of contact in the *Staging Mobilities* frame that I argue will be useful as an umbrella for the analysis.

Road systems and streetscapes: narratives of mobile semiotics

Here I shall present a few empirical examples of how the built environment hosting mobilities are staged with a prime concern of having signs and semiotics systems affording particular practices as well as preventing others. When the discussion is of road signage systems and the state's attempt to facilitate, order and orchestrate mobility, Wagner (2006) argues that increasing safety by making legible signage systems is the overarching rationale. As road signs often are fully visual and non-linguistic they rely on a high degree of cultural consensus and embedded values. Think of the 'intentio lectoris' meeting the 'intentio auctoris' at 140 km/hour or more! In their seminal work *The View from the Road* (1964), Appleyard *et al*. illustrate the connection between signs and movement related to 'the highway experience':

> The sensation of driving a car is primarily one of motion and space, felt in a continuous sequence. Vision, rather than sound or smell, is the principal sense. Touch is a secondary contributor to the experience, via the response of the car to hands and feet. The sense of spatial sequence is like that of large-scale architecture: the continuity and insistent temporal flow are akin to music and the cinema. The kinesthetic sensations are like those of dance or the amusement park, although rarely so violent.
> (Appleyard *et al*. 1964:4)

Movement on fast road systems is thus an embodied practice where mobile sense making is felt as well as perceived. The semiotic layer of the space is vital for the road user to manoeuvre safely but they also give orientation and have aesthetic properties, all combining into the 'highway experience'. In an analysis of the relation between the road signs and the underlying regulatory frameworks and the cultural appropriation of mobility semiotics, Wagner argues that road signage often is constructed so that 'people are treated as automata' (2006:314). The road signage system thus works from the outside in imposing or 'staging', as it were, preferred behaviour on the subjects. Seen from the perspective of the state a coherent and homogeneous system of road signs creates a system of 'simplifications' (Scott 1998), partly creating an ordered flow space 'staged from above' and partly a unified interpretive frame as acted out upon 'from below'.

With the advent of transnational auto-mobility at the end of the nineteenth century some demand for a unified system of easily comprehensible signs emerged (Wagner 2006:315). Most European countries signed the 'Convention of Paris of 1909' which may be seen as the first step towards regulation of road traffic. The internationally leading regulatory step was made with the 'Convention on Road Signs of Vienna 1968'. In this document it is specified which shapes, colours and texts are appropriate for different types of road signs (Wagner 2006:319). Furthermore, the 'Convention' distinguishes between three categories of signs: danger warning signs, regulatory signs and informative signs (Wagner 2006:320). From these early attempts to codify and stage the semiotic

Physical settings, material spaces and design 61

layer of national road space two key rationales were predominant: facilitation of mobilities and increase in safety (Wagner 2006:315). If we look at commercial signage in either cities or large terminal buildings and shopping centres we see that the circulation of people (i.e. the facilitation of mobilities) is a key feature of mobile semiotic systems there as well. Wagner points to an interesting clash of competing semiotic rationales with the conflict between metric and imperial sign systems in the United Kingdom (Wagner 2006:316). Although under the jurisdiction of the European Union and thus in principle under the regulatory framework of the 'Europe of Monotopia' (that is, the transnational space of seamless flow; see Jensen and Richardson 2004), the UK case is one of local resistance to give up, for example, miles and feet as measures on signs. And conversely, the Republic of Ireland's willingness to adopt European sign regulations is a symbol of its more positive attitude to European integration.

'Beautiful Roads': the staged semiotics of Danish road design

In the Danish Road Directorate's publication *Beautiful Roads* (2002), signage and the semiotic layer is clearly seen as something that road designers must use carefully. In particular, when it comes to roads in the open country, signs are tightly regulated:

> A characteristic feature of Danish freeways is a careful treatment of the landscape and terrain that rarely produces stark contrasts. Signage and other equipment are kept at a minimum and the absence of billboards, art, and other distracting and defacing elements in the road's immediate vicinity emphasizes the desire for clarity and simplicity. Lighting fixtures illuminate feeder lanes and exits, but otherwise there is almost no artificial lighting in the open countryside.
>
> (Road Directorate 2002:27)

In Denmark there has been some debate about the urban and semi-urban development alongside the motorway corridors (Nielsen *et al.* 2005). In general, one might say that there is strong commercial pressure for development and the accompanying semiotic codes that go along with this. However, such wishes for big-box retail spaces and huge billboards are kept down by a rather strict national regulatory framework (Road Directorate 2002:35). In other words there is a 'culture of semiotic restriction' on the most predominant sprawling features of the North American development (big-box retail, large billboards etc.) that seem to work against a full semiotic battle for attention in Danish road spaces:

> There is a firm tradition in Denmark of limiting the use of roadside equipment and the equipment used is standardized and simplified as far as possible. With design aimed at simple systematization and good readability, Danish road signs present clearly understandable messages. One special problem in the open countryside is the demand for readability at great

distances and high speeds. Information signs are consequently often quite dominating and special attention must be paid to where the signs are placed. It is important for how we experience the landscape, the road, or a building that signs be located appropriately in relation to them. We rarely associate suburban roads with design, but they usually do have standardized equipment such as bus stops, benches, fences, lighting fixtures, and bicycle racks.

(Road Directorate 2002:48)

As an important part of the theme of 'physical settings, material spaces and design', I will as mentioned include the networked technologies and ICT systems that are becoming ever more present in contemporary cities. More attention will be given to those in Chapter 6. Here I shall only mention that the software and hardware of complex computerised technologies are important dimensions of material settings for mobile practices. The digital semiotic layer is yet another dimension of the increasing complexity of the physical settings we need to explore when studying situated mobilities.

Concluding remarks

The topic of this chapter is so large and complex that I cannot claim to have dealt with it in a fully comprehensive manner. Rather I have attempted to illustrate that *Staging Mobilities* obviously takes place in physical settings and material spaces that are designed as well as practised. Seen in this way the staging from above as well as the staging from below becomes material and realised in the physical geographies of multiple mobilities systems and practices. I have chosen here to lean on literature less common to the 'mobilities turn' and social science since I believe that it enriches the theoretical perspectives that have developed so far. In the discussion I have established a few new concepts that need to be recontextualised into the *Staging Mobilities* framework. In particular I want to speak of mobile biotopes, mobile sociopetals and mobile sociofugals as illustrations of how the built environment and physical settings are encouraging as well as discouraging particular mobile practices.

Coming from the analysis of the material spaces of mobilities I shall speak of 'mobile biotopes' as the fully human-made inhabited, material and lived sites of mobile everyday life. The term 'mobile biotopes' is part of the language attempting to articulate that mobilities must be understood as meaningful social and cultural practices creating identities and cultures as well as material movement of bodies, goods and vehicles. When examining the concepts of 'mobile sociopetals' versus 'mobile sociofugals' we saw the former as sites and settings that are particularly adept at inducing people to go there and undertake their activities. In contrast the notion of 'mobile sociofugals' designates sites and settings that 'push' people away or distribute them from their centre of gravity. A fair amount of attention has been given to the semiotic dimension of mobilities and material spaces. From this springs the notion of 'mobile semiotics' by which is meant how signs (in the broadest possible sense) afford, process and coordinate (or obstruct) the physical circulation and movement of people, vehicles and goods in more or less codified systems of infrastructure. Moreover, I discussed a 'mobile geosemiotics' as a prolongation of the theoretical fusion of mobilities and semiotics in general (in the term 'mobile semiotics'). I find that the approach from 'geosemiotics' is even more appropriate in terms of analysing mobilities. By 'mobilising' geosemiotics, so to speak, I shall talk about the meaning of material locations as signs are interpreted in motion and that moving makes different interpretations possible. The notion of semiotics ties in with how agents make sense of their environment thus paving the way for a notion of 'mobile sense making'. Here I am thinking of how different mobile interpretations point towards the inclusion of signs into the analysis of mobilities in order to capture the very way mobile subjects understand the environment. I claim then that what takes place is a 'mobile sense making' where signs and meanings materially situated in the world and the moving human body create particular challenges and complexities in making sense of the world. Studying, for example, highway signs we find that there are underlying logics and rationales of specific mobile semiotics such as the quest for more flow, faster movement, coordinated mobility or increased safety which we may term a 'mobile semiotic grammar'. The 'intentio auctoris' (the intention of the 'author') cannot simply be 'read off', as it were, but must be understood in its specific material context. Having said so, an increasing number of semiotic techniques, designs, media, symbols and signs are coming together in an emerging 'mobile semiotic grammar'. Obviously more research is needed to determine how these generic conventions and practices work out but it seems clear that there are in fact a fair number of semiotic expressions that start working for a very large number of people regardless of whether they are international high-flying cosmopolitans, heavy truck drivers or sightseeing tourists. As such this may suggest the establishing of a general and generic 'mobile semiotic grammar'.

None of the empirical cases described in this book can be understood if we do not look at them from the perspective of a theory of assemblages. The systems and socio-technical networks that 'host' contemporary mobilities are complex and large material environments where technologies, humans, software, codes, semiotic and communicative systems, objects and artefacts are assembled in a specific combination facilitating and affording certain practices and restricting or preventing others. So 'mobile assemblages' specific to particular modes of transport mix and relate to the material design and manifestation of contemporary mobilities in ways that must be understood relationally and in semiotic terms. The key issue is how 'systems and networks' assemble human and non-human agents in an attempt to 'stage' mobilities. The semiotic system understood as a vital dimension of the 'mobile assemblages' modify and interact with the human body and sensations as the subject moves and thus affords particular motions, directions, speeds, modes and routes.

What is characteristic of all these concepts is of course that they lend themselves to the analysis of the physical and material settings of mobilities. Moreover, they are aimed at exploring the complex relationship between the way sites and settings afford and invite (or prohibit) particular mobilities through planning, design, regulations etc. as well as how they are appropriated and practised by human agents in their everyday-life mobilities. Returning to the *Staging Mobilities* framework I may summarise this chapter by recognising the very important element of the material and physical spaces of mobilities. This may sound strange or even trivial, but too much mobilities research has failed to be truly sensitive to this dimension. The mobile situations are performed in space and time within material and physical settings that either afford or prevent particular mobilities. The design of such sites of mobilities, the material infrastructures and the technologies working there must be seen as just as important as the social interactions to which I turn in Chapter 4.

4 Facework, flow and the city

> The Street is a stage, and the sense that an audience is watching pervades the gestures and movements of the players on it.
> William H. Whyte, *City: Rediscovering the Centre*, 1988, p. 21

> We exchanged glances on the 405: you were the cute, yellow beetle. I was the black mustang that let you in.
> LA personal ad, in Houben and Calabrese, *Mobility: A Room with a View*, 2003, p. 154

> What kind of social thing is Traffic? For there to be 'traffic' there must be at least two 'vehicular units' that encounter each other and are obliged to take each other into account, even if only to avoid collision … It takes two to traffic.
> Jim Conley, 'A Sociology of Traffic', 2012, p. 222

Introduction

In this chapter, one of the cornerstones of the *Staging Mobilities* framework will be explored in more detail as I engage with the social interactions and situated meetings of mobile subjects. The chapter will in particular relate to the work of Georg Simmel and Erving Goffman as the foundation of the framework (see also Conley 2012 for an additional theoretical framing of mobilities using Simmel and Goffman). The chapter foregrounds the mobile social interaction as a precondition to mobilities. The chapter is structured as follows: following this introduction the next two sections contain thematic re-readings of selected works by Simmel and Goffman. Thereafter, new concepts specific to the *Staging Mobilities* framework are presented. The chapter ends with a discussion and concluding remarks.

There is a strong sense that change is sweeping across the world whenever the topic of conversation is mobilities and global–local relations. Many people are travelling further, faster and more intensively. However, in the midst of this sense of global connectivity and place reconfiguration we still need to pay attention to the way interaction is facilitated in everyday life, as this is what makes up the globalised world. Whether we travel the flight-transit corridors between major city hubs, the mass-transit vehicles of metropolitan public transportation, the sidewalks of the city or the urban freeway we are in the process of engaging and interacting with our consociates. The aim of this chapter is, therefore, to offer a new perspective on mobility in the contemporary city by re-reading the two sociological 'classics', Simmel and Goffman. The point in so doing is that there is a need to comprehend and conceptualise the interaction and everyday level of flow and mobility in the midst of an intellectual climate dominated by grand theories of networks and globalisation (Bauman 1998; Castells 1996, 2002; Graham and Marvin 2001; Harvey 1996).

Approaching an issue like mobilities in the contemporary city from an everyday-life perspective seems to make a lot of sense as we struggle to ground the large and abstract concepts of contemporary sociological analysis in the ordinary life of social beings, where it all takes place. Or, in the words of Simmel:

> But in addition to these [definable, consistent structures such as the state and the family, the guild and the church, social classes and organisations based on common interests] there exists an immeasurable number of less conspicuous forms of relationship and kinds of interaction. Taken singly, they may appear negligible ... To confine ourselves to the large social formations resembles the older science of anatomy with its limitation to the major, definitely circumscribed organs such as heart, liver, lungs, and stomach, and with its neglect of the innumerable, popularly unnamed or unknown tissues. Yet without these, the more obvious organs could never constitute a living organism.
>
> (Simmel, in Wolff 1950:9)

So I shall attempt to shed light on the everyday mobility patterns of the contemporary city, releasing them from being 'unnamed or unknown tissues'.

A mobile reconfiguring of 'the person called I' and 'the place called home'

The new mobilities dynamics influence the practices, experiences and perceptions of place, subjectivity and identity (Kellerman 2006:57). An increase in movement makes us reconsider familiar sites of belonging and the relational geographies making up the near and the distant. This is hardly a new experience. The 'art of travel' (de Botton 2002) and its impact on human perception is widely recognised. However, there is a new dynamic and intensity to be heeded (e.g. due to faster mobility technologies and changed network relations).

To open up the analysis of the mobile reconfigurations of identity and place let us see it through the eyes of German cultural theorist Walter Benjamin. Benjamin's urban writings are not a homogeneous body of thought and neither is the reception thereof (Savage 2000). The main source of inspiration in this context is Benjamin's interest in the embodied practices of the strolling urbanite. Particularly relevant is the preoccupation with the chaotic city and the 'labyrinth' (staging from below) rather than the rational order superimposed on the city dweller (staging from above). To explore this, Benjamin coined the notion of the 'flâneur'. To Benjamin the streets of 1860s Paris indeed constituted a political space as Hausmann's project of demolishing housing blocks and paving the way for the 'grand boulevards' was to secure the city against civil war and the rioting masses (Benjamin 2002:12). In Benjamin's analysis of Paris in particular and the modern city in more general terms he developed the notion of the flâneur as the modern urbanite enjoying the freedom and cultures of the metropolis (for a critique of the gender bias of the flâneur, see Wilson 1991). The flâneur is a drifter in the metropolis, consuming the city with an aesthetic gaze. But the flâneur also embeds a subversive relation to the prevalent notion of urban circulation:

> Trade and traffic are the two components of the street. Now, in the arcades the second of these has effectively died out: the traffic there is rudimentary. The arcade is a street of lascivious commerce only; it is wholly adapted to arousing desires. Because in this street the juices slow to a standstill, the commodity proliferates along the margins and enters into fantastic combinations, like the tissue in tumours. – The flâneur sabotages the traffic. Moreover, he is no buyer. He is merchandise.
> (Benjamin 2002:42)

Pinder points to a similar subversive practice in the Situationist movement and its practice of drifting through the city – the so-called 'dérive' (Pinder 2005:150). So if the streets were populated with 'ordinary' citizens as well as the subversive and joyful flâneur, the armatures themselves also meant more than mere flow channels to Benjamin:

> 'Street' to be understood, must be profiled against the older term 'way'. With respect to their mythological natures, the two words are entirely distinct. The way brings with it the terrors of wandering, some reverberation of which must have struck leaders of nomadic tribes. In the incalculable turnings and resolutions of the way, there is even today, for the solitary wanderer, a detectable trace of the power of ancient directives over wandering hordes. But the person who travels a street, it would seem, has no need of any waywise guiding hand. It is not in wandering that man takes to the street, but rather submitting to the monotonous, fascinating, constantly unrolling band of asphalt. The synthesis of these twin terrors, however – monotonous wandering – is represented in the labyrinth.
> (Benjamin 2002:519)

This resonates with the way Jacobs (1961) saw the street as a site of social interaction as much as a space of circulation (for homage to the sensitivity of Jacobs, see Mikoleit and Pürckhauer 2011). Beyond the bodily movement through the city and thus the sensory experience of urban mobilities, the armature also carries the potential for interaction and culture as, to Benjamin,

> Streets are the dwelling place of the collective. The collective is an eternally wakeful, eternally agitated being that – in the space between the building fronts – lives, experiences, understands, and invents as much as individuals do within the privacy of their own four walls ... More than anywhere else, the street reveals itself in the arcade as the furnished and familiar interior of the masses.
>
> (Benjamin 2002:879)

Here we see an interpretation of the armature as a predominant space of interaction and meaning – a site of cultural expression and performance. The available space in this chapter prevents deeper explorations into Benjamin's analysis but he had a clear awareness of Parisians' 'techniques of inhabiting their streets' and how these made the street an interior (Benjamin 2002:421). The lived armature collapses the interior/exterior and the public/private distinction upholding a promise to become a space of political articulation.

Coming from a perspective like Benjamin's it becomes clear that there is a need to recognise that the impacts of mobilities to our understanding of place, identity and subjectivity has just as much to do with our mundane everyday-life experiences as with the exotic and heroic travellers' tales that make up cultural stereotypes of the meaning of mobilities. In the words of Patton (2004:21), mobilities offers particular 'subject positions' facilitating the construction of mobile subjects: 'People's subject positions are mediated by their habitual activities in moving about the city. The common practice of walking, bicycling, bus-riding, or driving constitute distinctive forms of urban life, each with characteristic rhythms, concerns, and social interactions.' What should be acknowledged is, therefore, the dialectic relationship between place and flow, between global movements and local relationships (e.g. Massey 2005; Morley 2000). In the words of Girot: 'a landscape seen in a variety of speeds and motions introduces a strong sense of relativity to our understanding of established identities' (2006:97). In contrast to the dichotomy of sedentary/nomad, I argue that the fluid and the fixed are relationally interdependent as mobile humans still need fixed enclaves of shelter and home (Mitchell 1999). Furthermore, critical human geography and cultural studies point in a direction of a different way of conceptualising identity and its spatio-temporal embedding. Thus some argue for a 'non-essentialist notion of identity' (Natter and Jones 1997) and a 'fictional status of the subject' (Game 1991:66). To Thrift 'the subject's understanding of the world comes from the ceaseless flow of conduct, conduct which is always future-oriented' (1996:37). Thus the embodied, situational, spatio-temporal and contextual practices create and recreate a sense of self and other. Drawing on the works of Foucault and Bergson, Game argues for a materialist, relational and mobile conception of the subject (1991:61). Accordingly meaning-generating processes are temporal as well as being embodied. When the subject is a relational entity, mobility becomes crucial to notions of identity, as 'the self–other relation is constituted in movement [and] ... movement is bodily' (Game 1991:11, 89). The thoughts of Simmel and Goffman precisely offer the opportunity to connect global flows to the everyday level of social practice, as well as linking more classical sociological theory to contemporary issues of mobilities. The reason to 'look back' is therefore to capture some of the peaks of the past's 'sociological imagination' and relate them to an important social phenomenon of the present. It is to add the insights of these classics to the growing body of research on mobilities.

Biographers of Simmel and Goffman seem to agree that Goffman did owe a lot to Simmel (Jacobsen and Kristiansen 2002; Kristiansen 2001). One very important common denominator was the interest in everyday life and the 'surfaces' of social life. Neither of the theorists was inclined to grand theory building, but rather focused on the level of interactions. Furthermore, they were both engaged in making sense of what Simmel termed the associational dimensions of society. That is, the way multiple and relational interactions make up society as a whole. The use of analogy is a method of reasoning that both thinkers frequently used, as is the attention they paid to the interaction and meeting of the eyes, the construction of trust and the importance of mobility practices to identity construction. Obviously, there are differences as well; Simmel's neo-Kantian notion of the pure and formal social forms being but one. Here, some would argue for a parallel between the two, since Simmel distinguishes between form and content and the search for abstracting actual content from its social forms could be said to have some affinity to Goffman's attempts to abstract and identify a finite number of forms of interaction (Jacobsen and Kristiansen 2002:40). Put bluntly, as Jacobsen and Kristiansen suggest the main difference between Simmel and Goffman is that the latter 'stays at the micro level' (Jacobsen and Kristiansen 2002:41). However, there are multiple connections to the wider normative systems and societal layers even in the smallest-scale accounts from Goffman. Clearly, the difference in scope and scale of the theorists is most evident when one turns to Simmel's work on larger societal structures such as the role of money in the development of Modernity (Simmel 1900/90).

Re-reading Simmel on mobilities

The works of Georg Simmel are of great importance to the discipline of sociology. Although he was a founding figure, Simmel's life and career were marked by his status as an outsider (Hansen 1991; Tonboe 1993, 2001; Wolff 1950). This status could be ascribed to the type of writing he practised (being known as the essayist par excellence in sociology) but also to his interest in the often (to his peers) 'obscure'-looking details of things (he wrote essays on the door, the bridge, the meal and fashion). Recently the value of Simmel's work on mobilities has begun to be realised, as here in the assessment of John Allen:

> Simmel's thinking on proximity, distance and movement can shed light upon how people make sense of today's complex networks of social interaction both within and beyond cosmopolitan city life ... modern times for

Simmel are experienced largely through *changing relations of proximity and distance* and, more broadly, through *cultures of movement and mobility*.

(Allen 2000:55; italics original)

The epistemological basis of Simmel's work was – despite his, at times, idiosyncratic approach – firmly anchored in neo-Kantian idealism (Lechner 1991:196; Tonboe 1993:192), which led him to understand the spatial dimension of social life as anchored in a subject-oriented perspective. However, some would find that Simmel, by arguing for the importance of the social 'association', took a third position in relation to the individualism and collectivism of main-stream sociology (Hansen 1991). Thus, space is seen as a formal category, or in Simmel's own words: 'The City is not a spatial entity with social consequences, but a sociological entity that is formed spatially' (Simmel, quoted in Frisby and Featherstone 1997:131). Here Simmel addresses the now-classic theme of 'spatial determinism', as he opposes such notions on the grounds of understanding space as a context for action, but also as a 'non-determining form', which leads Lechner to conclude that Simmel's position lies somewhere between spatial determinism and social constructionism (Lechner 1991:196). Others see Simmel's thinking as one of eminent dialectical reasoning overcoming dichotomous thinking (Ritzer 1992:160).

The key text of Simmel's work, when dealing with issues of urban mobilities, is the widely known essay 'The Metropolis and Mental Life', originally published in 1903. In this essay Simmel analyses the impact of urban life on the psychological and cultural aspects of sociality. The opening quotation of the essay illustrates how he makes a connection between the mundane activities of everyday life and the large epochal transformation processes of Modernity: 'The deepest problems of modern life derive from the claim of the individual to preserve the autonomy and individuality of his existence' (Simmel 1903/50:409). The tone of the essay is not exactly optimistic, as the city seems to sharpen the fight for survival amongst its inhabitants (a theme also to be found in the 'Chicago School' of urban sociology): 'It is decisive that city life has transformed the struggle with nature for livelihood into an inter-human struggle for gain, which here is not granted by nature but by other men' (Simmel 1903/50:420). Furthermore, the fight amongst fellow humans might be an expression of increased freedom and opportunity, but the flip side of the coin is that 'one nowhere feels as lonely and lost as in the metropolitan crowd' (1903/50:418). This metropolitan loneliness is linked explicitly to mobilities in some of Simmel's later work, as he portrays the crowded mass-transportation situation as the cradle of 'loneliness in togetherness':

> The feeling of isolation is rarely as decisive and intense when one actually finds oneself physically alone, as when one is a stranger, without relations, among many physically close persons, at a 'party' on a train, or in the traffic of a large city.
>
> (Simmel, quoted in Wolff 1950:119)

According to Simmel the hallmark of modern metropolitan life is the massive (over-)stimulation of the senses stemming from the environment in general: from traffic lights, masses of moving urbanites, commercials, sights and sounds. Indeed, it is hard to understand that Simmel knew a radically different form of cityscape than the contemporary ones of LED commercials covering whole façades of buildings and with the intensification of traffic in cities worldwide. The sensual over-stimulation of the urban dweller led Simmel to coin one of his most famous concepts: the notion of the 'blasé attitude' (a concept he had already presented in the *Philosophy of Money*, 1900/90:256ff.):

> The blasé attitude results first from the rapidly changing and closely compressed contrasting stimulations of the nerves ... An incapacity thus emerges to react to new sensations with the appropriate energy. This constitutes that blasé attitude which, in fact, every metropolitan child shows when compared with children of quieter and less changeable milieus.
> (Simmel 1903/50:414)

The city is also, according to Simmel, defined by a particular intellectual culture amongst its inhabitants. City 'man' (*sic!*) supposedly reacts using his head instead of his heart (Simmel 1903/50:410), as opposed to the less calculable and emotionally anchored psychological habitus of rural 'man' (the gendered language of both Simmel and Goffman calls for more attention in itself). The city thus nurtures a calculating behaviour and intellectual abstraction in its inhabitants. It is the predominance of intellectuality that serves not only to preserve subjective life against the metropolitan threat but also harbours the calculus of the money economy. Thus, city life is dependent upon punctuality, calculability and exactness, and it creates these features in its attempts to organise everything from the logistics of urban movement to the timetables of public transportation (Simmel 1903/50:413). This feature is precisely what is addressed by the *Staging Mobilities* framework and its sensitivity to 'systems' staging from above. Furthermore, to Simmel cities were primarily characterised by the highest economic division of labour (1903/50:420). According to Simmel, the increased flow of goods and people in the city was thus facilitated and enforced by the money economy: 'all things float with equal specific gravity in the constantly moving stream of money' (1903/50:414). The most striking illustration of Simmel's sensitivity to movement is to be found precisely in his understanding of the importance of the money economy to Modernity. As the circulating money flow in the city changes pace, so does the pace of life and, thus, the experience of space and time (Allen 2000:65). In many ways Simmel foresaw the intensification of the experiences in the modern economy that are nowadays hailed by the business gurus of the so-called 'experience economy' (Pine and Gilmore 1999). Simmel was of the opinion that money was not only abstract but also characterised by 'perfect mobility':

> Whereas the technical difficulty of transporting the values of a barter economy over long distances already restricts it to a relatively small number

of individual economic spheres, money, by virtue of its perfect mobility, forms the bond that combines the largest extension of the economic sphere with the growing independence of persons.

(Simmel 1900/90:349)

Furthermore, in Simmel's view the increasing impact of the money economy meant that the pace of life changed markedly (1900/90:498). In his analysis of the transformation processes of Modernity, Simmel is on a par with other major social thinkers such as Max Weber and Karl Marx in their interpretation of the domination growing out of large, instrumental systems. This Simmel termed the predominance of the 'objective spirit' over the 'subjective spirit' (1903/50:421) in which 'the individual has become a mere cog in an enormous organization of things and powers' (1903/50:422). This notion of the domination of the 'objective life forces' over the 'subjective life forces' was one of the key motives for Simmel's diagnosis of Modernity, and can be articulated with a spatial sensitivity to the way that the money economy not only facilitates flow and mobilities but also separates person and object (Simmel 1900/90:332–333). Seen this way, his analysis of the relationship between money and mobilities may also be said to run parallel to the notion of 'motility' as the capacity to move (Kaufmann 2002). As the power of money bridges distances it may also enhance potential for mobilities (i.e. motility).

The 'Metropolis' essay is considered not only to be exemplary of Simmel's particular way of analysing modern life, but also to be one of the founding texts in most urban theory curricula. On a more general level, the metropolis and the modern money economy depends on a new and extended form of trust. For one thing, money transactions would collapse without trust (Simmel 1900/90:17). Furthermore, the life and flow of modern Berlin (Simmel's case par excellence) would simply come to a halt, if, for instance, all the clocks went out of synchronicity (Simmel 1903/50). In other words, if a key feature of the staging 'from above' broke down. The identification of extended trust in systems as a precondition to urban mobility coordination is foreseeing the contemporary understanding of the modern individual's dependence on abstract 'expert systems' (Giddens 1990) in the 'risk society' (Beck 1986/96). However, the stereotypical opposition between the city and the small village seems today to be more of a caricature than a serious analysis. One example of this dichotomous thought is shown in the following passage:

> so today metropolitan man [sic] is 'free' in a spiritualized and refined sense, in contrast to the pettiness and prejudices which hem in the small-town ... The sphere of life of the small town is, in the main, self-contained and autarchic. For it is the decisive nature of the metropolis that its inner life overflows by waves into a far-flung national or international area.
>
> (Simmel 1903/50:418–419)

It is indeed debatable (and here the technological and infrastructural development excuses Simmel) whether a firm distinction between metropolis and small town makes sense, as today the urbanisation processes scatter built environment and urban symbolism in much less bounded ways (Graham and Marvin 2001; Soja 2000; Sieverts 2003). As Bouchet rightly points out, there were far fewer cars on the city streets of Simmel's Berlin, and public squares and market places still fulfilled the need of urban dwellers for interaction and exchange as opposed to the contemporary city with its specialised patchwork of flows and warehouses (Bouchet 1998:112). Furthermore, Bouchet argues that since Simmel wrote his analysis, cities have become even more challenging for the production and re-production of the identities of the urban dweller (1998:188).

In another essay 'The Stranger' (1908), Simmel qualifies his understanding of the relationship between the rooted group and the mobile visitor. In this essay, the co-existence of nearness and remoteness becomes a main feature of every human relationship (1908/50:402). Furthermore, the Stranger is an element of the group itself, is the person who 'comes today and stays tomorrow' (1908/50:408, 402). In other words, the stranger embeds a specific character of mobilities: 'If mobility takes place within a closed group, it embodies that synthesis of nearness and distance which constitutes the formal position of the stranger' (1908/50:403–404). Furthermore, in the essay on the 'Sociology of the Senses' (1908), Simmel has an interesting observation regarding the importance of mobilities to social interaction. Again the theme is based on the opposition between the small town and the metropolis. However, the argument is based on the power of sight as metropolitan dwellers meet and interact with larger quantities of people due to the influence of public transportation. According to Simmel, the emergence of public transportation in the nineteenth century (buses, rail coaches and trams) led to a new way of gazing at the fellow urbanite. Thus, before the entry of these mobility technologies, the urban dweller was neither able nor 'forced' to look at her or his consociate for minutes (or even hours) without speaking and communicating (Simmel 1908/98:78). Modern-life mobilities has an increasing effect on the visual senses, whenever we gaze at each other on the freeway or share a compartment on the subway.

In summary, I find in Simmel's analysis a sophisticated and complex relationship between modern society and its dependence on the effective and abstract money economy, the division of labour, the spatial organisation of flows within cities and the mental attitudes and cultures of urban dwellers. From here I now turn to the other thinker guiding this chapter: Erving Goffman.

Goffman and everyday-life mobilities

The exploration of everyday-life mobilities using Goffman as a guide makes us see that waiting in line for the bus, riding the subway, cycling to work or the freeway commute are by no means neither just instrumental practices of getting from A to B, nor are they trivial acts of physical displacement. Goffman's insights into the 'little practices' of social life substantiates the notion that contemporary everyday-life mobilities are produced by and re-produce culture and social norms. From the outset of Goffman's life as a social scholar he was interested in human interaction and how this may differ from the conceptions that people themselves typically hold. This was already his key concern in his master's dissertation (Goffman 1949). Goffman's concepts provide us with a rich vocabulary describing how everyday-life mobilities in the contemporary city are regulated both formally and informally.

Goffman and urban mobilities

Goffman has been declared to belong to many different theoretical corners or camps of the sociological landscape, from game theorist to carrier of the legacy of Émile Durkheim to symbolic interactionism (see Jacobsen and Kristiansen 2002:25–27 for a description and discussion of the 'war over Goffman'). Seen as part of 'symbolic interactionism', Goffman stresses the face-to-face interaction in everyday-life situations (Ritzer 1992). Still, he comes up with explorations of much more general phenomena than simple conversations or street encounters. Often this was done by creating and applying metaphors. Goffman's use of metaphors has given rise to a debate concerning his reception. Does the coining of metaphors lead to a conflation of methodology and theory, as some seem to suggest? Or is his working with metaphors to be understood as a creative and abductive approach enriching the capacity for social analysis and understanding? (See Jacobsen and Kristiansen 2006; Rigney 2001 for reports on this debate.) I subscribe to the latter of these interpretations and see the creation of metaphors within Goffman's vocabulary as one of the central and fruitful elements in his social analysis in general and in his understanding of everyday-life mobilities in particular.

One of Goffman's most important metaphorical tools for understanding the sociology of everyday-life interaction is his 'dramaturgical metaphor' (which is the basis for the *Staging Mobilities* framework) whereby social agents 'play roles' in accordance with more or less self-conscious 'scripts' for social action (Goffman 1959). In this way, social life is marked by the expressions we offer, as we attempt to control how these are perceived by others. As Goffman observes: 'the expressiveness of the individual appears to involve two radically different kinds of sign activity: The expression that he gives and the expression he gives off' (1959:2). The point is that we might intend not to express ourselves but we cannot (as soon as we engage in social interaction) avoid 'giving off' signs, signals and expressions that will be interpreted by our consociates. In the words of Goffman: 'performers can stop giving expressions but cannot stop giving them off' (1959:108). Furthermore, as shown in Chapter 1 the dramaturgical metaphor led Goffman to coin the concepts of 'front-stage' and 'back-stage' regions (Goffman 1959). In his PhD thesis on communication and interaction in a Shetland Island community from 1953, much of the ground is laid for the later perspective. This also includes sensitivity to the meaning of mobilities even though this never became articulated as an explicit focus of his theoretical efforts. Thus, from his studies in a remote and isolated island community Goffman already saw the importance of mobilities, for example to the way island inhabitants greet each other. So the particular mode of transportation and the particular infrastructure had repercussions on what he terms 'road salutations' (Goffman 1953:181–188). Furthermore, the physical location and movement of the interacting persons were seen as important to the definition of the 'sending positioning' of a communicating agent (Goffman 1953:202–203). However, these early writings only in a very indirect manner took on the issue of mobilities as a sociological field of investigation.

Behaviour in public places

One of the most obvious pointers from Goffman's work into the study of mobilities comes from the attention he directed to the fact that we manage to get around in busy and dense social settings without constantly coming to a halt or even colliding. The conceptual tool explaining this is the notion of 'civil inattention'. In his book *Behaviour in Public Places* (1963), Goffman defines the concept of 'civil inattention' in the following manner:

> What seems to be involved is that one gives to another enough visual notice to demonstrate that one appreciates that the other is present ... while at the next moment withdrawing one's attention from him so as to express that he does not constitute a target of special curiosity or design.
>
> (Goffman 1963:84)

With reference to Goffman, John Urry argues that meetings are especially important in 'face work' between people who interact (Urry 2007). The term 'face work' is precisely Goffman's terminology for how we, as consociates, both give and take impressions by means of our (bodily as well as facial) expressions in face-to-face interactions. Interestingly, the many transit spaces of our global network society facilitate meetings of all kinds. Thus, they are sites of mobile face-to-face interactions. Many of the empirical examples inhabiting Goffman's analytical universe in his book on behaviour in public places have to do with mobilities, as here in a comment on long-distance travel:

> Airplane and long-distance bus travel have here underlined some interesting issues. Seatmates, while likely to be strangers, are not only physically too close to each other to make non-engagement comfortable, but are also fixed for a long period of time, so that conversation, once begun, may be difficult thereafter either to close or sustain.
>
> (Goffman 1963:139)

This feature will be of some importance in the discussion of the 'mobile with' later in this chapter. Moreover, Goffman saw the practice of the street-meeting as more than just moving from location A to location B:

> One of the most significant infractions of communication rules has to do with street accosting. There are, of course, some legal restrictions placed

upon its varieties, upon begging, peddling, and pestering in public streets. But in the main, the force that keeps people in their communication place in our middle-class society seems to be the fear of being thought forward and pushy, or odd, the fear of forcing a relationship where none is desired – the fear, in the last analysis, of being rather patently rejected or even cut.

(Goffman 1963:140)

What on the surface looks rather trivial – a random meeting in the street – becomes in this perspective an important window into profound social processes that make up actual everyday-life mobilities.

The Individual as a Unit

In the essay 'The Individual as a Unit', Goffman articulates many thought-provoking arguments, much of which has inspired the *Staging Mobilities* perspective. Again the scene is related to that of mundane mobilities:

City streets, even in times that defame them, provide a setting where mutual trust is routinely displayed between strangers. Voluntary coordination of action is achieved in which each of the two parties has a conception of how matters ought to be handled between them, the two conceptions agree, each party believes that this agreement exists and each appreciates that this knowledge about the agreement is possessed by the other. In brief, structural prerequisites for rule by convention are found. Avoidance of collision is one example of the consequence!

(Goffman 1972:17)

This illustrates the dynamic interactions, the importance of relations and the ephemeral situational sensitivity that feeds into the mobile situation as it is staged from above and below. Moving about either as a pedestrian or as an airborne jetsetter is a symbolic act of identity construction as well as being an act of physical movement:

Take, for example, techniques that pedestrians employ in order to avoid bumping into one another. These seem of little significance. However, there are an appreciable number of such devices; they are *constantly* in use and they cast a pattern of street behaviour. Street traffic would be a shambles without them.

(Goffman 1972:6; italics original)

From this, it should be clear that the basic ways of getting around in the city are by no means trivial features of urban life. Goffman's understanding of such complex relationships pre-dates the now widespread 'actor network theory' or ANT (Latour 2005) and its dismissal of the agent as being isolated from environment and objects (not all agree on the sociological importance of ANT; see e.g. Dant 2004 for a critique of ANT, social agency and intentionality in relation to mobilities). Partly in parallel to the way ANT sees 'hybrid connections' between agent and object, so Goffman saw the mobile agent as both embedded in and embodying a so-called 'vehicular unit':

> A vehicular unit is a shell of some kind controlled (usually from within) by a human pilot or navigator. A traffic code is a set of rules whose maintenance allows vehicular units independent use of a set of thoroughfares for the purpose of moving from one point to another.
> (Goffman 1972:6)

Vehicular units (cars, planes etc.) are in Goffman's terms a sort of 'thick skin'. In this perspective, 'the individual himself, moving across roads and down streets – the individual as pedestrian – can be considered a pilot encased in a soft and exposing shell, namely his clothes and skin' (Goffman 1972:7). Material objects are, however, not only functional (or dysfunctional) but also symbolic and semiotic. Sign-giving in traffic is also about interaction. Much of it is codified and staged from above within legal frameworks specifying the meaning of various signs. However, as we saw in Chapter 3, mobile units, artefacts and objects also have semiotic properties. Thus, the meaning of seeing a Mercedes Benz in the rear-view mirror differs from seeing a Morris Minor. Visible and conspicuous car brands or high-end biking equipment becomes important mobile identity requisites.

As one of the central concepts to be developed later in this chapter is the 'mobile with', I will initially explore Goffman's own definition of a 'with'. Goffman defines a 'with' as 'a party of more than one whose members are perceived to be "together"' (Goffman 1972:19). As Goffman was less explicit in elaborating on this definition, I here follow Ron Scollon and Sue Scollon in their way of making the notion more operational. Accordingly, a 'with', in Goffman's sense, is characterised by civil inattention to non-members, proximity to members, the right to initiate talk and interaction amongst members, availability of interactions to members, ritual practices for joining and departing and greater latitude in behaviour than members would have as singles in a comparable situation (Scollon and Scollon 2003:60). Later, when I develop the notion of 'networked self', I shall have to be critical about the proximity requirement (as already illustrated in Chapter 2). The contemporary urban situation is marked by many groups that are connected-in-motion and where we are dealing with 'mobile withs' even though they are beyond close proximity. This is exactly the potential of the 'digital layer' that in a sense has been added to the physical city: that we can keep being related and even deepen our relationships despite being on the move and even moving in different directions and places in the city. Moreover, the notion of rituals for becoming a member might be more loosely defined. In some contexts there definitely exist rituals, such as when waiting in line for the bus in the United Kingdom (compared to the same practice in Denmark) or when sitting in a carriage.

In his presidential address to the American Sociological Association in 1982, entitled 'The Interaction Order', Goffman became more explicit in his articulation of the relationship between the interaction order, 'withs' and mobility:

> One can start with persons as vehicular entities, that is, with human ambulatory units. In public places we have 'singles' (a party of one) and 'withs' (a party of more than one), such parties being treated as self-contained units for the purpose of participation in the flow of pedestrian social life. A few larger ambulatory units can also be mentioned – for example, files and processions, and, as a limiting case, the queue, this being by way of a stationary ambulatory unit.
>
> (Goffman 1983:6)

In a longer essay entitled 'Remedial Interchanges', from the book *Relations in Public* (1972), Goffman explicitly acknowledges the 'mobile sense making' that takes place when everyday-life mobilities are being practised:

> When the individual is in a public place, he is not merely moving from point to point silently and mechanically managing traffic problems; he is also involved in taking constant care to sustain a viable position relative to what has come to happen around him, and he will initiate gestural interchanges with acquainted and unacquainted others in order to establish what this position is!
>
> (Goffman 1972:154)

From this short exploration of a few of Goffman's ideas I shall now briefly look into some Goffman-inspired research that centres on mobility before turning to the development of two central concepts.

The sociology of the familiar and the semiotic aggregate

A collection of articles inspired by the work of Goffman appeared in the publication *People in Places: The Sociology of the Familiar* (Birenbaum and Sagarin 1973). Amongst the many contributions to this publication, two chapters are of particular interest here. These are the chapter on the behaviour of pedestrians by Michael Wolff (1973) and the chapter on subway behaviour by Janey Levine *et al.* (1973). Both contributions deal with elements of urban mobilities seen through Goffman-inspired frameworks. In accordance with the aforementioned notion of the 'mobile with', Wolff's research found (though without using the term) that people in public transit constitute a co-acting group or a 'team' (Wolff 1973:35). The second contribution to the publication made by Levine *et al.* (1973) deals with field observations made on the subways of Boston and New York. One of the crucial elements in the informal regulation of subway behaviour seems to be the way one enters and finds a place in the compartments. The process of selecting a seat is governed by a principal need to sit alone that is only dispensed of in cases of shortage of free seats. The newcomer thus performs on a 'stage' already inhabited and symbolically inscribed by the passengers already there. Both the pedestrian study and the subway study indicate that Goffman's concepts are empirically very relevant to studies of urban mobilities.

More recently, from field studies in Vienna, Hong Kong, Beijing, Washington, DC and Paris, Ron and Sue Scollon map how we shape our 'interaction order' by means of reading discourses in place. For example, on the corner of Tat Chee Avenue and To Yuen Street in Hong Kong's Kowloon District, there is a major crossing point. Pedestrians mix with vehicular traffic in a complex setting termed a 'semiotic aggregate'. What is typical of semiotic aggregates is that they are full of signs and symbols within (at least) four general categories: regulatory discourses (e.g. municipal orders), infrastructural discourses (e.g. municipal signs), commercial discourses (e.g. street commercials or billboards) and transgressive discourses (e.g. graffiti) (Scollon and Scollon 2003:181). The regulatory discourse is formally present in all cases in the form of traffic lights (i.e. staging from above through infrastructure and design), but the informal 'mobility culture' (i.e. the interactive and cultural staging from below) differs immensely as people wait for the green light in an empty street in Vienna, whereas they walk as they please in Hong Kong. Furthermore, the way the mobile urban dwellers are integrated in the 'interaction order' means that there is a link between the way we move through the city and the way we perceive ourselves (and want others to perceive us). Thus, when we cross the street there is an intimate and important relationship between mobilities, social order and identity:

> The first consideration is the habitus of the social actor himself or herself. Am I the sort of person who waits for the walk light or do I cross when the road is free of traffic? Am I the sort of person who worries about whether others are watching me? Do I even notice?
> (Scollon and Scollon 2003:199)

Arguably, everyday-life mobilities are more than merely moving from location A to location B as we produce understandings of self and other whilst on the move.

The 'mobile with'

As we have seen, the interaction order of the social situation is the pivotal focus of Goffman's writings. Despite mentioning a number of examples related to mobilities and traffic Goffman did not, however, take his point of departure from the fact that much of what defines social situations and interactions is the dynamics of physical meetings and departures, or, in other words, mobilities. Here I explore the potential for including the mobile dynamics of the situation by focusing on how many social encounters develop by the simple fact that social agents move towards, pass by or come to stop due to their physical movement in space.

80 *Framing mobilities*

Still we remain, however, at the level of the individual. We saw Goffman's well-developed sensitivity to the 'individual as a unit' and needless to say much of our engagement with others must be seen from the vantage point of the personal embodied experience. Having said this, though, there is an under-theorised dimension in understanding how mobility with others makes an equally important feature of urban everyday life. So next to the 'mobile self' the 'mobile with' becomes an important analytical category (Figure 4.1).

Figure 4.1 A mobile with.

On the street, amongst our fellow moving consociates, we saw in Goffman the rich vocabulary of how individuals navigate and interact on their way through the city. However, rarely do we move about on our own in the sense that we meet no one (which may be why a late-night stroll or walking across town very early in the morning carries its own strange magic). Think of the way we walk down a pedestrian area – minding our own business and using all the civilised techniques Goffman so vividly explored. Facing a stop light we pause and, even though this might be for only a very short spell of time, we become 'the group of pedestrians waiting for the green light'. Needless to say, this rarely leads to any deep interaction of shared destinies, unless we include the marginal experiences of something very dramatic happening like a car veering off the road and hitting the group (often we hear about total strangers meeting under dramatic circumstances like a plane crash or shipwreck who later become intimately bonded by this shared existential experience). However, in mundane and ordinary everyday life we make multiple 'temporary congregations' as we slip in and out of different 'mobile withs'. So the 'mobile with' comes into being very quickly and can be dissolved equally swiftly. A 'mobile with' is to be understood as a group of two or more either co-presently moving together or in mediated contact 'stretched' across time and space facilitated by networked technologies. The everyday-life experience with 'mobile withs' thus carries a certain ephemeral quality. 'Mobile withs' might be exemplified as groups of recreational runners or cyclists (who might also be illustrative of the notion of the networked self if they carry GPS devices and mobile phones orchestrating their activities). They could be thought of as rowing groups of football supporters in cars cruising after a victory (or car-cruising youth in general). We also find 'mobile withs' engaged in much closer proximity doing 'body-work', such as people walking arm-in-arm. Such collective body mobility may be in the form of the 'escort', which again could be divided into helping less mobile persons, police arrests, practices of the pub bouncer 'performing mobility' to an unwanted customer or the loving couple strolling along. Hand-in-hand 'mobile withs' equally illustrate the collective body-work as in the 'parent–child with' or the couple performing mobilities, just as do two people riding a one-person bicycle.

Obviously, we may sustain the 'mobile with' over longer periods, as when Goffman illustrates the bus journey or the subway trip where we struggle to find our place and role within the 'mobile with' of, for example, the train compartment. This is similar when we engage in long-distance travel by train or plane where the complexity and requirements for presenting oneself and sustaining the order of the 'mobile with' becomes an even more delicate matter. For example, Goffman mentions the fact that there is a subtle balance to strike in opening a conversation with one's seatmate on a long-distance flight. Opening the conversation may imply a certain obligation to continue for the rest of the trip. Here I briefly pause to reflect upon some of the many potential 'mobile withs': the bus queue; pedestrians and cyclists waiting for green at the traffic lights; fellow travellers (on public transportation like planes, buses, trains and boats); fellow travellers in private means of transportation cruising down the highway (predominantly cars); fellow travellers not in same vehicle (bikes on a cycle path); groups strolling the city shopping, drinking or socialising; or the family Sunday drive. All these examples of 'mobile withs' have to do with 'temporary congregations'. They may occur on escalators, in lifts, on sidewalks, cycle lanes, freeway lanes, in flight waiting lines and all the other places where we meet and move alongside one another for a short period. However, these examples are thought of mostly by example of the non-aquatint (and thus unfocused interaction). But many times the 'mobile with' is composed of individuals familiar with each other (in focused interaction). We may arrange a trip with friends and family members where the movement itself becomes very central (as in the coast-to-coast US car vacation or the family holiday to distant places). But coincidental meetings with people we know can also turn into 'mobile withs', as when we meet an old friend we have not seen for a while and decide to keep each other company for the journey. Somewhere between this fully planned and very mobility-conscious set of practices (e.g. the family holiday) and the coincidental meeting we may find, for example, the night out on the town 'pub crawling'. Or the shopping trip with a friend or family. Here the 'mobile with' might have a prior established route (particular bars and pubs or specific shops) or the 'mobile with' may have no other rationale than to drift about aiming for either a drink or an unplanned shopping experience.

We can even speak of a 'stretched mobile with',[1] being the case when the 'with' on the move is coordinated and communicating in real time across distances (a concept I introduced in Chapter 1). The notion of 'mobile with' thereby comes in two variants: the 'co-present mobile with' (people moving together in time–space) and the 'stretched mobile with' (people linked as they move in different settings). In a research project applying Goffman to the study of the public spaces of the contemporary city, Buscher *et al.* (2010) argue that: 'New technologies like mobile phones, public screens, ubiquitous connectivity, GPS, new architecture, new policies and new social practices have changed how people involved in co-presence ... the compulsion to proximity – seems to be transmuting into a compulsion to be connected' (Buscher *et al.* 2010:4, 8). Or as I pointed out elsewhere: 'we are linked in motion' (Jensen 2010a:345). Likewise both Jenkins and Ling argue that Goffman in all likelihood would have included ICT and networked technologies in his work had he lived to witness the digital revolution (Jenkins 2010:259; Ling 2010:288). With an explicit reference to Goffman's work, Scollon and Scollon put the issue this way: 'New media technologies bring into question whether or not we should extend the concept of the with to people brought together into social interaction through a medium such as the cell phone' (2003:62). I completely agree and add to this that it is not only mobile phones that are affording new definitions of the situation but more generally what I term 'networked technologies' (and to which I return in Chapter 6).

Here we might pause and rethink the relation to Goffman's concepts. In fact, Goffman did develop the notion of the 'team', which has a very important relationship to the notion of the 'mobile with'. We might ask about the nature of the relationship between the 'mobile with' and the 'team' that Goffman coins in *The Presentation of Self in Everyday Life* (1959). Accordingly, he defines a 'team' as a set of persons who cooperate in practising a simple routine (Goffman 1959). This may seem like the notion of 'mobile with' presented here. However, Goffman stresses in particular that a 'team' put on a play and thus that there is an audience. In a sense one might see our fellow urban travellers as 'audiences' looking at the spectacle of urban mobilities. But as opposed to, for example, a 'team' of theatre actors, the 'mobile with' is not (consciously or collectively) working on 'giving off' a particular impression. Often the 'mobile with' is much more situational and spontaneous but can of course also be very planned and orchestrated as, for example, in the case of the family vacation or the business trip. However, the 'mobile with' can easily perform without an audience, such as when we ride across town very late at night in the company of friends without meeting anyone else at all. Returning to our discussion and development of 'mobile withs' we may expand this by examining the complicated nature of 'negotiation' that might take place when we move together, for example with friends and family. The situation may be one of deciding on the mode of transportation (e.g. 'Should we take the subway or walk?') or there may be an issue of routing (e.g. 'Let's pass the old square'). The point is that the very fact that the 'with' is on the move adds an immense level of complexity to the negotiation process. Sometimes we may witness arguments or even fights about where a 'mobile with' should go. At times this becomes a matter of either to follow or to break away. This could occur if, for example, someone in one's 'mobile with' stops for a red light whilst others cross the street. It is an example of a dynamic situational pressure and negotiation within the 'mobile with' and thus of the power relations manifest in any mobile situation and its staging from below.

Here I will look at two examples of 'negotiation in motion'. The first is related to an autobiographical experience, the second to an EU-funded traffic planning project. The first example of a 'mobile with' engaged in a 'negotiation in motion' springs from a family holiday in Paris. Some years ago, my wife, our two children – at that time aged 10 and 8 – and I were on a weekend vacation in Paris. In this context, I focus on an episode where the 'mobile with' walks along a busy Parisian street and approaches a red traffic light. The closing in on a street crossing illustrates how the 'mobile presentation of self' is negotiated not only with a keen eye to our fellow and co-present members of the 'order' of the street-corner interaction, but also with a focus on the social norms of parenthood. I described the episode in a paper from which I shall use the following excerpt:

> When I as a Scandinavian walk the streets of Paris with my children, I struggle between passing on to my children the legally prescribed respect for the 'red light' of our national mobility culture, and teaching them the more relaxed and pragmatic approach to such a regulative discourse – which they clearly spotted as the Parisian mobility culture! In the company of our children, we form a special 'with' in Goffman's sense, a 'with' where we negotiate the interpellation of the legal traffic control discourse with the social

norms of mobility performance of the particular street we walk. In a sense, we engage in a 'negotiated mobility identity' ... when we approach the traffic light or the zebra crossing which prompts a number of decisions about 'presentation of the self'. By coding and de-coding the urban mobility landscape, contemporary urbanites are constructing multiple layers of 'mobility meanings'. Clearly, some of these layers might be of more relevance to some than to others. Furthermore, such meaning selection might be situational depending on the situation one faces (avoiding a collision might be foregrounded to the issue of whether one violates basic traffic regulation by doing so).

(Jensen 2006:161–162)

The relevant issues around traffic safety, codes of behaviour and bringing up children are multiple and may often in more general terms work as windows into the actual process of socialisation. However, here I am more interested in showing that the family on foot in a big city becomes a 'mobile with' that is busy producing and re-producing normative codes of behaviour as well as making decisions about how to manage practical challenges such as crossing a street without being run over by a car (performing 'stretchy' control attempts). Add to this the discussion about national traffic behaviour codes, small-town versus big-city experiences as well as the simple fact that the 'mobile with' is trying to 'consume the place' as a group of tourists, we start to notice the complexity of the phenomenon. This Parisian experience thus illustrates the staging from above and below with a particular emphasis on the actual situation.

The other example of 'negotiation in motion 'and the 'mobile with' is the 'Shared Space' project. In this project a number of European municipalities have been experimenting with loosening the strict traffic regulations in order to explore what happens when people are forced to pay attention to their fellow travellers in the traffic rather than, for example, being guided by traffic lights or other publicly led mechanisms for mobility management (Shared Space 2005). Much seems to indicate that light regulation or dedicated lanes take away the mobile person's awareness of the mobile other and thus over time leads to less attention and awareness and thus ultimately to more accidents. Hence, the project on 'Shared Space' illustrates what might be learned from the 'mobile with' perspective: that we are, in fact, interacting when we engage in everyday-life mobilities and not just passively moving around (Jensen 2009a). Furthermore, the project is illustrative of how change in the staging from above (new regulations and different street layout) influences the staging from below with its mobile situational interactions.

The 'networked self'

Coming from the discussion of the 'mobile with', I want to point to the fact that contemporary urban mobilities mostly take place within networks of different sorts (here I will touch only briefly on this since it will be elaborated in Chapter

6). The movement of objects, signs and people constitutes material sites of networked relationships. However, as an increasing number of mobility practices are making up our everyday-life experiences, the movement is much more than travel from A to B. Mobile experiences in contemporary society are practices that are meaningful and normatively embedded. Furthermore, an increasing number of such mobile practices are mediated by technologies of tangible and less tangible types (Figure 4.2). In understanding the importance of mediation, global–local interactions, networks and the distributions of meaning, new ways of thinking about mobilities are called for. In particular, a critical awareness of how such technologies shape the foreground/background attention of social agents seems crucial.

Including networked technologies and 'ambient environments' increases our knowledge about the over-layering of the material environment with digital technologies. The presence of GPS (Global Positioning Systems), mediated surfaces, RFID (Radio Frequency Identification) and other technologies that all relate to contemporary mobility practices adds new dimensions to the notion of movement and constitutes new arenas and tools for identity construction and social interaction (as well as, of course, for commercial exploitation and state control). Analysts of the present state of affairs point to the fact that the previous obsession with the 'virtual' and cyberspace – where technology took off as it were from the physical environment – has come to be replaced with a beginning

Figure 4.2 The networked self.

awareness of the importance of the location, the placement and the situated technologies (Crang and Graham 2007; Manovich 2006; McCullough 2004). Rather than working within separate domains new media and technologies overlay the physical world of places, houses and infrastructures, thus creating a situation where the physical placement of social agency and the technology at hand becomes crucial. Much of this engagement with technologies we find in sites of transit and mobilities as we move across cities utilising numerous networked technologies to navigate, coordinate, communicate and facilitate our trajectories. Needless to say, new means of control and power also loom within these new 'augmented spaces' (Manovich 2006) as illustrations of the 'dark sides' of mobilities.

The argument thus far is that there is a new set of material and symbolic properties organising, facilitating, orchestrating and staging contemporary urban mobilities. One such new dimension concerns the mediated communication technologies that may be understood as 'another layer' to the hard infrastructure of, for example, the road systems with which we are already familiar. Two important points stem from this. First, we are 'linked-in-motion' and not (exclusively) dependent on locating at particular strategic sites of communication such as the telephone booth to communicate (as in Ling's (2010) notion of the 'unboothed' phone). Second, the fact that we are 'linked-in-motion' means that the way we engage with sites and places is altered as our embodied experience of the world changes. For example, we do not need to experience our environment in isolation as we may communicate our immediate experience online and in real time. Needless to say, there are also less positive dimensions to this instant online culture (for an early discussion of mobile communication, see Katz and Aakhus 2002). However, here I want to use this new field of experience to shed light on the fact that we are facing a mobile reconfiguration of 'the person called I' and the 'place called home' (Jensen 2009a). What this may mean in social-psychological terms is beyond the scope of this book to explore. However, it opens up to a discussion of the complex relationship between physical movement, social interaction and notions of self, other and place. In Jonathan Raban's *Soft City* (1974) we get a fruitful line of inspiration to open up an understanding of the issue of self, the city and movement (despite its publication being much prior to the development of these technologies). In the book Raban describes his own experiences of moving to London. In the book we learn to see that city life is about making sense of multiple interactions at more or less conscious levels. Raban too had an awareness of the importance of movement to the 'self' as he describes the fluid and mobile conditions for self-perception: 'During the course of a day, one passes from identity to identity ... Yet, in every contact with every stranger, the self is projected and exhibited – or, at least, a version of the self' (1974:84). This notion of multiple interactions as the hallmark of modern urban life is parallel to Simmel's 'Metropolis' essay (1903/1950). However, the mobilities perspective opens up for understanding the immense dynamism of the 'interaction order' when it is seen in motion:

My 'quarter' is a network of communication lines with intermittent assembly points; and it cannot be located on a map. Yet, place is important; it bears down on us, we mythicise it – often it is our greatest comfort, the one reassuringly solid element in an otherwise soft city. As we move across the square to the block of shops on the street, with pigeons and sweetpapers underfoot and the weak sun lightning the tarmac, the city is eclipsed by the here-and-now; the sight and smell and sound of place go to make up the fixed foot of life in the metropolis.

(Raban 1974:212–213)

The theoretical notion of the 'self' obviously becomes important in this discussion. In line with Anthony Giddens I shall speak of the 'capacity to use "I" in shifting contexts' (Giddens 1991:53) as a way of comprehending the reflexive and mediated conditions of the 'self'. On the same note, I find in Goffman a profound understanding of the 'self' as something always coming into being in a relational or situational context. So the 'self' in Goffman's understanding is 'networked', one might say. However, what I wish to point out here is the importance of new information and communication technologies and the digital 'layer' to the notion of the 'self'. Thinking about an ordinary, everyday-life commuting experience we will easily see that the 'classic' requisites that Goffman saw as important tools for establishing privacy and even non-engagement in public transit spaces (e.g. books, newspapers etc.) have today been supplemented by iPads, mp3 players, mobile phones, laptop computers and other technological devices. A fair amount of these technologies not only work as pass-the-time devices or artefacts that we may 'hide' behind, but they are networked and linked into the many other layers of communication and interaction that makes up the contemporary network city (Jensen 2008a). Today's spaces of mobilities are 'rooms' in which we live much of our life (Calabrese 2003). The moving urbanite engages with multiple mobile and electronic arenas during travel and 'being-on-the-move' is a significant contemporary everyday-life condition in the city. Therefore, we must comprehend transit places as sites of interaction and media flows that only become 'places' in so far as flows of people, ideas, symbols, goods and materials either positively flow 'into' these nodes in the network or conversely for all sorts of reasons do not flow into the nodes (Jensen 2009a).

If we add to the analysis the so-called 'social media' like Myspace, Facebook, LinkedIn, Twitter and all sorts of blogs and interactive Internet sites we see a growing number of new electronic forays in which 'social software' works as intermediary to a number of practices decoupled from time and place in a networked field of interaction. These phenomena are very dependent on infrastructures as well as personal resources, which means that they are not power neutrals (which, in fact, no technology is). As Bauman (1998) claimed, mobilities may be one of the most important stratifying dimensions to contemporary social life. Obviously, the capacity and will to move determines a host of social outcomes. Having said this, it also seems worth noting that (in the Western world at least) the networked technologies mentioned here are used across many social strata. Not so long ago I watched a homeless man on a San Francisco street sitting in his ragged clothes on a piece of cardboard on the pavement busy sending a text message on his mobile phone. Our understanding of 'self' and other becomes what they are not only as a reflection of social interaction (however important that may be) but also in a complex relationship to the material environment in which we live. This means that there is an intricate link between identification processes and the way we engage with the built environment and various technologies. Needless to say, multiple layers of identity production may have no primary spatial component. But the way we bodily engage with places through multiple ways of circulating in, out of and across them shapes an important part of the practical engagement with the world that ultimately constructs our understandings of self and other. Valorisation of the socio-spatial relation depends on the bodily experience of mediated practices in time–space. Identities do not solely reside in place (be it home, neighbourhood or nation). Rather, places are coded and de-coded in a complex valorisation process where the networked connections to multiple communities of interest and practice offer new layers of relational connectivity. However, identities, fluid as they may be, in relation to both the individual's subjectivities and collectives, are constructions made up of material and immaterial 'requisites' of more or less durable kinds. These requisites work as 'identity markers' that are continually being re-produced and re-negotiated. As we are linked-in-motion and thus not just passively being shuffled across town, such 'being-on-the-move' is an important contemporary everyday-life condition in the city and should be reinterpreted as such (Jensen 2009a:154–155).

The notion of the 'networked self' is a useful framing of the new mediated condition not only for communicating but also for experiencing urban mobilities. Furthermore, we very often see and hear in public transit spaces that communicating 'where we are' becomes a very significant dimension to contemporary everyday-life interaction. In buses, at the airport or in the queue in the supermarket often the report on 'where I am right now' becomes the entry point for much of the networked communication we engage in whilst on the move and constantly in contact with others. Such mobile and mediated network relations create new conditions for the 'self' and its ability to 'present itself' and will thus ultimately contribute to changed conditions for the relation between the 'self', mobilities and the network. Returning to Goffman, this means that the 'self' is becoming what it is not only in motion individually and collectively, but equally in new networked relations mediated by technologies that we did not have access to in Goffman's own lifetime.

Concluding remarks

In the following I shall partly recapitulate some of the main points from Simmel and Goffman's contributions to mobilities analysis, and partly exemplify how the concepts may influence our understanding of mobilities in the contemporary city.

This chapter has shown that through a re-reading of Simmel and Goffman's works we may establish a new vocabulary that makes the macro-societal conditions for contemporary mobilities comprehensible from the perspective of the 'little practices' of situational everyday-life mobilities. Seeing contemporary mobilities practices through Simmel and Goffman illustrates how social agents 'perform mobilities' as a significant cultural practice of everyday life. This amounts to seeing mobilities as a performative action. By this is meant an action producing and re-producing significant elements of the individual's self-understanding, perceptions of the material environment and the social networks within which the actor engages. Simmel and Goffman's insights into the 'little practices' of social life substantiate the fact that contemporary everyday-life mobilities are produced by and re-produce culture and social norms as they connect staging from above and below in situations of mobilities. Goffman's analysis provides us with a rich vocabulary describing how everyday-life mobility in the contemporary city is regulated formally as well as informally. I have aimed at exploring the usefulness of the concepts of the 'mobile with' and the 'networked self' whereby the legacy of Goffman is put to use in analysing contemporary everyday-life mobilities. Needless to say, this chapter cannot in full depth and detail unfold the argument behind these notions. Hopefully, I have managed to raise awareness of an important sociological phenomenon and point to an insightful source of inspiration. From the two cases of 'mobile withs' (the family trip to Paris and the Shared Space project) it should be clear that our movement in the city is a dynamic and socially complex affair that may have more repercussions than 'just being traffic'. The fact that we are 'moving animals' and that we make sense of our environment as we move means important things to the way we engage with our consociates, whether we know them or not. What may seem like trivial moving about are expressions of highly complex and dynamic situations of 'negotiation in motion' as they embody the 'temporary congregations' of urban mobilities.

On the notion of the 'networked self' I first of all want to emphasise that the notion demands a much deeper theoretical underpinning than it has been given here. The main feature I want to stress is the contemporary situation where urban everyday-life mobilities are deeply embedded in all sorts of networks (from 'hard' infrastructure to 'soft' digital communication systems). Some of these are the 'channels in which we move', so to speak. Others are pass-the-time communication and entertainment systems (e.g. commercials or digital gaming). And, finally, it seems that more and more of the networking in digital systems become mobile, meaning that the social agent to a large extent is becoming what he or she is whilst being on the move. As we are linked-in-motion the ways this plays out in socio-technical systems, sorting software and new interactive practices need investigation. The notion of the 'networked self' is a first beginning at providing a theoretical concept for such investigation.

The importance of the disciplining and normative regulation of the everyday-life interaction within the realm of urban mobilities cannot be under-estimated. However, it is important that the 'civilising element' of both Simmel's and

Goffman's perspectives does not overshadow the fact that not all mobilities interactions are civilised. This is in part what I want to address by including the 'dark sides' of mobilities into the analytical framework. Clearly, bumping into a fellow pedestrian might be 'solved' in a civilised and non-violent manner, but most urbanites would know of examples of how 'the bump' is a technique deliberately used by people looking for conflict or even fights. Also, the increasing number of reports on 'road rage' (or 'driving anger' as the scientific discourse has it; see Dahlen *et al*. 2005) bears witness to a less civilised form of mobility interaction. The examples of 'uncivilised attention' would contain everything from 'road rage' and violent conflict over accidents to traffic jams. Obviously, traffic jams will only count as uncivilised in the cases where they lead to open social conflict. The Hollywood film *Falling Down* (1993) starring Michael Douglas might qualify as a caricature of this example. The down side to any form of 'uncivilised inattention' is the loss of care for the 'other' – in this context one's fellow mobile subject (Levine *et al*. 1973:213).

Looking more broadly at the relationship between mobilities research and the vocabularies of Simmel and Goffman, it should now be clear that there are a number of well-defined modes of mobilities, all of which have repercussions for life in the contemporary city: walking, skateboarding, cycling, motorcycling, car driving, bus driving, train riding and aeroplanes and boats (as inter-urban mobility forms) – in other words, multiple categories of 'corporeal travel' (Urry 2004a:28). Each of these mobilities domains involves a set of practices and normative regulating principles that one needs to either master for practical reasons or deliberately contest by counter-practices (e.g. skateboarding on park benches or on busy streets). There are 'walking codes', 'cycling codes' etc. Clearly, these are ways of acting that we could see as more or less explicitly articulated cultures. Such 'mobility cultures' are linked to official and legal sanctions and mobilities regulations (staging from above). However, they are also embedded in the body as tacit mobilities cultures (staging from below). Some are more global generic mobility codes, whilst others are locally anchored and as such are expressions of local mobility norms and customs. Scollon and Scollon (2003) show how such 'clashes of mobility norms' and cultures can be seen when, for example, a Finnish person walks the streets of Hong Kong, or vice versa. Beyond understanding these mobility practices as embedded in legal and cultural contexts, they express particular 'ways of knowing'. In other words, there is 'cycling knowledge' and 'aeroplane knowledge' etc. to be accumulated. In an accelerating mobile society this process starts with the way parents teach their child to take care in traffic. But the learning goes on for the rest of our 'mobile lives', as we continue to be exposed to ever more sophisticated webs and networks of mobility practices that demand a continuous upgrading of our 'mobility knowledge'. This is the case when, for example, new technologies regulate the flow of urban traffic by means of GPS equipment or when airports are connected in ever more complex systems of access regulation and logistics (Graham and Marvin 2001; Jensen 2006; Urry 2003).

In order to understand this complex process, it has been my intention to show the value of applying the perspectives of two sociological theorists who are 'untimely' in relation to the latest technological innovations and mobilities systems, but nevertheless seem to offer a helpful perspective for understanding the facework and flow in the contemporary city. From this chapter I will in particular point towards the concepts of 'mobile with' and 'networked self' as key contributions to understanding the processes of *Staging Mobilities*. After this exploration of the second theme of the *Staging Mobilities* framework (social interactions), I shall proceed in the next chapter to discuss the third dimension of situational mobilities: mobile embodied performances.

Note

1 Here I would like to acknowledge the work of Paul McIlvenny who coined the notion of 'stretching' in his analysis of communication between two fellow cyclists (McIlvenny 2010). However, in this work the notion will be even more 'elastic' and include stretching to the other side of the globe as is the case when satellite communications mediate 'mobile withs'.

5 Mobile embodied performances

> When I think of my body and ask what it does to earn that name, two things stand out. It moves. It feels. In fact, it does both at the same time. It moves as it feels, and it feels itself moving. Can we think of a body without this: an intrinsic connection between movement and sensation whereby each immediately summons the other?
>
> Brian Massumi, *Parables for the Virtual*, 2002, p. ix

> [T]he city comes alive through movements and its rhythmic structure. The elements are no longer merely inanimate. They play a vital role: they become modulators of activity and are seen in juxtaposition with other moving objects. Within the spaces, movement flows, the paving and ramps become platforms of action, the street furniture is used, the sculpture in the street is seen and enjoyed. And the whole city landscape comes alive through movement as a total environment for the creative process of living.
>
> Lawrence Halprin, *Cities*, 1963, p. 9

> The pedestrian is a social being: he [sic] is also a transportation unit, and a marvellously complex and efficient one ... In fractions of a second he responds with course shifts, accelerations, and retards, and he signals to others that he is doing so.
>
> William H. Whyte, *City: Rediscovering the Centre*, 1988, p. 56

Introduction

This chapter explores the relationship between the body and mobilities by looking into a number of modes of transportation and their ways of constructing particular engagements with embodied mobilities. The 'mobile embodiments' are significant to material and symbolic relations between human agents and material artefacts. The chapter targets the complex relationship between the moving, sensing body and the material and built environment of infrastructures and mobility modes in order to explore what norms, meanings and everyday-life cultures are being produced and re-produced in this process. By looking into walking, running, cycling, driving and mass-transit mobilities, different modes of embodied mobilities are identified. Theoretically it is based on a re-reading and reinterpretation of Gibson's theories of visual perception and motion, Lynch's theories of the mobile experiences of the city and Goffman's notions of 'presentation of self' and elaborations on ideas about interaction in motion. The theorists engaged with are all rather 'old', meaning that they are re-read in order to explore their under-used potentials. However, this obviously also mean that more contemporary theorists understanding bodily movement, material sites of mobilities and social interactions must be consulted along the way (e.g. Latour's work on objects and actor-network theory, Thrift's work on the body and 'non-representational' theory and Massumi's notions of affects and emotions related to bodily mobilities). I am looking for the new insights that may be provided by a theoretical framing connecting perception and bodily motion with an understanding of face-to-face interaction and an explicit awareness of the meaning of the physical design of the sites and places of the bodily mobilities and interaction. The argument is thus that understanding embodied cultures of mobilities from the perspective of this chapter lends itself to new interpretations, explorations and understandings of what it means to move between other social agents, in particular material and physical environments – in other words to understand the embodied mobile performances of *Staging Mobilities*.

The chapter is structured into two more general and theoretical sections on the issue of mobile bodies, perception and emotions/affects (second section) and mobile bodies, infrastructure and the cultures of mobilities (third section). In the rest of the chapter I explore the relationship between the mobile body and different modes of mobilities (walking, cycling, running, car driving and mass transit). Needless to say the human practices of mobilities cover a wider set of practices that are not described in this chapter (e.g. flying, horse riding, sailing etc.). This is not because they are of less importance; rather it is a simple effect of delimitation. The chapter ends with a concluding section where I focus on the creation of embodied cultures of mobilities and the new key concepts developed throughout the chapter.

Mobile bodies, perceptions and emotions/affects

Humans are mobile animals and as such we share a number of conditions with many other species. The physical movement in natural as well as human-made environments is a further common denominator. Finally all moving species perceive and orient themselves in the world by sensual perceptions (Gibson 1986:7). Humans, however, have made an extraordinary imprint on the material environs and habitats in which they move, as the creation of complex technologies, mobilities networks and 'mobile biotopes' bears witness to. Next to the creation of artefacts of mobilities our species also creates meanings and cultures related to these complex and dynamic engagements. From the perspective of 'classical' anthropology one may say that:

> Man's [sic] entire organism was designed to move through the environment at less than five miles per hour. How many can remember what it is like to be able to see everything nearby quite sharply as one walks through the

countryside for a week, a fortnight, or a month? At walking speeds even the nearsighted can see trees, shrubbery, leaves and grass, the surfaces of rocks and stones, grains of sand, ants, beetles, caterpillars, even gnats, flies and mosquitoes, to say nothing of birds and other wildlife. Not only is the near vision blurred by the speed of the automobile but one's relationship to the countryside is vastly altered.

(Hall 1966:76)

The central claim in this chapter is thus that by looking at the embodied movements of humans we are not only studying moving animals, so to speak, but also the creation of cultural significance and social practices. In this section the theme will revolve around the body, movements and perceptions of the environment and the emotional from the perspective that 'mobility is something we feel in an emotional and affective sense' (Adey 2010:162). Embodied and sensed mobilities are creating particular cultures as well as relying on complex technical assemblies. In the words of Elliott and Urry:

> physical travel involves lumpy, fragile, aged, gendered, racialized bodies. Such bodies encounter other bodies, objects and the physical world multi-sensuously. Travel always involves *corporeal* movement and forms of pleasure and pain. Such bodies perform themselves in-between direct sensation of the 'other' and various 'sensescapes'. Bodies are not fixed and given, but involve performances, especially to fold notions of movement, nature, taste and desire into and through the body. Bodies navigate backwards and forwards between directly sensing the external world as they move bodily in and through it and experiencing discursively mediated sensescapes that signify social taste and distinction, ideology and meaning. The body especially senses as it *moves*. Important here is that sense of movement, the 'mechanics of space', of touch, such as feet on the pavement or the mountain path, hands on a rock face or the steering wheel. There are thus various assemblages of humans, objects, technologies and scripts that contingently produce durability and stability of mobility.
>
> (Elliot and Urry 2010:16; italics original)

Arguably the settings for mobilities are dependent on a number of elements interlinking. Furthermore, such 'sensescapes' are like stages where the affordances of complex mobile scenographies that are staged from above meet and mingle with bodies performing mobilities in choreographies staged from below. The staging from above combined with the individual's staging from below has the sensing body as the pivotal locus and lends itself to an investigation into how systems and stages are creating affordances to particular practices: 'Locomotion and behavior are continually controlled by the activities of seeing, smelling, and hearing, together with touching' (Gibson 1986:32). So mobilities are embodied practices that are not only highly sensorial but, from a cognitive perspective, also very complex information-processing events. Here Gibson explains the notion of 'affordance' with a reference to the different dimensions of the material environment and how it affects human activity in general and bodily movement in particular:

> Air affords breathing, more exactly, respiration. It also affords unimpeded locomotion relative to the ground, which affords support ... water is more substantial than air and always has a surface with air. It does not afford respiration for us. It affords drinking. Being fluid, it affords pouring from a container ... a horizontal, flat, extended, rigid surface affords support ... the affordance of what we loosely call objects are extremely various ... sheets, sticks, fibers, containers, clothing, and tools are detached objects that affords manipulation ... the richest and most elaborate affordances of the environment are provided by other animals and, for us, other people. These are, of course, detached objects with topologically closed surfaces, but they change the shape of their surfaces while yet retaining the same fundamental shape. They move from place to place, changing the postures of their bodies, ingesting and emitting certain substances, and doing all this spontaneously, initiating their own movements, which is to say that their environments are *animate* ... when touched they touch back, when struck they strike back; in short, they *interact* ... Behavior affords behavior.
> (Gibson 1986:129–135; italics original)

In this lengthy quotation the body, mobilities, affordances and interaction connect. But more importantly, seen from an interaction perspective the claim that behaviour affords behaviour is crucial. From this discussion of affordance I should aim at clarifying and specifying notions of 'mobility affordances' created by the natural environment as well as the human-made infrastructures and transport technologies. As argued by Lynch:

> Spatial forms are only partly sensed from one viewpoint, and require movement and a succession of views to be fully enjoyed. The fluctuations in space as you move about, the sight of the same objects in different relations, the sensations of near and far, closed and open, turning and straight, over and under, are one of the delights.
> (Lynch 1990:145)

So from the point of view of the city planner and designer the body and the perceptions afforded by mobilities are keys to the urban experience. This was seen by city planner and urban designer Ed Bacon, originator of the famous master plan for Philadelphia:

> The problem of the city designer is to deal simultaneously with the different speeds of movement and different rates of perception, to create forms which are as satisfying to those in an automobile as they are to those who travel on foot.
> (Bacon 1967:35)

What is crucial here is an understanding of the importance of mobile bodies to the meaning of the city.

The city and the mobile practices within it are therefore related to the mundane and everyday-life practices where the body and the cultural codes we navigate by create a situation where we are being 'staged' as well as 'staging' ourselves in what looks like banal practices, such as crossing a street (Goffman 1963:140). As Goffman rightly illustrates, mundane and ordinary embodied mobility practices are 'cultivated' into particular ways of moving, interacting in movement and bodily 'coordination-in-motion':

> Take, for example, techniques that pedestrians employ in order to avoid bumping into one another. These seem of little significance. However, there are an appreciable number of such devices; they are *constantly* in use and they cast a pattern of street behaviour. Street traffic would be a shambles without them.
> (Goffman 1972:6; italics original)

Elsewhere I have termed these practices of navigating and manoeuvring in spaces 'negotiation in motion' (and I return to this in more detail in Chapter 7) and this, I would argue, has a certain affinity with Cullen's notion of 'serial vision' as we see the importance of bodily mobilities to the perception of place and environment. The perspective thus applies to all other sorts of motion and mobilities, since what is the key is the moving, sensing and perceiving human body. Moreover, the notion links to 'jump cut urbanism' (Ingersoll 2006) and the 'cinematic' understanding of mobility and mobility design (to which I shall return to in Chapter 9):

> Let us suppose that we are walking through a town: here is a straight road off which is a courtyard, at the far side of which another street leads out and bends slightly before reaching a monument. Not very unusual. We take this path and our first view is that of the street. Upon turning into the courtyard the new view is revealed instantaneously at the point of turning, and this view remains with us whilst we walk across the courtyard. Leaving the courtyard we enter the further street. Again a new view is suddenly revealed although we are travelling at uniform speed. Finally as the road bends the monument swings into view. The significance of all this is that although the pedestrian walks through the town at a uniform speed, the scenery of towns is often revealed in a series of jerks or revelations. This we call SERIAL VISION.
> (Cullen 1996:9; emphasis original)

In a similar vein Laurence Halprin proposed that 'the essence of our urban experiences is the process of movement through a sequential and variegated series of spaces' (1963:196). The body on the move is therefore a mode of being in the world that is as profound and basic as the immobile and fixed body. Casey argues that:

The vehicle for being-in-place is the *body*. The body is indispensable here not just as a 'practical operator' of habitudinal schemes or as the 'body schema' that is the format of receptacle of such schemes ... the body's role is much more basic. In matters of place, as Henri Lefebvre claims, 'the body serves both as a point of departure and as destination'.

(Casey 2001:413; italics original)

Understanding such 'habitudinal schemes' as more than scripts and roles is of course essential. In line with thinkers such as Heidegger (1927/62) and Merleau-Ponty (1945/94), the body must be seen as the existential point of departure as well as the destination. Leaving aside a certain anthropocentrism in this perspective, the existential dimension of embodied cultures of mobilities must be reflected in its relationship to the technologies and artefacts affording and creating embodied mobilities. As the post-phenomenologist would claim:

The matter may be put simply: there is no bare or isolated micro perception except in its field of a hermeneutic or macro perceptual surrounding; nor may macro perception have any focus without its fulfilment in micro perceptual (bodily sensory) experience. Yet in the interrelation of micro- and macro dimensions of perception, there may lie hidden precisely the polymorphic ambiguities which most particularly emerge in the later work of Merleau-Ponty and Foucault in particular.

(Ihde 1993:77)

The technological artefacts and networks affording mobilities are to be understood as bodily and sensory extensions:

A tool or machine enlarges a person's worlds when he [sic] feels it to be a direct extension of his corporeal powers. A bicycle enlarges the human sense of space, and likewise the sports car. They are machines at man's command. A perky sports car responds to the driver's slightest wish. It opens up a world of speed, air, and movement. Accelerating over a straight road or swerving over a curve, momentum and gravity – these dry terms out of a physics book – become the felt qualities of motion.

(Tuan 1977:53)

The idea that technologies should be understood in their relation to the body and often as 'extensions' of the body and its senses was noticed by McLuhan (1964) and is very much in accordance with Ihde's post-phenomenological analysis, as he claims that: 'The I-world relation is changed to the window-I-world. This is more than a formal change; the way the world is experienced is changed *ontologically*' (1990:47; italics original). This means that the body's capabilities are enhanced (as 'motility') by technologies (as well as it obviously could be restrained by technologies): 'Only by using the technology is my bodily power enhanced and magnified by speed, through distance, or by any of the other ways in which technologies change my capacities. These capacities are always *different* from my naked capacities' (Ihde 1990:75; italics original). Ihde uses the distinction between 'Body I' as our immediate being-in-the-world versus the notion of 'Body II' as the experiential world mediated through artefacts and technologies (Ihde 2002:xi). 'Body I' is the existential body, so to speak, and 'Body II' may conversely be thought of as the cultural or social body. Schusterman further argues that

> To focus on feeling one's body is to foreground it against its environmental background, which must be somehow felt in order to constitute that experienced background. One cannot feel oneself sitting or standing without feeling that part of the environment upon which one sits or stands. Nor can one feel oneself breathing without feeling the surrounding air we inhale. Such lessons of somatic self-consciousness eventually point toward the vision of an essentially situated, relational, and symbolic self rather that the traditional concept of an autonomous self grounded in an individual, monadic, indestructible and unchanging soul.
> (Schusterman 2008:8)

So any technology may be thought of as a filter or an extension depending on the nature of the relationship and the affordances created by it. Inserting this understanding into the mobilities analysis we start to see that mobile technologies of all kinds (from bikes and cars to Blackberrys and smart phones) are altering our perception of the world at the most profound level and reconfiguring our bodily enactment with objects and environs: 'The experience of one's "body image" is not fixed but malleable, extendable and/or reducible in terms of the materiel or technological mediations that may be embodied' (Ihde 1990:74). Such insights are in accordance with Maurice Merleau-Ponty when he writes that

> One cannot therefore say that our body is *in* space and by the way neither that it is *in* time. It *inhabits* space and time ... I am not in space and time, I don't think space and time; I am existing in space and time, my body connects and embraces them.
> (Merleau-Ponty 1945/94:93–94; italics original, my translation)

To quote McCullough: 'Place begins with embodiment. Body is place, and it shapes your perceptions. Embodiment is not just a state of being but an emergent quality of interactions' (2004:27). As most of the above-quoted scholars agree, this is partly related to sensing but equally importantly it is related to effect and emotions.

Affect/emotions

Before moving towards the meaning of embodied cultures of mobilities to larger sets of socio-technical systems as well as cultural norms let us end this section with a discussion of emotions and affects related to bodily mobilities. Mobilities are performative acts as well as being embodied and relational practices that are creative (and at times playful) acts of affective and emotional character (Vannini 2012). I will return to this issue as I touch upon the specificities of the various ways of moving. Before that, however, I will reflect upon the deeper sensations and ultimately emotional relationships that bond bodies and movements. Feeling is relating to the world, and relating to the world is emotional. As Massumi stated in the opening quotation to this chapter:

> When I think of my body and ask what it does to earn that name, two things stand out. It moves. It feels. In fact, it does both at the same time. It moves as it feels, and it feels itself moving. Can we think of a body without this: an intrinsic connection between movement and sensation whereby each immediately summons the other?
>
> (Massumi 2002:ix)

If moving and feeling are two key dimensions of our bodily engagement with the world then perhaps also the moving body is a window into even more profound and ontological relations between world and body:

> When a body is in motion, it does not coincide with itself. It coincides with its own transition: its own variation. The range of variations it can be implicated in is not present in any given movement, much less in any position it passes through. In motion, a body is an immediate, unfolding relation to its own nonpresent potential to vary.
>
> (Massumi 2002:4)

What happens when we move is obviously that we negotiate, handle and orient ourselves in the world, making some sort of sense of it. Often this is done with a very instrumental set of goals like getting from A to B or using the least effort. But beneath this instrumental surface our bodily engagement with the world in motion also sustains an emotional relation that unfolds affects as much as reasons. There is no reason to believe that just because our systems, technologies and artefacts affording mobilities represent highly sophisticated achievements, we should have skipped the emotional and affect-based experiences of successes and failures in the everyday-life mobilities practices. Thrift theorises the emotional and affects under the heading of 'spatialities of feeling' (2008:171–197) and thus become a central theoretical figure in acknowledging the emotional geographies related to contemporary mobilities. According to Thrift there is no single definition of affect. However, for Thrift affect should be thought of as a 'form of thinking' or even as a different form of intelligence about the world (2008:175). So we relate with feelings, emotions and affect as different ways of both engaging with but also knowing the world. Affects may even be thought of as containing a potential for actions and practices: 'Affects are more than mere feelings and emotions; they also constitute *action-potential*, or an individual's dispositional orientation to the world' (Duff 2010:5; italics original). Situated mobilities are thus affective and performative at their core (Schechner 1988). From this discussion of mobile bodies, perceptions and emotions/affects I now turn to the mobile body and its relationship with systems and infrastructures as a way into understanding the cultures of mobilities.

Mobile bodies, infrastructure and the cultures of mobilities

From this discussion of the body and its senses in relation to mobilities I turn to the systems, governing rationalities and emerging cultural practices relating to these. The basic assumption behind this is that as we engage with the many stages of mobilities we are enacting scripts that either have become anchored into the systems and recurrent practices or which have been developed over time with the embodied experiences in a complex relationship of staging from above and below. To the various domains and stages of mobilities I claim there are linked certain rationalities and cultural norms. The bodily appropriation of the built environment by means of different mobility practices means that the subject is immersed not only in material hardware and infrastructures but also that 'mobile subject types' (Jensen and Richardson 2007; Richardson and Jensen 2008) are being created as imaginary entities within various policy and planning frameworks (staging from above):

> What we are exploring within these complex nexuses of physical infrastructures and technology, cultural norms and legal regulations, design codes and architecture, social practices and interaction are in fact the creation of what might be termed 'mobile subject types'. By this is meant the production of relatively clear and well defined categories of imagined mobile citizens in the socio-technical nexus of infrastructure systems ... mobility systems are designed for certain imagined types of citizens, and urban and regional maps are drawn to fit with planners' and policy-makers' imaginaries of how these particular types of citizens will want to move in time and space.
> (Richardson and Jensen 2008:218, 220)

Politics and planning together with hard infrastructure is only one dimension to contemporary urban mobilities practices. These may facilitate the production of particular mobile subjectivities and identities. Moreover, the embodied practices of mobile subjects are acts of 'culture production' as the way we move signifies who we are, our norms, aspirations and dreams:

> The first main point to observe is that even if we study the physical movement of 'objects' like people, cars, bikes, or goods we are simultaneously dealing with social issues of norms, power, identity and *culture formation*. It is fairly evident that mobility as a specific social practice may be related to cultural norms and regulations (as for example in the case of traffic regulations or local customs of movement). One might come to think of

mobilities as determined by cultural contexts. However, more importantly, mobilities and culture are not external to one another. Rather performing mobilities *is* culture. So the claim is that the mobile practices are more than physical practices as they also are signifying practices.

(Jensen 2009b:xv; italics original)

In an analysis of cars and auto-mobility reshaping American culture and individual identity Seiler finds inspiration in Foucault's notion of the 'Dispositif' (often translated as 'apparatus') and argues that 'More than a set of policies or attitudes cohering around cars and roads, automobility comprises a "multilinear ensemble" of commodities, bodies of knowledge, laws, techniques, institutions, environments, nodes of capital, sensibilities, and modes of perception' (Seiler 2008:6). So the ways we are moving are 'staged' from above by political doctrines and planning schemes, and we bodily 'stage' ourselves in myriad mobility practices. Such a 'dramaturgic' model of understanding mobilities fits closely to the notion of 'subject position' (Patton 2004:21). The 'staging' of mobile subjects is in this respect illustrative of how larger systems 'work on the bodies' of subjects in various regimes of circulation. Regimes regulating the movement of bodies in space (or confinement on the movement of bodies) have a long history. The making of state territories and the control of subjects' mobility in and out of the territory (Scott 1998) is one thing. But also the modern preoccupation with the rational organisation of social life from 'Scientific Management' with the control of the worker's bodily movements (Cresswell 2006) to the organisation of urban infrastructures and mobilities practices of moving subjects (Richardson and Jensen 2008) are examples of the inherent relationship between the mobile/immobile body and power. With the advent of new information technologies the power-holder's strategies of mobility impairment (e.g. incarceration and imprisonment) are being supplemented with the strategies of simply knowing the location of the subject (Jensen 2009a), adding new technologies of mobile governance as well as suppression illustrative of the 'dark sides' of mobilities.

From these explorations of the relationship between mobile bodies, perceptions, emotions, infrastructures and cultures of mobilities I move towards much more tangible and situational examples of embodied mobile performances.

Mobilities practices: walking

The point of departure for this exploration is the practice of walking seen as a very basic dimension of a mobile relationship to the material world. A very important point to underline here is that walking is in one sense the most basic form of mobility practices since it relates to the important event in human development, namely when humans started to walk in a bodily upright position. As such we may say that walking is a 'mode of being' (Lorimer 2011:27). Setting aside the evolutionary aspects of this mobility practice, it is less fortunate to describe walking as more 'authentic' than other mobility forms. A quick glance at the human mobilities practices of the contemporary world certainly suggests that walking is but one of a number of practices shaping our mobile engagement with the world. There is a deeper debate here about the understanding of walking and running as somewhat more 'authentic' forms of mobilities than motorised ones (e.g. car or plane). However, the study of technologically mediated and afforded mobilities practices points to the problematic assumption of identifying a natural and 'true' primordial mobility form. When it comes to walking this seems to be the understanding amongst scholars such as Augoyard (1979/2007), DeCerteau (1984), Gehl (2010), Hall (1966) and Schmitz (2006). According to these theorists walking is the primordial model of perceiving the world as well as the most authentic experience of the world. Rather than looking for an original and unmediated form of mobility we should understand the qualitative and different forms of sensing that each specific combination of human bodies, mobility technologies and infrastructures affords. Moreover, even a walk is mediated by objects like shoes and pavements! An entry point to this debate is the now-classic text by DeCerteau on walking and the critical comments from Nigel Thrift thereto. DeCerteau saw walking as a 'pedestrian's speech act' by which the pedestrian appropriates the city (DeCerteau 1984:97–99). Moreover, as briefly mentioned in Chapter 1, DeCerteau made a distinction between 'strategy' and 'tactics' and argued that 'moving about is tactical in character' (1984:xix). DeCerteau thus saw a progressive and political potential in walking that was not to be found in other modes of mobilities. Countering this, Thrift criticises DeCerteau's notion of walking as the authentic expression of embodied mobilities by pointing out that 'research on automobility shows the world of driving to be as rich and convoluted as that of walking' (2008:79). Having positioned ourselves at a critical distance from the idea that walking is more authentic than any other form of mobility I shall of course have to acknowledge that the body is differently centred in this particular practice since it becomes its own driving force, so to speak, as we are dealing with what I in Chapter 2 termed a 'muscular powered mobility mode' as opposed to a 'machine powered mobility mode'. Walking is acknowledged here to have a central and pivotal place in relation to how the body moves and how it senses movement and the environment, as well as how perception is triggered (Ingold and Vergunst 2008:1). This shall not be disputed. But it is disputable that walking is more authentic and 'real' than other forms of mobile embodied performances. The notion of 'authentic walking' ties into a moral geography that clouds the insights of 'critical mobilities thinking'. Duff argues that walking does have a profound relationship to the self and our understanding of place:

> To walk in the city is to be affected by the city, just as one's walking affects the city that this walking produces. The poetical of place generated in this walking is as much a function of practice, of a doing and making, as it is a function of feeling and affective modulation ... To walk is to be affected by place and to simultaneously contribute to the ongoing co-constitution of self and place.
>
> (Duff 2010:4, 7)

From a case study of an urban transit space where pedestrians mix with cycles, buses and lorries I found that walking as a mode of mobility carries a different and much more unfiltered communicative dimension (Jensen 2010c). People passing through this space 'negotiate in motion' and perform mobilities with the usage of a large number of detailed embodied tactics that are best perceptible between fellow pedestrians. Needless to say the car driver also has to guess whether the person standing at the kerb will walk or not, but the amount of available information is much higher amongst the pedestrians themselves when they are making their way through urban spaces. As I show in Chapter 7 in more detail, pedestrians negotiate with other pedestrians for the space, but mostly on the sidewalk. Moreover, a number of 'mobile negotiation techniques' are applied by the pedestrians whose bodily interactions in motion are the primary 'interface' to mobile situations (Jensen 2010b:397–398).

Much of this discussion of walking is biased towards the urban situation. Needless to say, other dimensions like the relationship between walking and the perception of pastoral landscapes or great open spaces may stimulate other reflections on the meaning of moving by walking. Likewise, the notion of the underpinning rationales for walking is of importance: 'Walking within a place produces meaning and constructs understanding, and the rational walking has altered from different times, as has the aesthetic of the park where people walk' (Moles 2008:41). As the mobilities practices of walking are so closely wedded to the individuals' habitus and identity, 'the way you walk' also signals issues of identity:

> People have different rhythms of moving while walking, and the sense of their own gestures is varied and noticeably different ... Even when designing for pedestrians who move at comparatively slow speeds, the environment relates to the person constantly in motion with a varied view point and a constantly changing position.
> (Halprin 1963:193, 194)

This is being utilised by sophisticated surveillance technologies where software systems detect 'suspicious' ways of moving, such as those in airports or other spaces of surveillance (Graham 2011). Also Scollon and Scollon (2003) find that the way a person walks and negotiates traffic lights is significant to questions of identity and self-understanding. Much more could be said about walking but I wish to move on to a closely related practice, namely that of running, as it in many ways shares similarities with walking as well as having its own particular dimensions.

Mobilities practices: running

In many respects the practice of running may be seen as so closely related to walking that we need not discriminate between these two sets of bodily mobilities practices. However, here I want to put emphasis on running as a particular cultural practice that opens a different set of issues next to many of those already discussed in relation to walking. In this section I look at two different dimensions of running (acknowledging that there are many other reasons to run, such as the deeply embedded flight instinct; see Hall 1966). The first is related to the recreational practice of running. This practice will be discussed on the basis of my own experiences and engagement with running. The second dimension that I touch very briefly upon is the practice of 'free running' or 'parkour'. The first dimension of running as a bodily mobility practice is, as mentioned, based upon my own experiences with running. I hope for the reader's forgiveness for this self-centred account (see Letherby 2010 for a reflective discussion of autobiography in mobilities research). However, it does strike me as being of quite some relevance to the discussion of embodied mobile performances as this is a phenomenological account of a practice that has been developed partly in relation to ideas about health and fitness, and partly from the experiences of how hard body-work frees energy and promotes relaxation over many years. So I shall make clear that this account sees running as less of an instrumental act of 'hard work' being increasingly rationalised (Bale 2011). This surely may also be the case, but that diverges from the aspects of running that are engaged with in the following account. However, as with all other modes we must take care not to romanticise or naturalise running (Vannini 2012:51).

One of the first things to notice when my autobiographical account of running is broached is the decision of routing. For me, choosing the urban tracks or the woods offers two very different ways of 'staging' a mobility experience. Needless to say, the perception of the woods is different from that of the city, but contrary to some runners I enjoy both options. In the woods nature, trees and the hilly and often uneven surfaces are the key elements to an embodied experience. Conversely I like the perception of the city when I see it from the perspective of the hard-working body. Sites and places I often experience on a bike, on the bus or in my car are perceived in a different light altogether when they become points on a physically laborious route. The woods (which I just as often visit as a walking person) are experienced as a network of paths and habitats for different species and vegetation, and can actually be said to be much more dynamic in its transformation from time to time than the city. Seeing how a tree has collapsed or parts of a path have been expanded due either to 'forest cultivation' or the imprint of BMX bikes illustrates this point. The social meetings of various users of the woods are very different from the meetings as one runs across town. There is a sense not of community (there are plenty of conflicts between runners, dog walkers, BMX riders, young families etc. in the woods) but of 'chosen co-presence' in a site where everyone has deliberately (and some with a lot of effort) chosen to move about. In the city running is obviously conspicuous if one chooses to run around the pedestrian areas, but my preference is along larger arteries of roads. One of the most significant differences in terms of bodily engagement with the places is that running in the city means negotiating a number of involuntary stops, most often in the form of traffic lights. The embodied mobility is mediated and negotiated by the traffic-light system coordinating larger flows of traffic in the city. I thus feel part of the big 'circulation machine' when I am exposed to systems processing (staging from above) mixed with my personal attempt to navigate and control my movements in the urban context (staging from below). In the woods there is much less restriction on movement as the physical topography is the main modifier. The staging from above is thus more vividly felt when I am running in the city.

Leaving aside the discussion of the context of running, there is the element of social interaction that is vital if one is running alone or as a 'mobile with'. Seen from the perspective of *Staging Mobilities* an interesting example of mobile front staging/back staging materialises as one engages in running. The sudden appearance of people on benches as an 'audience' for my staged mobility creates a dynamic situation where an attempt to negotiate a front-stage perspective takes place (i.e. upping the pace and thinking about running style). Some might argue that they do not pay attention to the presence of others when running, but several decades of running on my own and in organised races suggest that this is a marginal standpoint. Most runners notice 'audiences', whether they are other runners potentially outpacing you, pedestrians or sitting spectators. The key point in this context is that the embodied practice of running draws upon a culturally embedded reservoir of practices as well as the material and physical environment. Having participated in a number of organised races over the years I would say that it is clear that there are 'communities of running'. One meets many familiar faces, and along the route one learns to spot the experienced runner whom one might try to 'hook up' with and the novice that you know you will overtake in due time thanks to his or her speedy start.

The technologies and artefacts in play related to recreational running is a field on its own (and signifiers of what Bale (2011) considers the instrumental and rationalised practice of running). The material that running shoes are made of, the latest pulsar wrist watch with built-in GPS and real-time uploading of one's performance on the Internet are but a few of the elements of a culture of gizmos and objects. To paraphrase Latour (2005), 'assembling the runner' is a complex process involving human and non-human objects as well as including the material environment in a sensed embodied mobile experience where, for example, the steep hill is an 'agent' to be felt as much as the fellow runner. Similar to other recreational fields of activities like hiking, running has its own sub-cultural divisions of social groups. There are people uploading and sharing running routes and results. In particular I find that the watch is an interesting device to discuss in relation to running as a bodily practice. I cannot remember having gone for a run without setting the stop watch and making a note of the time in my little notebook afterwards (or, as it is now, uploading my route and speed to my PC from my GPS watch). I keep a time record of official races each time I participate, but for the ordinary routes I only note a time that is faster than earlier times. This is clearly a rationalisation and instrumental approach to running as the subjective and embodied experience is being 'disciplined' or measured as it were by the quantitative clock time. However, it is also this keeping track that makes it challenging to 'compete with oneself', so to speak (this can also be done using the 'virtual opponent' function on the GPS watch).

So by measuring the bodily mobilities performance my practice becomes objectified and thus set apart from my body as something external that I can challenge and compete with. The interesting thing here, however, is that all of this merges into the bodily experience of running. The different objects and technologies as well as the different routes and sites for running come together in a perception of the environment that is markedly different from strolling in the woods or the car drive across town. My central claim from this more phenomenological and autobiographical investigation is that the moving body inscribes a logic into our perception of the material sites as well as it is being afforded by certain materialities (from asphalt paths to traffic regulation systems or rough and difficult rural terrain).

The idea that the mobile body 'measures' and draws up the meaning of buildings and sites is no more clear than in the special discipline of free running, or 'parkour' as it is termed. So ending this section on the body and running I shall discuss this fascinating embodied cultural practice. Parkour was initially invented by military people and the perspective is to see the mundane and ordinary urban environment as a race track that can be overcome and challenged by running, jumping and climbing. Furthermore, by running, jumping and crawling on buildings and objects, the parkour practitioner 'draws up' the architecture and spaces with his or her own body. The mobile sense making creates experiences with designed and staged spaces. The practice of parkour is thus in accordance with the way Pels *et al.* see the relationship between architecture, buildings and mobile bodies: 'People perform objects, but especially buildings, by moving through and around them; but these objects also perform people by constraining their movements and by suggesting particular encounters between them and others' (2002:13). In a very explicit sense parkour thus sheds light on the staging from above in terms of architecture and urban design as well as the staging from below in the running and jumping bodies. According to Smith (2010), parkour represents a mobile and embodied engagement with the built environment that opens up new opportunities for understanding urban spaces and furniture as the practitioners of parkour explore the city by moving their bodies in a very radical and 'at the limit' way.

After this focus on running that took a very different direction in terms of 'evidence' and academic references, I now get back on track discussing the embodied mobilities practice of cycling.

Mobilities practices: cycling

The next mode of transport is equally within the realm of 'muscular powered mobilities' (Figure 5.1). Much has been written about the cultural history of the bike (Furness 2010) but here I will shape our attention by looking into the way that a specific mobility technology becomes a cultural artefact: 'The bicycle, like the automobile, is an object that becomes meaningful through its relationship to an entire field of cultural practices, discourses, and social forces' (Furness 2010:9). Furness makes a distinction between three different modes of cultural

Figure 5.1 Cycling as an embodied mobility practice.

appropriation of the bicycle, which are the recreational, utilitarian and political practices wedded to cycling practices (Furness 2010). North Europeans are far more likely than Americans to cycle for practical, utilitarian purposes (Pucher and Buehler 2008:499). Studies in China put emphasis on cycling as a recreational practice in relation to the sites of the new booming economy (Chang and Chang 2009). Until recently the utilitarian rationale has, however, been dominant in large Chinese cities like Beijing and other metropolises where the car is slowly pushing the bicycle off the streets, as it were. Elsewhere in a study of cycling in the United States I argued for the same three dimensions of recreation, utility and political voice, but also that large differences are being brought out if we look at the United States versus Denmark in relation to cycling (Jensen 2007c; Mikkelsen *et al.* 2011).

Obviously it has a lot to do with the whole nationwide transport system and the physical morphology of cities that are very different between these two settings. However, the particular cultural appropriation of the bicycle is also related to the bodily practices that in the United States are mainly catered for as a recreational or even political practice whereas in Denmark these are mundane everyday-life mobilities practices naturalising the bicycle. This creates a different socio-cultural underpinning to the embodiment of the bicycle:

> In Denmark most children will be given a bike (of sorts) shortly after they learn to walk. Even though there are many adult Danes that do not cycle at all, it seems fair to claim that there is an almost universal taken for granted understanding of bikes and their potential for mobility that is grounded in the early years of childhood. As the child grows older the bike represents the main expression of self-determined mobility and thus symbolizes freedom of movement as an important cultural signifier. One could argue that on this background the bike becomes almost invisible to most Danes. Not in the sense of it being inconspicuous in the everyday streetscape – the bike is predominantly visible as part of Danish mobility culture. But in the sense of becoming as familiar a mobility technology as say knife and fork is to everyday life's eating practices. Therefore it must be understood as less of a manifestation to see bikers in a Danish context than in an American. Until very recently the practice of cycling in the US has mostly been considered either a recreational activity or a political statement. This may be changing these years and is one of the reasons why the study of cycling practices in the US is such a fascinating topic. What is at stake is not only new ways of moving in the city, but also new ways of perceiving the city, new ways of producing and re-producing the city and ultimately new ways of constructing identities and meaning.
>
> (Jensen 2007c:1)

Comparing the cultural appropriation of the bicycle in Denmark to the usage of knife and fork may seem strange, but I mean it quite literally. As we do not pause and reflect an awful lot about the eating practice involving the artefacts of knives and forks, so very many Danes do not consider cycling to be an exotic practice. There is a multitude of reasons for this, but one inevitable in this context is that by becoming familiar with the technology from the early years of childhood the cycling practices of many Danes have become a tacitly embodied culture of mobilities. Pesses, who is a US-based scholar, also notes the differences between American and European experiences with the bike:

> Bicycle touring has existed in Europe since the Industrial Revolution ... American workers did not take to this form of recreation so quickly, and it wasn't until the 1950's that bicycle tourist organizations began to form. This cultural difference is reflected in the bicycle industry.
>
> (Pesses 2007:2–3)

According to Pucher and Buehler (2008), policy and planning in the 1970s and onwards have changed Dutch, German and Danish cycling culture and practices. The assessment is that 'cycle planning works', so to say, but more interestingly in this context is that these nations are all affluent societies suggesting that cycling in these countries is something other than an economical necessity (which seems to be the case in other parts of the world). However, if we broaden out the debate from just being a comparative discussion between North America and Western Europe we may note that

> An embodied understanding of the bicycle, affected by and affecting its users and their perception of the urban has not yet reached the thinking of transport geographers and policy makers ... cycling, 'sustainable' but marginalized, sits in between the two predominant means of moving around cities – by motorized vehicle and on foot as a pedestrian.
> (Jones 2005:815–816)

Turning to the political dimension, one may of course think of the street-clogging practices of 'Critical Mass' as a political manifestation of cycling practices (Furness 2010; Jensen 2007c). But Alred (2010) has an even more basic point linking cycling to the notion of political rights and ultimately an idea of 'cycling citizenship'. Interestingly and significantly Alred involves the body in the analysis when she argues that 'cycling as a body practice could thus be seen as a means of displaying one's identity as a healthy, low-carbon subject' (2010:36). Becoming a 'healthy, low-carbon subject' requires a set of bodily and culturally significant practices. Alred identifies four dimensions of cycling citizenship: being responsive to environmental issues, taking care of oneself, being rooted in one's locality and responding with openness to the social environment as a 'model of cycling citizenship' (2010:39). Halprin, whom we saw put specific effort into understanding and mapping the mobile body, notes the hybrid or in-between character of the cycle compared to other modes of mobility: 'halfway between the pedestrian and the motorist, bicycles give a mobility, an ease of negotiating traffic quickly, and an individuality of choice to motion which mass transportation cannot equal' (1963:77). The embodied cultural practice of cycling furthermore opens up to a particular embodiment and appropriation. The 'view from the saddle' is a sensory and embodied experience mediated by the interplay of cycling infrastructures and cycling technologies ('cycling hardware') and a more or less coherent set of cultural norms and guiding principles that may vary from explicit legislation or tacit and embodied cycling practices and norms for 'good cycling behaviour' (Andrade *et al.* 2010):

> Bicycling is a form of life in that the relations between the equipment, infrastructure, and people's practices shape what is socially possible. Getting someone on a bicycle creates the possibility of that person seeing the city as a cyclist. Unfortunately, the 'view from the saddle' is often ugly: most city streets do not adequately support cycling and safety is the major obstacle for those who are otherwise willing to ride. While economically inexpensive, bike lanes are politically expensive because they require the reallocation of roadway capacity on streets with finite rights-of-way.
> (Patton 2004:18)

Let me turn to a more fully fledged example of 'bike phenomenology', namely that of US-based scholar Jen Petersen, who argues that

> Travel by two human-powered wheels is an active choice to encounter urban elements that often go unnoticed and unappreciated by people of privilege. To commute by bicycle, for example, is a choice to breathe in the dangers of diesel pollution, which the city's poorest dwellers take in by design. But such a choice also, ten minutes hence, gives access to a completely unfiltered and breathtaking view of a quintessential monument to modernity – the Brooklyn bridge – stretched out in masoned extravagance. And what is more precious than to be treated, on a late night ride along the Hudson River, to a private showing of lights reflecting in the water from tall buildings on the palisades of the opposite bank, while sailboats rock in the river's currents? Cycling also promises encounters with pedestrians and other cyclists. Greetings and reassurance, not glassed in by power windows or drowned by the noise of idling engines, can replace the sometimes violent spatial competition that plays out between travellers who move by other means.
>
> (Petersen 2007:37–38)

Even though the tone is rather enthusiastic, what is well described here is the emotional and affect-based sense of power and self-determination that most cyclists will recognise. This is certainly a feeling that sits in the body mediated by the bike. Petersen goes on to argue:

> Bicycling provides us with an unbuffered range of sensory experiences of the monumental urbanity we have created, and a view into the spaces of hope in its cracks, fissures, and contradictions. To bicycle through frenetic and congested cities is a work of beauty, one that can redraw the often discriminatory boundaries of neighbourhoods, redeem strained social relations, and rehabilitate a suffocating natural environment, together with the ways urban inhabitants become crippled by it. Inherently human-scaled, it is one path to an alternative understanding of the urban.
>
> (Petersen 2007:37)

Whether the bike paves the way for an 'alternative understanding of the urban' must depend on the context, and here the US bias in my selection of texts surfaces again. The key point to derive from this section is that the embodiment of cycling makes a significant contribution to the perception of the city in movement. The 'view from the saddle' is, however, different not only as a function of 'cycling hardware' but equally importantly of the 'cycling software' – the latter relying on the embodiment as much as on intellectual schemes and plans.

Mobilities practices: car driving

Addressing the car is to engage with one of the most influential mobility technologies that has been the key transforming agency of urban experiences worldwide. Many scholars have pointed to the car as a destructive force in urban transformation (e.g. Gehl 2010; Jacobs 1961). However, beyond this focus on the hardware and physical morphology there are cultural and aesthetic experiences with the 'software' that are understandable only if one looks without prejudice at the bodily experiences of car driving. It should be noted at the outset that I do not endorse the many 'negative externalities' such as accidents, pollution and environmental monotony caused by the car (i.e. the 'dark sides' of auto-mobilities). However, understanding the embodiment of auto-mobilities must reach into the ordinary and positive everyday-life experiences that millions have with the car. In a critical piece, Urry writes about car culture that 'the car is the literal "iron cage" of modernity, motorized, moving and domestic' (2004b:28). This is a nice play on Max Weber's (1968) notion of Modernity as the 'iron cage' of rationality. However, it also only point towards the 'dark side' interpretations of auto-mobilities.

Car embodiment and emotions: the hybrid human–technological mobile event

It should be acknowledged that the car affords different car cultures leading to a new sense of the 'auto-self' performing in a 'fluid choreography' (Featherstone 2004:5–8). Seen from the perspective of *Staging Mobilities* and in accordance with Tim Dant I argue that: 'the motor car affords the human being locomotion and mobility, and it affords the driver motility (the capacity to move spontaneously and independently)' (Dant 2004:65). So Dant sees the 'cyborg' dimension of the car–human relationship very clearly as he states that 'the human driver is habitually embodied within the car as an assemblage that can achieve automobility' (2004:73). Therefore he ceases to see the artefact of the car and the body of the driver as two separate entities. Rather he speaks of the 'driver-car' which is 'neither a thing nor a person; it is an assembled social being that takes on properties of both and cannot exist without both' (Dant 2004:74). Dant's point may obviously be generalised to other modes of mobilities as well. Sheller adds to this perspective by including the emotional side of car driving as she argues for an emotional sociology of automobility and speaks of 'automotive emotions' (Sheller 2004:223). Needless to say, such emotive experiences cover a wide range of ways of being emotional: 'Pleasure, fear, frustration, euphoria, pain, envy: emotional responses to cars and feelings about driving are crucial to the personal investments people have in buying, driving and dwelling with cars' (Sheller 2004:224). This range of emotions, I would argue, could be broadened from being specific to cars to concerning all modes of transport. But of more importance is that the emotive and sensing relations between human and non-human is what puts the body in the centre of the analysis: 'Emotions are felt in and through the body, but are constituted by relational settings and affective cultures; they are shared, public and collective cultural conventions and dispositions' (Sheller 2004:226).

Here we are at the precise bridge to my claim that mobilities are embodied, affect-related practices that are also cultural and collective expressions. They are 'staged' and felt by a much more rich and differentiated bodily register than the dominating view of the instrumental rationality governing much transportation and city planning – the 'iron cage' of Urry as mentioned above. As a consequence of the sensed and embodied engagement with the car, Sheller speaks of a kinaesthetic investment: 'Kinaesthetic investments (such as walking, bicycling, riding a train or being in a car) orient us toward the material affordances of the world around us in particular ways and these orientations generate emotional geographies' (2004:228). Obviously this may apply to all modes of mobilities, but the notions of 'kinaesthetic investments' and 'emotional geographies' are important pointers and are an expression of 'driving the car [that] becomes much more closely wrapped up with the body (or at least, a naturalized view of embodiment) via the active intermediaries of software and ergonomics' (Thrift 2008:85). Urry continues to say that

> The driver's body is itself fragmented and disciplined to the machine, with eyes, ears, hands, and feet all trained to respond instantaneously and consistently, while desires even to stretch to change position, to doze or to look around are being suppressed.
>
> (Urry 2004b:31)

Here Urry takes side with what I term the perspective of 'de-sensing' the car (see also Sennett 1994:18). Many seem to support this interpretation but in light of the theoretical framing here I would prefer to speak of the car as 'filtering' sensations. By this is meant that the car, rather than inhibit sensations, filters them and accentuates other combinations of senses.

Thus the sensation of heat and cold is heavily mediated as is smell, but a different sense of acceleration and deceleration is also afforded. It is by no means a new discussion as, for example, Hall has pointed to the fact that humans were equipped in sensory terms for moving through the environment at less than 5 miles an hour, and that increasing beyond this speed involves sensory deprivation (Hall 1966:177). Besides naturalising the pedestrian this 'de-sensing argument' seems to appeal to critics of car-based urban developments in general (Gehl 2010). This is important since on some dimensions Urry and others are correct in claiming that the car takes away elements of sensation like the smell and sound of the city. On the other hand I think it is safe to say that no one who has been pushed back in the seat due to instant acceleration would claim that they felt and sensed nothing. So the car (and also mass transit and all other 'capsular' mobilities devices) does change the senses but they very often substitute with others and different bodily registers meaning that a more accurate way to describe the human–car relationship is that of 'filter' rather than lack of sensations. In Katz's terms, we trade a set of competencies or the opposite as we shift between the mobilities modes of, for example, driving and walking:

> When a person moves from being a pedestrian to being a driver, he or she trades in one dialectical complex of interaction competencies and

incompetencies for another. For the same reason that the vision of drivers is relatively unencumbered, the driver's ability to speak and, more generally, to express his or her understanding and intentions to other drivers is severely impaired.

(Katz 1999:25)

The car reconfigures our sensing experience of mobilities but it does not take the sensing experience away and the more reasonable interpretation is thus that car driving is what Olesen terms a 'plurisensorial' mediation where a very large part of the way we appropriate and perceive the material environment is shaped and influenced by this global technology:

> Driving a car is noteworthy as a more complex example that involves whole-body motility. Driving involves several senses at once, that is *plurisensorial* mediation. The joy of driving is normally connected to the total range of embodiment relations. The driver experiences the road and the surroundings *through* the activity of driving the car, the movement being the focal activity. The bodily experience is expanded to include what can be experienced by a (driver-in-a-car) body. In respect to several other kinds of experiences, many instruments, technologies, and a more composite learning process are involved here, but the involved knowledge is fundamentally embodied ... our sense of our body is polymorphous: our body experiences are not predetermined but rather malleable and reducible in correlation to those technological mediations the body is able to take in. The sensing body may just as well be a (listen-with-the-stethoscope) body as well as a (drive-in-the-car) body, or something entirely different. It depends on the situation and the already constituted technologically mediated relations. The body can thus be described as *multistable*.
>
> (Olesen 2006:241–242; italics original)

From this debate on how the car changes perceptions and how humans and non-humans interact mediated by bodies let us look at the car from the 'outside', so to speak. What do the transformational capacities of the car amount to when we start exploring the spaces and sites of 'car rule'?

Car spaces: the sites of cars and their aesthetics

In architecture and urban design there has for some time been a critical discussion about the knee-jerk reaction seeing all car infrastructures as ugly and bad (I return to this theme in Chapter 9). Needless to say some truly are, but one misses the finer grains of the importance to our embodied mobilities cultures if one does not see these sites as stages for human life and experiences as well (Appleyard *et al.* 1964:3). So from this perspective we learn that there is a phenomenology and bodily perception of mobilities to be developed for each new technology affording mobilities. There is a new aesthetics and perception that leans more on the effectual, the embodied and the experiences that moves beyond instrumental necessities or inconveniences. Writers as diverse as Appleyard *et al.* (1964), Banham (1971/2009), Halprin (1963), Ingersoll (2006), Katz (1999), Lynch (1990) and Waldheim (2006a) are exponents of this shift in perspective. When it comes to the car and the highway we may think of this as a phenomenology of the embodied highway experience:

> The sensation of driving a car is primarily one of motion and speed, felt in a continuous sequence. Vision, rather than sound and smell, is the principal sense. Touch is a secondary contributor to the experience, via the response of the car to hands and feet. The sense of spatial sequence is like that of large-scale architecture; the continuity and insistent temporal flow are akin to music and cinema. The kinesthetic sensations are like those of the dance or the amusement park.
>
> (Appleyard *et al.* 1964:4)

Here we see affect, body and sense inherently related to mobilities and even though this over-emphasis on vision might be said to under-state that cars have smells, ambiences and tactile dimensions when they are operated, the position is clearly within the phenomenology of car driving. Rather than de-sensing or sealing off the car user, the car is understood as a 'filter' (Appleyard *et al.* 1964:4). This is in accordance with Ihde's post-phenomenology of objects–humans–worlds and also opens up to understanding the particular sensational quality of the 'filter' rather than condemning the car as an isolating 'capsule' (DeCauter 2004). So the car is a performative technology that alongside other mobilities technologies is assembled into networks and relationships with human agents affording it to perform mobilities (and, of course, it may contribute to barriers and social exclusion): 'Driving, I have argued, enables an affirmative performance of energy, speed, and motion even as it emplaces the subject in social relations and environments not of her making and decreasingly malleable by democratic, collective will' (Seiler 2008:144).

Very much as Lynch argues that travel may be suffered or enjoyed, but will be remembered, so Merriman argues that the contemporary experience of motorway driving constitutes an important cultural, embodied and emotional experience:

> The practice of driving or being a passenger in particular cars, travelling to and from particular places, along particular stretches of motorway, provoke a range of emotions, thoughts and sensations: from feelings of anxiety or excitement about being in motorway traffic, to emotions surrounding one's departure and arrival at another place. We may get bored, feel strangely alone, or feel quite excited or relaxed on the motorway, but our movements and actions are still implicated in the working and performance of the motorway landscape, the ongoing 'placing' of these driving environments in a myriad of different ways.
>
> (Merriman 2007:218)

The speed potential, the sensations and the aesthetics of car spaces are seen by some scholars as the hallmark of our time (even though its time may in fact be running out):

> the automobile on the freeway is symbolic of the intense dedication of our age to motion. No other combination gives the same sensation of speed ... Freeways which carry the automobile in its adventures are among the most beautiful structures of our age ... these vast and beautiful works of engineering speak to us in the language of a new scale, a new attitude in which high-speed motion and the qualities of change are not mere abstract conceptions but a vital part of our everyday experience.
>
> (Halprin 1966:11, 16)

Despite this overly positive language, Halprin was not an uncritical apologist for urban car mobility and stated that freeway design has paid little respect to urban design values. However, Halprin saw this 'dark side' of mobilities as something owing to architects, planners and designers' lack of ability to unfold its true potential. A number of architects and designers (Appleyard *et al.* 1964; Halprin 1963; Ingersoll 2006; Lynch 1990; Venturi *et al.* 1972) compare urban auto-mobilities to a cinematic experience. Halprin writes of urban mobility as similar to frames in a motion picture (1963:199) and Ingersoll (2006) uses the term 'jump-cut urbanism' to capture the cinematic 'staging' of auto-mobilities as well as the creative 'editing' that is the architect, planner, traffic engineer or urban designer's job.

An concluding note for this section on the car is that I fully endorse the scholars that see the future extrapolation of existing car system developments as unsustainable and without a safe future (Dennis and Urry 2009). Alternative visions for a world 'after the car' as we know it will not, however, change the fact that the car has shaped the mobile experiences of millions of people since its invention and in particular in the post-war period. On top of this, experiments with alternatives to the car as we know it still need to be close to the embodied experiences of car driving (for example, the MIT project *Reinventing the Automobile*; Mitchell *et al.* 2010). As space is restricted, however, I move on to the last mobilities mode in this chapter, namely that of public transportation or mass transit.

Mobilities practices: mass transit

This theme is treated very briefly here since the practice of 'metro riding' is the topic of Chapter 8. Bodily sensation is not the same in all public transport systems. There is, for example, a world of difference between riding a bus without air conditioning or the Sky Train in Bangkok (Jensen 2007a). Likewise, the rural bus experience on a hilly countryside is very different from the urban subway. Here I lean on earlier research and its focus on how the mass-transit systems of the Bangkok Sky Train and the urban metros of Paris, London and

Copenhagen engage with users and their mobile bodies (Jensen 2007a, 2008b, 2012a). Moreover, I should note that in some contexts riding a public bus is a signal of lack of resources and social status (like the non-air-conditioned bus in Bangkok), whereas no one would claim that London's 'Tube' users are of lower social income and status groups altogether. This goes to show that an infrastructure is being inscribed into a particular material context as well as, of course, affording particular experiences that are all embodied and sensed.

One of the key experiences with mass transit that most people are familiar with is that the itinerary and routing is not made by individual choice. Small wonder mass transit is also termed 'public transportation'. This covers the fact both that the providing of mass-transit services is often seen as a public job, but also that we are sharing the spaces and technologies with our fellow mobile citizens. Thus the second experience many people have is that one often has to share a very limited space with other mobile bodies. Goffman used this to analyse how people produce and sustain the order of public space (Goffman 1963). But also the very bodily sensation of overcrowded buses and train compartments can be part of the experience. So it is not surprising that the creation of the now-classic term 'personal space' was actually created in relation to analysis of public transportation:

> I introduced the term 'personal space' to describe the emotionally-tinged zone around the human body that people feel is their space ... the personal space concept has been applied in the design and layout of many things, but its greatest applicability is in mass transit and institutions with fixed seating and little opportunity for personal mobility.
> (Sommer 2007:2–3)

Often the crowded experiences with mass transit are used as an argument for not using it (Næss and Jensen 2005). This definitely has to do with the feeling of transgressing 'personal space'. But mass transit also solves huge transportation challenges in many global metropolises and they are often iconic and identity-giving systems and artefacts that signify whole cities – think of the London 'Tube' or the New York City Subway, to mention a couple of the more well known. Looking at an investigation of three major subway systems in Europe (or what I termed 'European Metroscapes'), namely those of London, Paris and Copenhagen, the hybrid and networked dimension of human/non-human interaction and the moving subject as an embodied subject opens up to seeing a very complex field indeed (Jensen 2012a). I will return to this in more detail in Chapter 8.

Another example of mass transit that I briefly look into is the Sky Train in Bangkok (BTS). In some respects it is like the one in Copenhagen with its smooth systems and shiny aesthetics. But the main difference in a bodily sense is that the Sky Train in Bangkok has air conditioning! This sounds trivial but it is not. The humid and smog-clogged streets of Bangkok stand in stark contrast to the quiet and almost frictionless flow many metres above in the cooled and controlled environment of the train compartments. The story of the Bangkok Sky Train is both a story of mass transit providing new layers of socio-spatial segregation to a city, and the story of how a new mass-transit system may alter the time regimes and the cultures of meetingness (Urry 2007) by establishing a new culture of punctuality (Jensen 2007a:402). I will explore the Bangkok Sky Train in more detail in Chapter 8. Here the key thing to notice is the difference the BTS makes in relation to creating a very different bodily feeling by being smoothly transported over the clogged and polluted streets in an air-conditioned train. The coupling of almost seamless travel and cold air is noticeable in a city like Bangkok and is illustrative of how the staging from above may afford a set of very distinctly sensing embodied experiences.

The Highway Code: a short illustration of 'mobile body semiotics'

As we saw in Chapter 3 the semiotic dimension of the material environment is important to understand the processes of *Staging Mobilities*. In this chapter on embodied performances I will briefly mention the special case of the situation where the mobile body becomes a sign. In Britain the emergence of mass motorisation led to a large increase in traffic accidents and deaths. Therefore the government issued the first *Highway Code* in 1931 and the very language accompanying and legitimising the code was one of an appeal to the interest in one's fellow mobile citizen and the common good (Highway Code 2008). The way this code is illustrative of a 'doctrine' and a 'normative manifesto of mobility' has been described elsewhere (Jensen 2010c). Here I focus on one particular dimension of the code (and obviously this is just one example that could have been elaborated with other national regulatory frameworks), namely the way it addresses the body as a sign-giving vehicle and a mobile semiotic entity. The body as a sign mediating mobilities is a well-known phenomenon in general, such as in the 'walk' and 'stop' signals to be found in most cities across the world today (Figure 5.2)

The *Highway Code* targeted the body and the practices of the mobile citizen in a very direct manner as an object of disciplining and 'ordering'. This is seen in the way the code recommends particular bodily practices and gestures related to the communication of 'mobile intentions' on the road. There are a number of very detailed gestures and bodily postures that one can find meticulously described in the code. Besides being a key illustration of how state powers work in a very direct way on the subject's bodies inscribing them in a set of practices that must be obeyed in order to 'perform correct mobility', the case of body signs is interesting since the 'sign' itself is moving. Moreover, there is much less control with the 'sign' both in terms of whether the human body will in fact perform the sign correctly at the given time and place, as well as whether the 'sign' will be 'read' with the precise intention of the 'intentio auctoris'. The person giving signs by bodily expression may do so in an idiosyncratic way leading the 'reader' to misunderstand the message of the situation. The 'mobile body semiotics' is therefore an illustration of a sign-giving situation and

Figure 5.2 Mobile body semiotics.

'staging' where the discretion room for alternative interpretations is present at a much higher level than, for example, in an airport or the road-side where a well-known and always identical sign informs the mobile subject about particular restrictions or opportunities (from speed limits to car park guidance). Moreover, the collective practices can be sensitive to locality, as is the case in Copenhagen where cyclists have invented a local sign variation for communicating intentions of directional change by using the hand pointing out from about the hip.

Concluding remarks

It is not possible to do justice to the many differences and alterations working their way through the many mobility modes discussed. However, it should be clear that embodied cultures of mobilities and their relationships to the infrastructures, spaces, technologies and artefacts affording these is a complex discussion. The 'staging' from above of mobile bodies as well as the way these mobile bodies 'stage' themselves with repercussions for experiences and cultures lends itself to the development of new theoretical concepts and nomenclatures.

The discussion so far has put the mobile body at the centre. Therefore I want to end this discussion with a perspective that may be termed a new 'mobility aesthetics'. The realm of aesthetics becomes highly relevant as we engage the wider production of subjectivity and the meaning of movement to perception. We are looking at 'experience in motion' and the body, as shown in the chapter, plays the pivotal role in creating the touch points for the creation of cultures and practices related to mobilities. From understanding the moving body in its many different subject–space–object configurations like walking, running, cycling etc., I argue that two essential outcomes are being created. First, the mobile body produces and re-produces a mobile aesthetics that creates particular subjectivities and particular ways of perceiving the world. This is the case regardless of whether the embodied mobility practice we study is walking or driving. Following from this is the second point. This has to do with the way mobile embodied perceptions are creating systems, patterns and models of moving and being moved. That is to say, embodied mobilities afford particular normative and social interactions that aggregate into cultural patterns of mobilities meaning. Such embodied cultures of mobilities are at one and the same time very specific to particular modes of mobilities (cars afford different experiences than walking shoes) and similar (our body and senses interact with systems, technologies and artefacts that have the same body 'interface' regardless of whether we are driving, sailing or flying). The self–world relation is enacted differently as our bodies are either fixed or moving through spaces that may be familiar or unknown, local or global, generic or specific and increasingly being mediated, afforded and created by technologies, artefacts and systems of mobilities. The mobile body is the entry point to understanding the individual's engagement with the world as well and is the key to seeing the way meaning and norms are created in embodied cultures of mobilities. This is particularly relevant to notice when the epicentre of the analysis is the mobile situation.

There is a new 'mobility aesthetics' that in this context is defined as the production of subjectivity and the meaning of movement to perception. Here I should mention that the notion of 'aesthetics' is related to everyday life as a(n) (art)work and the creative practices social agents perform to 'create life' rather than the classical notion of judgements concerning 'the beautiful' (Nielsen 2001; Turner 1982; Vannini 2012). To this links a notion of 'mobile sensations' meaning that the human body senses the world visually and corporeally by moving in it. The physical and almost 'mechanical' part of this relates to a 'mobile kinaesthetic', by which is meant that the human body experiences the world as it moves, but also refers to, for example, the way temperatures are sensed and the efforts and the 'work' the body has to perform to become mobile. These come together under the notion of 'mobile embodied performances' focusing on the fact that humans experience the world in bodily mobility but equally important that they act in the world by mobile embodied practices. Such practices may be thought of as performative in the sense that we stage and act in front of 'others' but also in the sense that the mobile body enacts and creates identities and relationships by its movement. Embodied mobilities have performative capacities. The material sites and technologies that bodies negotiate in mobile practices may then be thought of as 'mobility affordances'. By this is meant how the specific relation between the moving body and its material environment opens up (or narrows down) to particular modes of mobilities, different speeds, trajectories etc. 'Mobility affordances' illustrate the very specific and material dimensions to mobile situations. As the body in motion is working hard to orient itself, make complex decisions and interpret the motives and intentions of other bodies we may say that what is taking place is 'coordination in motion'. This relates to the more instrumental feature of continuous monitoring and more or less self-conscious work by mobile bodies aiming at preventing physical contact with fellow mobile subjects as well as avoidance of collision with physical obstacles or 'dangerous' mobile objects (e.g. cars, trains).

Across all cases of mobilities research the moving and perceiving body is crucial. However, what becomes even more interesting under the notion of a 'mobile body semiotics' is that not only do human bodies move and sense the material and semiotic environment; the body on its own also becomes a 'sign vehicle' communicating intentions and norms targeted at orchestrating mobilities. Therefore the codified regulatory principles governing the gestures of the mobile bodies as they move in the traffic become an interesting and illustrative case of a 'mobile body semiotics'. In almost direct connection to the 'mobile body semiotics' is therefore the idea of a 'mobilities choreography'. Many urban scholars have reflected upon the orchestration and the notations capturing both the intentions from above as well as the signifying practices from below. This tension I argue can be understood as the key dimension to *Staging Mobilities* but there are also interesting lessons to be learned if we start thinking with these very specific dramaturgic metaphors drawn from the world of dance and theatre. As we look at how the environment's semiotic layer instructs and affords particular mobile practices it makes sense (to a certain extent) to think of these in terms of 'choreography', such as when we study a busy street crossing or an airport space processing passengers.

The mobile embodied performances are thus a crucial dimension to the *Staging Mobilities* framework as we are embodied in any material practice in the world. I want to conclude by stating that the body assembles or 'collects' the mobile situation in time and space. I have now laid out the three key areas of the framework in this section: the physical settings, material spaces and design; the social interactions; and the mobile embodied performances. After this general framing we shall look into practices of mobilities in the third part of the book.

Part III
Practices of mobilities

6 Networked technologies and the will to connection

> The people who first built a path between two places performed one of the greatest human achievements. No matter how often they might have gone back and forth between the two and thus connected them subjectively, so to speak, it was only in visibly impressing the path into the surface of the earth that the places were objectively connected. The will to connection had become a shaping of things, a shaping that was available to the will at every repetition, without still being dependent on its frequency or rarity. Path-building one could say, is a specifically human achievement; the animal too continuously overcomes a separation and often in the cleverest and most ingenious ways, but its beginning and end remain unconnected, it does not accomplish the miracle of the road: freezing movement into a solid structure that commences from it and in which it terminates
>
> Georg Simmel, 'Bridge and Door', 1909/97, p. 66

Introduction

This chapter puts forward the argument that mobilities research needs to pay increased attention to the way network technologies and location-aware media are influencing movement in everyday life. Georg Simmel argued more than a century ago for the importance of understanding the 'will to connection' as a defining human feature. Since then much technological development has taken place and today we need to engage with this from the perspective of the 'mobilities turn'. Crucially, 'visibly impressing the path into the surface of the earth' is no longer sufficient evidence of connections and interactions since networked technologies create connections by 'invisible' linkages (Willis 2008:23) across time and space, suggesting that we need to add 'digital connectivity' to 'physical proximity' in order fully to comprehend contemporary mobilities. This chapter foregrounds technology as a precondition to mobilities, arguing for a situational and everyday-life perspective as part of the *Staging Mobilities* framework. The chapter puts focus on the dimension of network technologies in particular, which is understood to be nested within the theme of 'physical settings, material spaces and design'. Here the chapter engages with notions of 'Net Locality' (Gordon and Silva 2011), 'Code/Space' (Kitchin and Dodge 2011), 'Digital Ground' (McCullough 2004), 'Splintering Urbanism' (Graham and Marvin 2001) and the

'Sentient City' (Shepard 2011) in order to qualify the technology dimension of the *Staging Mobilities* framework.

The mobile experiences of contemporary society are practices that are meaningful and normatively embedded. That is to say, mobility is seen as a cultural phenomenon shaping notions of self and other as well as the relationship to sites and places. Furthermore, an increasing number of such mobile practices are mediated by technologies of tangible and less tangible kinds (Wilken and Goggin 2012; Vannini *et al.* 2012). Thus by focusing on the complex relationship of networked technologies within the sphere of mobilities it is shown that we need to move beyond the dichotomies of global or local, nomad or sedentary, digital or material. The chapter investigates the meaning of mobilities and the potential in mediation and technologies. In particular a critical awareness of how such technologies shape the foreground/background attention of social agents seems crucial. By studying embedded technologies and 'ambient environments' we increase our knowledge about the over-layering of the material environment with digital technologies. The presence of GPS (Figure 6.1), mediated surfaces,

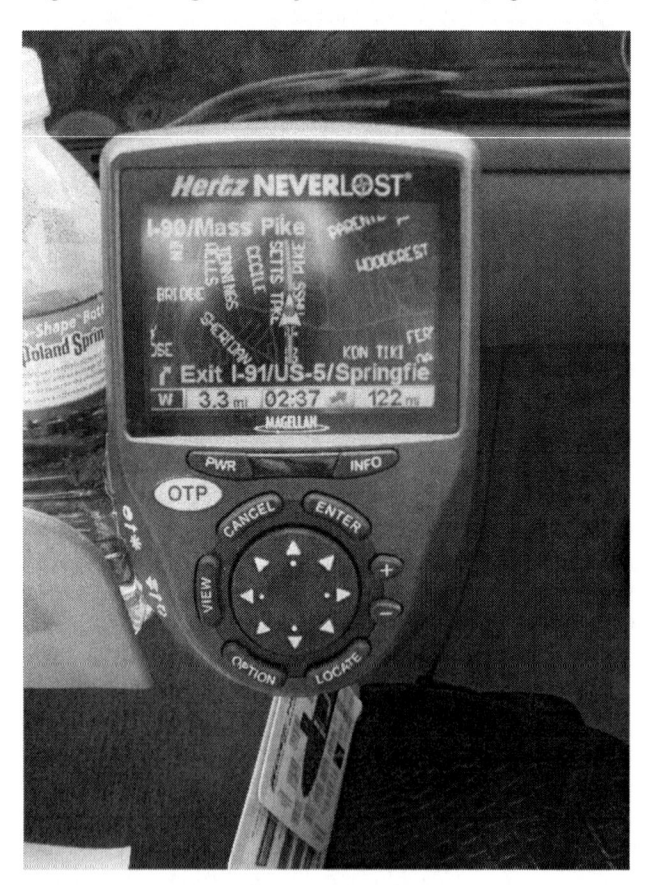

Figure 6.1 Hertz car rental 'never lost' GPS.

mobile agents (robots), RFID and other technologies that all relate to contemporary mobilities practices adds a new dimension to the notion of movement and constitutes new arenas and tools for identity construction and social interaction (as well as, of course, commercial exploitation and state control). Networked technologies constitutes a field of exploration into broader issues of democracy, multiple publics, privacy issues, forms of segregation and new mobile (electronic and material) agoras pointing towards a critical reinterpretation of contemporary politics of space and mobilities.

The structure of the chapter is as follows: after this introduction I discuss how mediated and networked technologies must be included in the *Staging Mobilities* perspective as a key feature of physical settings and material design. In the following section I engage with three specific perspectives on the networked technologies that are particularly important, namely those of Net Locality, Code/Space and the Sentient City. In two shorter sections to follow this I point at how lived mobilities are produced within socio-technical mobility systems on an everyday-life basis and how power may be conceptualised as a movement from 'enclosure' to 'tracking', illustrating a reconfiguring of the public and the political. The chapter ends thereafter with a few concluding remarks.

Mediated and networked technologies

If we see mobilities as being afforded by networked technologies as well as understanding these to be effects of multiple mobile interactions, a key category like 'place' alters. As I showed in earlier chapters this means thinking in terms of a 'relational and mobility-oriented sense of place' that merges assemblages and mobilities as an analytical perspective. This is a deepening of the perspective discussing places and mobilities in the light of relational assemblages from Chapter 2, but with an explicit focus on networked technologies as a key feature of the *Staging Mobilities* framework.

We are facing an understanding of place as something that has more to do with mobilities than stability, more with 'becoming' than 'being' (Casey 1997:317; Dovey 2010:13). In this chapter I connect this relational and mobilities-oriented sense of place to the networked technologies of the contemporary city. Shepard describes the urban situation where digital and material space and technologies overlay each other as one where the city becomes 'sentient': 'a sentient city, then, is one that is able to *hear* and *feel* things happening within it, yet it doesn't necessarily know anything in particular about them. It *feels* you, but doesn't necessarily *know* you' (Shepard 2011:31; italics original). In a city that 'feels' (or at least records, stores and recycles data and tracking information), the relationship to place becomes more ephemeral and less tied into classical notions of fixed belonging. Physical space is being over-layered with mediated technologies of all sorts, creating 'augmented space' (Manovich 2006). This, however, is by no means related to the 'end of geography' or the seamlessness and frictionless utopias analysed in the literature (Jensen and Richardson 2004). Rather, we see a situation where sites are mediated by 'local protocols' (McCullough 2004) and where 'spatially dispersed yet coordinated, fluid collections of wirelessly interconnecting individuals – perhaps assembled, from the beginning, in cyberspace rather than at any physical location – are becoming a crucial fact of urban life' (Mitchell 2003:161).

An understanding of the interdependence of technologies and mobilities is essential to understanding how place increasingly becomes mediated and thus 'produced' by technologies. Furthermore, such an understanding must include a notion of a relational geography which lays a stress on movement, fluidity and 'mixity' (Massey 2005). The situation may be described as one of 'emergent urbanism' (Pinilla 2007). It is a situation where the fixed hierarchy of global and local becomes blurred and the notion of 'scale' becomes more a question of mediation, networked selection and mobilities. Thus we may say that we move from a situation of homogenous and fixed conceptions of spatial configurations to a situation of heterogeneous and fluid conceptions of spatial configurations. The key point being that in the heterogeneous model proximity is defined by selective and filtered mediation. In other words, the networked relationship and the layers of communication may (to a certain extent) compensate for a lack of physical proximity. At least it is safe to say that in the heterogeneous model sites become defined by the degree of mediation and networked links – or bypasses. So rather than subscribing to a notion of 'end of geography' and footloose visions of cyberspace, I want to point to the increasingly (but clearly transformed) important relationship to material and physical sites. So place is defined by the flows and fluids either crossing through it or for various reasons bypassing it (e.g. powerful software selection or physically decoupled sites). However, this does not mean that we should cease to include the fixed and the permanent in our theoretical understandings. Rather, flows need fixity (McCullough 2004) or, as we saw Urry argue, 'it is the dialectics of mobility/moorings that produces social complexity' (2003:126).

Within such new hybrid system of place and flow we may start to think of the notion of 'Hertzian landscapes' (Mackenzie 2006:141) as a way of understanding the mediated ground condition for networked urban mobilities. However, just as I do not see the value in thinking about a placeless understanding of the new media and technologies, so an unrestricted and information-flooded condition makes no sense. Only by selection, placement and channelling does it make sense to think about mediated places and technologies. In the words of McCullough, there is a need for 'local protocol' and grounding. Analysts of the contemporary situation point to the fact that the previous obsession with the 'virtual' and cyberspace where technology 'took off' as it were from the physical environment has come to be replaced with a beginning awareness of the importance of location, placement and the situated (Crang and Graham 2007; Manovich 2006; McCullough 2004). Rather than working within separate domains, new media and technologies overlay the physical world of places, houses and infrastructures. Thus creating a situation where the physical placement of social agency and the technology at hand becomes crucial. Much of the engagement with these technologies is to be found in sites of transit and mobilities. As we move across cities utilising numerous networked technologies to navigate, coordinate and facilitate our trajectories, potentials for new experiences might occur in these sites of mediated interaction. Needless to say, new means of control and power also loom within the 'augmented spaces' (Manovich 2006). In other words, the 'dark sides' of mobilities may equally be sustained by these new technologies as will new potentials for social interaction and coordination.

In this chapter I argue that it is important to understand how the networked technologies relate to contemporary urban mobilities, and offer potentials for transgressing mobilities as a 'waste of time' or instrumentalism at the same time as they are power-laden and oscillate between state control and market consumerism. Such a discussion should try to point to the third space for meaningful social interaction mediated by networked technologies that goes beyond state control and market commercialism. Furthermore the critical dimension to this discussion addresses the issue of 'qui bono?' or who wins? (Flyvbjerg 1996). As mobilities is a socially differentiated phenomenon, new networked sites of interaction potentially favour some groups whilst disfavouring others. What really matters is how to empower people by exploring the potentials of the new mediated technologies. But being critical also means to problematise the taken-for-granted notion that infrastructures always host instrumental practices and that they are generic 'non-places' (Augé 1995). Here I subscribe to a 'politics of visibility' in the sense that new experiments and explorations of augmented spaces and mediated networks become crucial when discussing the pros and cons of these often 'invisible' technologies (Crang and Graham 2007). In terms of not only 'thinking mobilities' (analysis) but also 'designing for flows' (intervention) it seems pertinent to explore the opportunities for transit spaces to become more than venues for instrumental mobility practices. The issue of how to develop and design 'public domains' in these spaces and with the help of multiple and layered technologies is at the forefront here. The temporal and often 'messy' transit spaces need to be seen as sites of interaction between multiple publics and social groups – the very definition of public domain (Hajer and Reijndorp 2001). Today's spaces of mobilities are 'rooms' in which we live much of our life. Beyond that the meaning of mobilities is more than circulation as it becomes a culturally significant practice. Therefore sites of mobilities and infrastructures facilitating these could become sites of cultural production, enhanced experience and democratic pluralism (Calabrese 2003). Meeting points, exchanges and flows of communication may be commercial and less oriented towards building public spheres (like the commercial billboards alongside the urban freeway). However, this does not rule out a potential for rethinking the relation of infrastructures to notions of the public realm. The moving urbanite engages with multiple mobile and electronic agoras during travel. We are, as mentioned, linked-in-motion and thus not just passively being shuffled across town. The new mediated spaces are unfolding between many different normative ways of engaging with the social production of mobilities and interaction. Assessing whether they are socially inclusive or exclusive, environmentally sound or destructive, creative or mindlessly reproducing established ways of thinking, if they are

Net Locality, Code/Space and the Sentient City

In this section I aim to qualify the understanding of how networked technologies afford and affect contemporary mobilities. In particular I draw on recent research that sets up a vocabulary containing key terms like 'Net Locality' (Gordon and Silva 2011), 'CodeSpace' (Kitchin and Dodge 2011), 'Digital Ground' (McCullough 2004), 'Splintering Urbanism' (Graham and Marvin 2001), the 'Militarization of Urbanism' (Graham 2011) and the 'Sentient City' (Shepard 2011). Even though much research is being conducted on the importance of understanding mobilities in relation to the geographical and social realms of society (Cresswell 2006; Graham and Marvin 2001; Jensen 2006; Urry 2007), I would argue for an understanding of mobilities as particularly dependent on interactive technologies and socio-technical systems, since 'the powers of "humans" are always augmented by various material worlds, of clothing, tools, objects, paths, buildings and so on' (Urry 2007: 45). So what we are confronting may be thought of as a 'multi-layered technological negotiation' (Wasiak 2009:357) as the interactions of everyday life increasingly are mediated and redefining the spaces of interaction (Marchetti 2011:22).

Gordon and Silva argue that the notion of 'Net Locality' implies a ubiquity of networked information as a cultural formation where we no longer enter the web, but where it is all around us (Gordon and Silva 2011:2–3), or as van't Hof *et al.* put it, we have moved 'from being on the Net, to being in the Net' (2011:14). As such the term describes a situation where urban space has become hybridised towards a convergence and overlapping of material and digital realms and thus strikes a chord with the description made by McCullough (2004). Furthermore, experiencing 'Net Locality' transforms our understanding of 'near and far' and affects our understanding of the co-presence of others. The way we meet these new changes and technologies are by using GPS tracking devices helping us navigate through space, by downloading apps that make us aware of the location of particular features in the city (shops, services, sights), or with travel information being fed back in real time to the mobile subject. In all of these ways (and multiple others) the networked technologies facilitate, orchestrate and afford particular mobile practices and as such are illustrative of the mobile staging of everyday-life mobilities. The fact that much technology creates the opportunities for mobilities to take place in the first place is due to the fact that computing has become ubiquitous (McCullough 2004) as not many areas of human activities are outside 'code' (i.e. regulation and staging by means of software). In light of this we may start to speak of 'code/space' as a term for the situation where software (written in 'code') becomes intertwined with space and the material world in such a manner that the strict distinction between these collapses (Kitchin and Dodge 2011). In a thought-provoking statement Kitchin and Dodge embark on the thought experiment of imagining 'life outside code':

Living beyond the mediation of software means being apart from collective life: not appearing in government records; not employing any utilities such as water and electricity or banking services; not using any kinds of household appliances that rely on digital code to control functions, ranging from bathroom scales to washing machines; not watching or taking part in commercial entertainment or recreational activity (e.g. watching television, reading a newspaper); excluding oneself from professional healthcare, avoiding all manner of everyday life activities such as shopping (thereby eluding the significant role of software in barcode systems, computerized cash registers, credit cards, and the like); and not travelling anywhere by any mode of transport (pedestrians are registered on digital surveillance camera networks). In fact, even nonparticipation is often still logged; passivity is as easily monitored by software as activity is.

(Kitchin and Dodge 2011:ix)

Obviously the effects of being enmeshed in 'code/space' may both be liberating and oppressing. Here the key point is that it seems to have become so all-embracing that it has broad repercussions for all dimensions of life including mobilities. There are people starting to criticise this situation from the perspective of 'off-grid living' and other attempts to deliberately avoid engagement with 'the system' as it ranges from infrastructure and technologies to government regulations etc. (see Rosen 2010; www.off-grid.net or www.livingoffgrid.org). It seems fair to say that the 'off-grid' philosophy is clearly challenging the key point of 'code/space' and eventually leads to the questions of whether it is possible to live outside the code (and the grid), or if the omnipotence of code and grid makes this impossible? In political terms the question is partly what influence the subject has on these systems, but also whether there is an 'outside'? This is not the place to engage with political philosophy, but the logical end of such thinking seems to point at strategies for change that either seek to place themselves 'outside' (like off-grid living) or, conversely, engage with the political change 'from within'. In terms of the latter I believe a strategy like the 'politics of visibility' becomes crucial.

According to Gordon and Silva the presence of location-aware technologies is not sufficient in itself to create 'Net Localities'. Rather these are practised spaces and rely on co-present individuals. Thereby the 'Net Locality' shapes the experiences of those present who are not networked, online or attached to a networked communication device (Gordon and Silva 2011:86). People without network connectivity living in spaces over-layered with networked technologies for one thing seem to 'live in a different city', as they are not engaging with the digital layer operative for networked subjects. This, of course, suggests that the so-called 'digital divide' must be addressed. However, in the context of *Staging Mobilities* we would argue that this is only one dimension of a whole set of other 'mobilities divides'. These are the socially stratifying practices related to mobilities that either come about as a function of economic resources, intellectual and knowledge capabilities, practical skills or cultural frames, all contributing to the fact that some people know how to, can and will be mobile and connected whilst this is out of range for others. Gordon and Silva counter the criticism of seeing mobile technologies in public spaces as inherently socially exclusive by arguing that urban spaces are always mediated by technology, and that 'Net Locality' may or may not create further social divides (2011:87). And, further, that

> Traditional metropolitan public space is perhaps becoming like the small town, where pure physically co-present seem oppressively small. Not being connected to a network, not having access to information about where you are, is tantamount to being closed off to a space's potential ... Mapping has changed from something that can spatialize social information to something that can socialize spatial information. Once information is geolocated, it becomes the context and content for social interaction.
> (Gordon and Silva 2011:89)

In relation to the *Staging Mobilities* frame one of the most important perspectives coming out of 'Net Locality' is the way we need to redefine the 'situation' as something that may now reach across the immediacy of physical co-presences (as, for example, when I am talking to friends elsewhere on my mobile phone as I ride the bus). This I termed 'non-proxemic' and 'stretched' interactions in Chapters 1 and 4. Clearly Goffman did not speak of networked technologies and how they change the dynamics of the interaction and situation. But he did provide us with a framework from which to approach the problem (Gordon and Silva 2011:91). Like in all other situations, 'Net Localities' are inscribed into the whole dynamic setting of focused and unfocused attention, interaction orders and rules for expected behaviour etc. Networked technologies become part of this mobile situation and add new dimensions of complexity to the situation, but they are as material and real as any other object, artefact and person in the situation. Put differently:

> In net localities, the local space is the dominating involvement; however, the local space is not always solely physical. In the physical spaces of the street, the technology is brought to bear on one's assessment of the 'situation' ... Net localities are spaces where one can shift their attention outside of the physical situation, because the situation is understood to be larger than what is physically near.
> (Gordon and Silva 2011:93)

In this perspective the definition of the situation leans predominantly on where the attention is, rather than who is physically co-present. This is very important as one of the key shifts that an analysis of mobile situations is facing after the advent of networked technologies. Moreover, this is very much in accordance with the relational- and mobility-oriented sense of place advocated earlier. And this fits the shift from thinking about proximity alone towards understanding the intertwinement of proximity and connectivity. A key expression of this shift is the way that digital and material elements fuse into whole ecologies staging practices like mobilities. Such environments may be highly dependent on software and thus work as 'coded assemblages' (Kitchin and Dodge 2011:7), which are when several differently coded infrastructures converge and work together in becoming integral to one another as in the case of many transportation systems. Importantly, the visible or invisible presence of code or software is not only about technologies, since coding relies on a wider underpinning of cultural values, normative beliefs, habits and discourses of right and wrong (Kitchin and Dodge 2011:75). Thus we may speak of a particular 'mobility code' as the specific software staging of mobilities. 'Mobility codes' may be considered from above as when code stages movement through the city by means of ITS systems as well as from below when we stage our movement by means of personalised technologies such as location-aware smart phones.

The mobilities 'staging' by means of code is prevalent in a number of modes. One of the more conspicuous ones is related to air travel and airports in particular. The code/spaces of airports are understood by Kitchin and Dodge to be elements of large coded assemblages of global reach, where code performs with agency and the material setting itself becomes staged by means of software. Even the static and solid object of a house is networked and permeated by multiple flows of information- and software-regulated systems (Kitchin and Dodge 2011:169), drawing a straight line back to Lefebvre's pre-code/space understanding of the house as: 'permeated from every direction by streams of energy which run in and out of every imaginable route: water, gas, electricity, telephone lines, radio and television signals, and so on' (1974/91:93).

Also urban public spaces are increasingly being influenced by code as when squares and plazas in many Western cities have become sites of digital display and interactivity (Kitchin and Dodge 2011:198). Code may be seen as the 'glue' that binds distributed and distant activities together (Kitchin and Dodge 2011:200) as it works to mediate the 'proximity–connectivity nexus'. The 'proximity–connectivity nexus' is here to be understood as the new dialectical and dynamic relationship between physical co-presence and mediated connections across time and space and how this effects the mobile situations. The omnipresence of code inspires Kitchin and Dodge to refer to the now well-established notion of 'everyware' as a word play on the all-encompassing distribution of software:

> Everyware is the notion that computational power will soon be distributed and available at any point on the planet ... however, everyware in its contemporary deployment is highly partial in nature, uneven, and unequal in distribution, density, penetration, sophistication, and form. Access is dependent upon economic resources, knowledge to use technologies, location, and whether appropriate infrastructure is available, and devices and networks being interoperable.
>
> (Kitchin and Dodge 2011:216)

132 *Practices of mobilities*

If our mobile lives are staged by the omnipresence of 'everyware', this will have direct repercussions for the situations and sites of lived mobilities that we experience as we enter into a relation to socio-technical systems.

The production of lived mobilities within socio-technical systems

The analytical understanding of mobility systems and how they shape the conditions for mobile urban subjects has much bearing on the new development of theories dealing with power, politics and mobilities. However, to understand how this produces on-the-ground mobilities we need to add the perspective of seeing these as forming a socio-technical system (Galis 2006). Only by understanding how the assemblage of human and non-human elements within a larger socio-technical system works can we claim really to have understood the production of lived mobilities (Valderrama and Jørgensen 2008:203). The profoundness of the assembling of urban mobilities reaches well beyond the ordinary as it carries repercussions to ontological assumptions of space and time:

> Newtonian conceptions of space and time determine a commonsense notion that transport systems are the means to achieve mobility in a certain space, which is defined by natural principles and boundaries. Such conceptions are often found in the literature on transport systems and transport planning and translated into models of transport behaviours and needs. However, more sophisticated conceptions invert the relation and state that space is the outcome of different ways of being, affecting and organizing others.
> (Valderrama and Jørgensen 2008:215)

Movement in the city is social to the extent that we need to pay attention to the 'mobile other'. Certainly the mobility practices of everyday life are related to 'ways of doing' in the sense of particular practices, norms, codes, rationalities, cultures and knowledge forms (Jensen 2006). This understanding grows out of an attempt to revalorise the 'numb objects' and technologies that afford mobilities: 'Our collective is woven together out of speaking subjects, perhaps, but subjects to which poor objects, our inferior brothers, are attached at all points. By opening up to include objects, the social bond would become less mysterious' (Latour 1996:viii). Like the 'sociogram' may chart human interests and translations we have to add the so-called 'technogram' in order to chart the 'interests and attachments' of non-humans (Latour 1996:58). The report on the conditions of technology in producing mobilities should be held against the insight that 'a technological project is not in a context; it gives itself a context, or sometimes does not give itself one' (Latour 1996:133). As inspired by Latour's way of thinking I want to add a particular way of seeing the 'subject' within such a socio-technical system (Richardson and Jensen 2008:218). The 'mobile subject type' imagined within plans and policies may be manufactured to a certain extent. However, it should become increasingly clear that the social cannot be 'closed' and thus completely determined. Armature spaces might work as 'heterotopias' (Foucault 1997) in the interpretation, valorisation and practices of the everyday life of mobile urbanites where their imagined mobilities are predicated upon, and are used to make new technologies of mobility thinkable and normal (Jensen and Richardson 2007; Richardson and Jensen 2008). So the creation of 'mobile subject types' unfolds in this dialectical space between the state's will to orchestrate urban mobility, and the multiple actual coping practices and strategies of the individual in his or her daily movement through the city. The introduction of new transport infrastructure, then, creates new conditions for social 'condensation' as socio-technical systems create interfaces between the view from the state (staging from above) and the practices of everyday life (staging from below). Accordingly, the production of mobile subjects takes place between the policy and the everyday-life level and is mediated by infrastructure and technologies (Richardson and Jensen 2008:221–222).

From enclosure to tracking: reconfiguring the public and the political

Exploring the potentials for mobile practices within armatures does not per se point at liberating and interesting, socially or aesthetically stimulating experiences. The new mobility practices and infrastructures indeed offer new means of control and power as a potential 'dark side' of mobilities. In accordance with the shift in understanding of mobilities advocated so far we might also want to explore alternative notions of the role of power and its relationship with mobilities. In the 'disciplinary societies' of the eighteenth and nineteenth centuries, power, according to Deleuze, manifested itself by means of enclosure, concealment and boundedness (the enclave symbolising confinement par excellence). However, as Deleuze (1992) argues, we may now describe the contemporary social formation as 'societies of control'. Accordingly, we are witnessing a new form of power, which arguably is inherent to mobilities and flow as the notion of 'tracking' overlays the notion of enclosure. One has to say 'overlay' due to the fact that enclosure has not vanished as an expression of power but has been supplemented with the technique of tracking. With a reference to Guattari, Deleuze argues that 'what counts is not the barrier but the computer that tracks each person's position' (1992:312). The new face of power is, in other words, related to the attachment of data to 'particles' (that being humans, goods or signs) in a global networked flow system. Thus the shift from enclosure to tracking is an indication of a new mediated notion of power being immanently related to fluids, movements and mobility (Graham 2011). This should be seen within an analytical frame arguing that 'power is not some "thing" that moves, but an effect that is mediated, and such effects may mutate through relations of successive or simultaneous reach' (Allen 2003:37). Or, as Amin and Thrift argue, power should be understood as 'a mobile, circulating force which through the constant re-circulation of practices, procedures self-similar outcomes, moment by moment' (2002:105).

In the contemporary mediated city of armatures we need to rethink the political and the notion of the public. In new hybrid relationships between technologies and humans, potentials arise (as well as dangers). In understanding the potentials of performative urban architectures we may start by reinterpreting the notions of 'public' spaces (van't Hof *et al.* 2011). The investigation into whether sites facilitate interactions between different social groups and thus constitute a 'public domain' (Hajer and Reijndorp 2001) is more important than keeping alive the fictitious vision of just one public space. In the city of armatures a new discussion about interaction and mediated spaces must be opened:

> The expanded and mobile city implies a new agenda for the design of public space, not only in relation to the urban centres or in the new residential districts, but especially in the ambiguous in-between areas ... Furthermore, we seem to think too much about public space in the sense of fixed and permanent physical spaces, and we give insufficient consideration to the way in which public domain comes into being in flux, often extremely temporarily.
> (Hajer and Reijndorp 2001:14, 16)

This suggests itself as an idea relatively compatible with the critique of the modernist notion of the city as one of homogeneous communities. From their engagement with mediated urban spaces and the new situation of political articulation, Crang and Graham (2007) argue for the above-mentioned 'politics of visibility' in which performative installations and art forms experimenting with technologies in the city may become a political platform for exposing the pros and cons of mediated and situated technologies. Seen this way, the 'politics of visibility' is about using the new performative urban architectures and networked technologies as windows into a discussion shaping awareness about the opportunities and threats that cities face (Graham 2010). The technologies themselves need to become visible to the communities for them to realise the field of action they offer (Sheller and Urry 2006:8). There is a new dynamic between place, mobilities, technology and the political that needs to be taken into consideration. It is a notion of thinking about this relationship as mediated and open indeed, but equally as related to ideas about belonging and identity. In the words of McCullough:

> at least to the more mobile and networked of us, place has become less about our origins on some singular piece of blood soil, and more about forming connections with the many sites in our lives. We belong to several places and communities, partially by degree, and in ways that are mediated. With the rise of pervasive computing, more applications must enhance, and not undermine, our perceptions of grounding place.
> (McCullough 2007:388)

The socio-technical systems orchestrating and mediating mobilities are important sites of the production of lived everyday life that need attention. Moreover, the networked technologies discussed in this chapter are also new planning tools that city planners, architects and urban designers must show an interest in. Or, in the words of Jørgensen:

> It is widely believed that personal media technologies remove us from what is important. This idea is based on the assumption that meaningful relationships can only occur in face-to-face meetings. Such an approach leads to urban planning strategies that focus solely on physical space, and neglecting the virtual. I do not agree with that assumption. In modern society personal media such as smart phones are the interface between our social networks and the physical world. When this interface is mobile and context-sensitive, we can weave together these various spaces in new ways. It adds another dimension when the city begins to 'respond' to its citizens, through more or less visible technologies embedded in urban spaces. Examples of this can be when traffic lights are optimized for traffic surveillance, cameras tracking criminals, and pollution sensors and dynamic signage allows you to divert heavy traffic. You could say that the city itself, to a far greater extent than previously, is to be understood as a living, sentient entity.
>
> (Jørgensen 2011:19; my translation)

Moreover, the networked technologies are potentially emancipating (or at least useful) for civil society groups and non-governmental organisations trying to understand their neighbourhoods and city quarters (Knudsen *et al.* 2011; Nold *et al.* 2008). Urban applications of tracking technologies carry ambivalent potentials that are explored in a great deal of research (e.g. Schaick and Speek 2008; Pae *et al.* 2006). The point is that these technologies stage lives and carry the potential for people to voice decisions related to their cities. But they need to be exposed, and their potential as powerful tools of surveillance and suppression also need to be brought into the open. The 'politics of visibility' is in demand. In other words, there is a need to confront the 'dark sides' of mobility technologies. Another way of thinking about the new networked technologies and participatory powers is to speak of 'urban markups' which 'turns the privileged reader into an active tagger', to use the words of McCullough (2008:63). Accordingly, some new technologies are now being tested for their abilities to inscribe public visions of the just city, rights to places and territorial appropriation in the city. Some, however, also lend themselves to the power-holders and their agendas of command and control. Like it or not, a society of pervasive computing is a pervasive surveillance society (Wood 2008:93) in which we should speak of 'spatial protocols' as highly restrictive and controlling rules embedded within the materiality of urban space, which produce all kinds of new liberatory and repressive possibilities (Wood 2008:94).

In this short chapter I have only lightly touched upon the importance of networked technologies for everyday-life mobile situations. More theoretical and empirical work needs to be undertaken, but the key motivating force underpinning the chapter looks to be correct: that networked technologies create, afford and alter mobile situations in new and important ways.

Concluding remarks

Within the key themes of *Staging Mobilities* the dimension of networked technologies has been the focus of this chapter. As an increasing number of practices are regulated, monitored, surveyed and afforded by mediation and technologies we must seek to explore an adequate theoretical framework and vocabulary for dealing with this condition. So added to the increasing new mobilities vocabulary aimed at situated mobilities are the notions of 'mobilities divides', 'mobility code' and the 'proximity–connectivity nexus'. I therefore turn to these and their relationships.

The differentiations made and afforded by networked technologies are targeted with the notion of 'mobilities divides'. These are the socially stratifying practices related to mobility differentials that come about either as a function of economic resources, intellectual and knowledge capabilities, practical skills and geographical location or as cultural frames, all of which contributes to the fact that some people know how to, can and will be mobile whilst this is out of range for others. 'Mobility code' is the specific software staging of mobilities. 'Mobility codes' may, as with all other situational mobility, be considered from above as when code stages movement through the city by means of ITS systems as well as from below when we stage our movement by means of personalised technologies such as location-aware smart phones. The outcome of 'mobility code' is protocols for organising and choreographing mobile practices. The 'proximity–connectivity nexus' is the new dialectical and dynamic relationship between physical co-presence and mediated connections across time and space and how this effects the mobile situations. Connections and distances have been influencing each other for a long time, but now the networked technologies described in this chapter create a new and dynamic interface and mediation, or what I term a 'nexus'. This equals the distinction between topography (proximity) and topology (connectivity).

If we think back to the title of this chapter and Simmel's notion of 'will to connection', the complex interrelationship between 'mobility codes', 'mobility divides' and the 'proximity–connectivity nexus' suggests new ways to think about these matters. First of all, the 'imprint' of humans and the ways to find connections obviously has moved beyond the visible imprints on hard surfaces that could be seen with the naked eye. The multiple mobile practices that are being organised and orchestrated by mobility code across a vast 'Hertzian' landscape of scales and technologies means that knowing what to do and how in terms of making connectivity work as a facilitator for mobilities becomes quite a complex endeavour. Ultimately this potentially contributes to social stratification, mobility segregation and new mobility divides. Not in an automatic way, though, like notions of 'one person's mobility, is the other's immobility' (Graham and Marvin 2001). Such thinking is too simplistic to grasp the complexities of contemporary networked technologies and their impact on the process of *Staging Mobilities*. As these technologies are part of the complex assemblages we call cities, practising situated mobilities in everyday life may be seen as a constant juggling of material spaces, social interactions, embodied performances and networked technologies. As we move across time and space we may find ourselves placed at different levels of the mobility skills ladder. At times struggling with opening a gate or finding our way, at other times having difficulty paying or entering certain spaces. Not rare, of course, are social agents with good social, economic and cultural capital capable of organising the mobile situations in very close accordance with their imagined trajectories or their 'will to connection'. But there is no formal logic at work here. The unemployed or the homeless may navigate as seamlessly and smoothly across town as any Young Urban Professional. Moreover, both ends of the social spectrum might fall victim to failure, breakdown and fragilities (Graham 2010) of the 'systems' facilitating movements in everyday life (a metro breakdown might hit the stockbroker on her way to work as hard as any other traveller, one might say). This is not to suggest that the networked technologies are contributing to a more equal or just distribution of mobility skills and options per se. Rather I want to point to the complexities of situated mobilities and warn against motor interpretations. Likewise we see great differences in the way different age groups deal with daily mobilities mediated by networked technologies. Here, younger people may have an advantage (Fisker 2011).

In relation to the notion of the city as a 'sentient' space collecting and distributing data and information in complex systems either to the immediate user (e.g. real-time travel information or location-based services on a mobile phone) or to some level of systems surveillance and monitoring (e.g. the traffic-regulation system or the police tracking suspects), we come to see that the virtual/digital and the physical/material realms need to be reconnected in our conceptual frameworks and theories. The advantage of taking a point of departure in the *Staging Mobilities* framework thus becomes one of setting the practical situation at the centre and then exploring how material/non-material, human/non-human and digital/physical realms are constantly being enacted in complex processes of mobilities. Regardless of how much scholarly research within disciplinary boundaries we may consult, and regardless of the many different government bodies and departments at work, the individual mobile subject does not experience life (and thus mobilities) in either scientific disciplines or municipal jurisdictions. Rather we move more or less effortlessly through our everyday life practising mobilities and experiencing them in concrete and complex situations. *Staging Mobilities* offers a clear gaze at the situational mobilities of everyday-life practices by foregrounding analytically distinct themes (material space, embodied performance and social interaction) helping to understand how networked technologies are *Staging Mobilities* and thus ultimately affecting our will to connection.

Coming from this increased awareness of the importance of networked technologies to everyday-life mobilities, I want to move closer in the next chapter to the direct and co-present physical interaction of public transit spaces as another but equally important dimension of *Staging Mobilities*.

7 Negotiation in motion
Unpacking a geography of mobility

> Traffic Culture [is] how people drive, how people cross the street, how power relations are made manifest in those interactions, what sort of patterns emerge from the traffic. Traffic is a sort of secret window onto the inner heart of a place, a form of cultural expression as vital as language, dress, or music.
>
> Tom Vanderbilt, *Traffic*, 2008, p. 216

> City streets, even in times that defame them, provide a setting where mutual trust is routinely displayed between strangers. Voluntary coordination of action is achieved in which each of the two parties has a conception of how matters ought to be handled between them, the two conceptions agree, each party believes that this agreement exists and each appreciates that this knowledge about the agreement is possessed by the other. In brief, structural prerequisites for rule by convention are found. Avoidance of collision is one example of the consequence!
>
> Erving Goffman, *Relations in Public*, 1972, p. 17

Introduction

In this chapter I will be engaging with understanding public transit spaces as sites of multiple dynamic interactions. In accordance with the *Staging Mobilities* framework I explore the potential usefulness of concepts related to interaction, mobility and transit that focus on notions of the 'mobile with', 'negotiation in motion', 'mobile sense making' and 'temporary congregations'. The theoretical approach aims at seeing public transit spaces as sites where cars, pedestrians, mopeds and bikes on a regular basis 'negotiate' not only routes in and across the space but also express dynamic flows of interaction in motion. The claim is that what seems like ordinary urban movement patterns are more than this. By moving in the city amongst buildings, objects and people we interact with the 'environment' making sense of it and ultimately producing culture and identity. Empirically Nytorv Square in Aalborg, Denmark is analysed through field studies. The chapter aims at unpacking the geography of mobility at the site of Nytorv by applying the two perspectives of the 'river' and the 'ballet' to the mobile practices of the site. The case study presented in this chapter is both a story about a particular design and a story about a more generic set of requisites and cultural practices developed through the daily urban mobility performance. The object of study was the actual movements in and across the square of Nytorv (Figure 7.1). The reason for studying these mobile interactions was to uncover the meaning of movement to social interaction and cultural production. So this is a study of the very concrete sites of movements and actual practices within a realm sometimes considered self-evidently a matter of technical design and traffic optimisation only. The Nytorv study is therefore to be seen as an argument for a much wider understanding of the meaning of movement in the contemporary city.

The structure of the chapter is as follows. After the introduction the site is briefly presented and the public debate at the time of its redesign in the mid-1990s is discussed. Thereafter follows the empirical findings based upon quantitative traffic counting and ethnographic field observations. The chapter ends with some concluding remarks.

Setting the scene

The actual site of study is a crossing between three streets and their accompanying sidewalks for pedestrians in the centre of a Danish city. The public space of Nytorv is more than just a random street crossing as it has come to carry a highly symbolic importance amongst the inhabitants as the de facto city centre. The site

Figure 7.1 Setting the scene – Nytorv, Aalborg.

is located in the fourth-largest city in Denmark, namely the city of Aalborg which is a municipality of approximately 200,000 inhabitants. The city used to be an old shipyard and industrial city, but has since the establishment of the regional university in the early 1970s seen cultural and economic changes of similar magnitude to those of many other lower-tier cities in Europe.

Nytorv is located at the historic centre of Aalborg and under its pavement runs the old river. The site is a central traffic node to pedestrians, cyclists and buses (only cars with a business purpose are permitted to transit). The symbolic importance of Nytorv is seen in the fact that many young people designate Nytorv as the most obvious meeting point when they go to town. The site connects the two pedestrian zones of the city and thereby hosts a number of pedestrians and people on bicycles. Nytorv has been designated different roles in municipal traffic plans through the years. In the mid-1990s it was changed from a heavily car-dominated node of intersecting traffic arteries into a dedicated bus and slow-traffic area, where the clearly visible demarcation between asphalt lanes for cars and brick sidewalks for pedestrians was abolished, and Chinese granite was used for all surfaces. The public debate that took place around the transformation in the mid-1990s in the local newspaper *Aalborg Stiftstidende* is illustrative of the political significance of the site (the following extracts are my translations):

> Nytorv Will Become a City Square Again
> (Headline in *Aalborg Stiftstidende*, 4 May 1997)

> We naively thought that we would get a square with very little traffic. Instead you must jump for your life because buses, cars, bikes and motorbikes drive in all directions.
> (Jørgen Andreasen, Chairman of Aalborg Tourist Association, statement issued at the General Assembly 26 April 1999)

> The New Nytorv Is Lethal
> (headline in *Aalborg Stiftstidende*, 5 May 1999)

> The weak road users in the re-built Nytorv/Østerågade will be subject to a false sense of security. In particular the T-junction outside McDonalds is very dangerous.
> (Citizen interviewed by *Aalborg Stiftstidende*, 5 May 1999)

To further put this public discourse in perspective I contacted the local police to hear their story. According to the Police Department in Aalborg, there have been no major accidents at Nytorv in the period 2006–9. In the period from 2007 to 2010, however, four incidents with personal injury were reported. But in relation to the number of people and vehicles passing through Nytorv these figures must be considered very modest. Clearly there is a dissonance between the actual occurrences at the site and the public perception thereof. This seems to be a general issue when well-established codes of design are suddenly abolished, such as the clear demarcation between street and pavement. Such staging from above takes some time to become internalised into everyday mobile practices as mobile subjects start appropriating and negotiating the site in a process of staging from below.

Mapping mobilities

I carried out the field study with the help of a research assistant over four weeks in February and March 2009. The traffic counting conducted in this research was carried out in accordance with the methodologies set out by the Danish Road Directorate (DRD 2006). Accordingly, the counting is termed 'manual counting' with clocks, paper and pencil. The calculated Daily Year Traffic (Årsdøgnstrafik, ÅDT in Danish) is calculated from the aggregated daily (DT) and weekly traffic counts (UHDT). Counting was done at 15-minute intervals and multiplied by four to produce the traffic flows per full hour. The counting was conducted on Tuesdays, Wednesdays and Thursdays in the timeslots of 7–10 a.m., 11 a.m.–2 p.m. and 3–6 p.m. In terms of registration a simplified system of notation was inspired by Low (2000). The mobile subjects were observed from two places. One site was a bench at the square (the 'ballet' viewpoint) and the other was from a second-floor window in an adjacent building (the 'river' viewpoint).

The mapping uncovers the mobile dynamics and rhythms of the site. Here I find that there are patterns of significant time intervals. From 7 to 9 a.m., growth is slow in numbers of mobile action. From 9 to 11 a.m. there is a strong and rapid increase in the activity pattern. From 11 a.m. until 4 p.m. the volume is fairly high and stable. Then follows a period of steady activity decrease from 4 until 6 p.m. when the registration stopped. Due to the fact that the specific time when the registration started coincided with a national holiday, registrations was made for both the holiday and an ordinary working week. From this was found that the growth of activity patterns and number of people at the site keeps increasing until noon. Furthermore the total volume of activity is (unsurprisingly) higher in the area during the holiday season. Given the location of Nytorv in the city it is also not surprising that the job commute and the shoppers' mobile patterns within the regular working and shop-opening hours are what gives the site its main impulses. Given the weather conditions in this North European country a summer study might have provided more volume, but there is no reason to believe that the trend would look significantly different if the study was done at another time of year. Many types of streets cater to different speeds and modes of transportation and the literature is rich on recommendations on how to plan and design these (Marshall 2005). However, here I shall pay particular interest to a site that (on an almost continual basis) is negotiated and appropriated by multiple modes and speeds of mobility at the same time as it functions as a meeting place and a 'public domain' (Hajer and Reijndorp 2001). Seen this way Nytorv is the city's 'living room' and 'transit space' at one and the same time.

A place full of speed changes

In this section I briefly summarise the quantitative empirical findings for the different vehicular units at Nytorv. For the sake of clarity and overview I will present these in terms of 'volume' and 'mobile action'. In terms of volume, buses are constantly present at Nytorv during the daytime (at least from 7 a.m. to 6 p.m.). They form a pulse of large vehicular units and they dominate the space and fill it with their presence. On an hourly basis about 60–65 buses pass Nytorv in the daytime, resulting in a fairly steady pulse. At nighttime only half as many or fewer pass the square. A calculated ÅDT (Daily Year Traffic) gives a number of approximately 940 buses in 24 hours. In terms of mobile action the buses travel in all directions, and turn both left and right. When two buses pass each other they take up the whole driving lane. The buses slow down when entering the actual square due to the design. The bus drivers all follow the legislation, and respect other buses, holding back in the blocked street etc. But there is a sense of 'mobile with' between the buses as they often form groups of three. This creates free passage for all of them, and makes pedestrians cross either before or after the 'chain' of buses.

In the case of trucks and volume the trucks are mostly present on Nytorv during the morning and at midday, delivering goods to the stores and offices around Nytorv and in the pedestrian streets. After 3 p.m. they almost completely vanish. In the morning, approximately 22 trucks pass the square within one hour. During daytime (7 a.m.–6 p.m.) the volume spreads out and approximately 18 trucks pass in an hour. A calculated ÅDT gives 175 trucks in 24 hours. In terms of mobile action the trucks that deliver goods act as if they own the square, and do not always follow the traffic regulations. They drive fast, and they go back and forth. They travel in all directions, and also use the sidewalk to dump goods or park close to the stores. When they park they have the largest impact on the square. Like a 'rock in the stream' they influence the flow for all units travelling at Nytorv. Other trucks or buses have to radically slow down, and their driving becomes more restricted as they have to move around the parked truck. Bicycles and pedestrians also have to pass the parked trucks and their visibility becomes delimited.

When I look at the cars in terms of volume the first thing to notice is that cars at Nytorv are present all day. In the morning the cars are driven to work, and taxis bring people to meetings etc. At nighttime the taxis take over, and almost no other cars are seen. On an hourly basis about 75 cars pass Nytorv in the daytime (7 a.m.–6 p.m.). A calculated ÅDT gives a number of approximately 1,050 cars in 24 hours (compared with the amount on a relatively busy street like Jyllandsgade in Aalborg where 10,900 cars are counted, the number of cars at Nytorv is low). In terms of mobile action the cars travel in all directions, and do not need to slow down at Nytorv. Therefore they are potentially the most dangerous vehicular units on the square. Yet no major accidents have been recorded, according to my enquiry to the police. A number of different types of cars travel through Nytorv: cars as postal service, cleaning service and others that drive to and from different places as part of their job. There are cars like taxis and minibuses that are used only for transporting people. And there are private cars moving from A to B or just cruising in the city. The mobile action is fairly similar, but small differences have been detected. The taxis that are looking out for customers drive slower through Nytorv, and the 'illegal' private cars drive a little faster to get through, except for the 'cruisers' that drive slowly to be seen – and heard! In terms of mopeds and volume, it should be noted that mopeds are poorly represented at Nytorv. Mopeds are more or less only present in the hours from 9 a.m. to 5 p.m.. On an hourly basis about ten mopeds pass Nytorv in the daytime (7 a.m.–6 p.m.). A calculated ÅDT gives a number of approximately 100 mopeds in 24 hours. Due to the very small number, mopeds also have very little influence on the traffic situation at Nytorv. In terms of mobile action, the mopeds use the whole square, including the pavement, either to park or to drive to the entrance of a bank or store. They are either driven by young men, as they are cruising in the city in small groups as 'mobile withs', or by older men travelling alone. The small size and number makes them less significant when considering the general situation at Nytorv.

When it comes to bicycles, these are present all day. Their presence is concentrated in a morning and afternoon rush. On an hourly basis about 255 bicycles pass Nytorv in the counting period from 7 a.m.–6 p.m. on working days. A calculated ÅDT gives a number of approximately 3,460 bicycles in 24 hours (compared with the amount on the relatively busy street Jyllandsgade, this only holds 2,000 bicycles). In terms of mobile action the bicycles travel in all directions, and use the whole square when turning. Some are more careful than others, especially those turning towards or from the east. In this turn they sometimes establish a 'mobile with' and 'temporary congregations' when they stop to wait for traffic passing or just to orient themselves. This is actually one of the few places where bicycles stop at Nytorv and not just slow down. In other situations they simply slow down and slip through a small 'hole' in the pedestrian flow. Bicycles may be considered to be the most vulnerable group in the traffic at Nytorv due to several factors. They are travelling at relatively high speed, especially those going downhill. They do not have any reserved space and are not as flexible as pedestrians and cannot stop or re-route as quickly. Almost every bicycle passing Nytorv will experience a need to negotiate the space actively. However, only rarely do we see bicycles as 'mobile withs' in such numbers that they 'call the shots'. This is often seen on some of the more busy streets in lager Danish cities and corresponds to the notion of 'safety in numbers' (Vanderbilt 2008:86). When this really takes off the mobile practices of large numbers of cycles seem like an emerging swarm (which is the case in Copenhagen, for example). However, at Nytorv I saw no such emergent properties for cyclists.

Finally we shall look at the pedestrians who in terms of volume are present all day. From the early morning the number of pedestrians rises, reaching the highest level between 9 a.m. and 4 p.m.. The counting of pedestrians was made only for the pedestrians crossing the square. This was done for two reasons. First, it is practically impossible to count all the people walking at Nytorv.

Second, to give an actual picture of the relation between the different vehicular units, the counting should be carried out within the same field – that is the actual road space. On an hourly basis about 1,155 pedestrians cross Nytorv in the counting period from 7 a.m. to 6 p.m.. A calculated ÅDT gives a number of approximately 14,670 pedestrians in 24 hours (the calculation is based on the factors and categories from bicycles). The biggest volume of pedestrians is found during the business opening hours from 10 a.m. to 5 p.m., and therefore we must expect a significant proportion of shoppers in that group. From the counting, the numbers also show an over-representation of women (approximately two-thirds of those counted). In terms of mobile action the pedestrians, especially amongst the locals, indicate a very relaxed attitude to moving across the square. They cross the street wherever they feel like, even if they have children or baby strollers with them. From the traffic counting there was registered an almost even number of crossings at the zebra crossing and across the square on the east-to-west axis.

So Nytorv is full of speed changes. All vehicular units slow down, speed up, stop and start here. Buses slow down to pass and they stop to let off passengers and set off again. The taxis also let passengers off and take new ones in, and the trucks park to unload goods. The bicycles slow down to turn and avoid pedestrians. They stop here and start from here either to park or visit the shopping street. Pedestrians are found moving at all kinds of paces. They stroll, walk or run as they shop, talk or simply cross the street. The traffic flows in a relatively unhindered manner at Nytorv, which might be due to the fairly small amount of signage and regulatory interventions. This would be in accordance with the findings of the 'Shared Space' design principles (Shared Space 2005). Also, in accordance with this I find that the road users become more alert and attentive. At least the different users quickly adjust to each other. They work to develop a level of mutual trust which is vital to get Nytorv performing as a well-functioning transit space.

The 'river' and the 'ballet': two perspectives on mobilities

From the inspirational insights gained from Goffman and in line with the *Staging Mobilities* framework I will zoom in on an operational and methodological interpretation. The following is thus a presentation of a very simple conceptualisation used to interpret and understand the meaning of moving at the site of study.

In social science in general there is some debate about the epistemological status of using metaphors (Czarniawska 2004; Rigney 2001). Furthermore, there is a particular position within cognitive psychology arguing for the ontological status of metaphors to the way we think, perceive and inhabit the world as human beings (Lakoff and Johnson 1980). Here I cannot engage deeply with these discussions. But just as Goffman saw the metaphor as a strong and powerful tool to theorise the social (Goffman 1959), I find metaphors to be useful interpretative tools leading to new insights. This is evident in the usage of the dramaturgical key metaphor of the 'stage' in the *Staging Mobilities* framework.

But the use of metaphor as a methodology and framing device has advantages and disadvantages. On the productive side of things, metaphors help frame and shape what we see. Thus we get closer to the understanding of what actually takes place at Nytorv when we start 'seeing through' the metaphor of the 'river' and the 'ballet'. On the other hand, the coining of metaphors carries the risk of over-simplifying the issue. And furthermore metaphors are always setting certain issues in the foreground and others in the background. In other words, metaphors have 'blind spots' that might cloud our analysis. Having said this, the coining of the two metaphors of the 'river' and the 'ballet' have been found very useful for the analysis at Nytorv as long as one remembers that the flow of the 'river' and the interaction of the 'ballet' are only two dimensions of the complex transit space called Nytorv. For example, the notion of the 'river' reduces individual mobile subjects to a homogeneous flow of identical entities. Equally important, the metaphor of the 'ballet' does not do away with power issues. People are not 'dancing' in one happy performance. Rather there are many direct and indirect manifestations of power and its relationship to mobility at Nytorv.

The term 'ballet' has been used in urban studies before, most notably by Jane Jacobs in her notion of the 'sidewalk ballet' as a way of describing the complex interactions on city streets (Jacobs 1961). Also I find in the work of Lawrence Halprin an interesting relationship to the notion of dance and choreography of flow being influenced by his collaboration with his wife who was a dance choreographer (Halprin 1963). Here, however, I am using the term in a different manner. Thus seeing the mobility practices at Nytorv 'as a ballet' means to be at the eye-level of the moving urbanites. Seeing the mobility practices 'as a river' means then to aggregate and 'look down' at the mobile urbanites from above and thus create more abstract and generalised understandings and interpretations. When seeing Nytorv 'as a river' what becomes most clear is that objects (the actual layout of the site with kerbs, basins and urban furniture) create a 'riverbed' shaping the flows of people as water in a stream. Once accustomed to this perspective we start to see how we may discriminate between permanent 'sedimentations' that are lasting and enduring conditions shaping the flows and the more temporary 'sediments'.

From time to time we might experience the parking of a large truck, for example in front of McDonald's unloading goods. With the arrival of such temporary 'sediments', the flow of the 'river' will be changed briefly but with immediately observable consequences for the orchestration of movement patterns and interactions. We might speak of permanent versus temporary 'sediments' of the 'river' and people themselves might, of course, also be seen as 'sedimentations' of the temporary sort. At Nytorv the presence of the global burger chain McDonald's has made a permanent impact on the 'riverbed' as the site in front of the restaurant is widely recognised as the central meeting point amongst young people in the city. Seen from the perspective of the 'river' the sidewalk in front of McDonald's has become an island of meetings and interactions.

As we shift to the perspective of the 'ballet' we come to be at eye-level with the mobile subjects at the site and thus are able to actually see the gestures, gazes and embodied negotiations and interactions that take place ever so swiftly as people move into and out of Nytorv. Studying the 'ballet' it becomes clear that there are certain patterns and types of moving (tactics). These concern the nature of mobile interaction and power, and may be illustrated by the traditional 'power of speed' tactics as, for example, when cars gain predominance over bikes or pedestrians as a function of their relative 'speed advantage'. However, more subtle interactional patterns emerge. One such example is the 'I pretend not to have seen you' tactic or what I term a tactic of 'seeming unawareness' which is used in particular by pedestrians and cyclists. Such tactics have to do with 'the burden of responsibility'. By this is meant that a mobile subject may deliberately give the impression that she or he has NOT seen the follow urbanite moving into this person's zone. The notion has been discovered elsewhere and is described in the literature by Vanderbilt with reference to Mexico City (Vanderbilt 2008:32) and also corresponds with the report by Kingwall stating that 'running is a sign of failure' when one performs as a pedestrian on the streets of New York (Kingwall 2008:41). Running across the street is considered 'uncool' and is a bodily illustration that gives away that one has seen the 'mobile other' and accepted their dominance. By adhering to the tactics of 'seeming unawareness' the mobile subject puts the responsibility for stopping or diverging on those who have seen them. Needless to say this may be a risky tactic as people in fact might not have seen you! With reference to Schelling's analysis of bargaining power Goffman gives this the label of 'avoidance of cooperative claims':

> If a pedestrian wants to ensure a particular allocation of the street relative to a fellow pedestrian, or if a motorist wants to ensure priority of his line of proposed action over that of a fellow motorist or pedestrian, one strategy is to avoid meeting the other's eyes and thus avoid cooperative claims.
> (Goffman 1963:94)

The situation at Nytorv is highly dynamic as many cyclists and pedestrians in fact check and double check the 'mobile other' a number of times and adjust accordingly (a mobilised and sped-up version of Goffman's 'body check'; Goffman 1972). Interestingly though, this only means that those who have perfected this tactic of 'seeming unawareness' often come out of the power struggle even more convincingly. I return to this particular tactic later. The perspective of the 'ballet' is also what makes us realise the 'mobile withs' and their interactional dynamics. Here the number seems to have importance. Two friends shopping perform a very different 'ballet' than that of the family or the group of youngsters out on the town. The latter often deliberately try to occupy as much space as possible to 'claim territory' whereas the others use a wide array of 'sliding and evasion techniques' to not interfere with the flow in direct bodily contact.

Negotiated mobilities and interactions: mobile ethnographies

There are different types of negotiations taking place at Nytorv between different road users and in different situations. The types found at Nytorv are not unique to this site, but they can be observed here in particular because the square forms a space where all types of road users meet. Considering how the users meet and the situation they have to negotiate, three situations or set-ups are interesting. The first one is the 'frontal meeting'. This situation is very common as the traffic is two-way, but besides the buses and their internal system of negotiation it is most interesting amongst the pedestrians. Second, I speak of the 'orthogonal meeting'. This situation is also common at Nytorv since the square functions like a T-junction. Since the square works like a large crossing for pedestrians, the orthogonal meeting is a particularly interesting form of meeting between pedestrians and other road users. The third typology of meeting is the 'parallel meeting'. This situation is best seen when buses overtake bicycles or when one bicycle overtakes another.

Different types of negotiations are possible. First of all, between pedestrians there is a 'reading' of body language and possible eye contact between the two parts meeting – that is a direct negotiation. Second, when the meeting is between pedestrians and cyclists it is a matter of 'reading' and evaluating body language, though not so much a direct negotiation as a swift estimation of the situation. And third, there is the situation where no negotiation in terms of 'reading' is taking place. If we look more closely into the mapping details we can focus on the different road users and their negotiation situations at Nytorv. The pedestrians negotiate with other pedestrians for the space, but mostly on the sidewalk. A number of 'mobile negotiation techniques' was observed as part of the study. Here I will present the six most predominant ones (Figure 7.2).

The first one, or 'type A', I term 'group passing other pedestrians'. In this case the group will come closer together to pass, in order to make room for the 'strangers'. 'Type B' is 'group letting in stranger'. I find here the same situation as in Type A, but with a different reaction. The group splits, and lets the 'stranger' in between them. Type C is what I term the 'the classic dance'. This could also be termed 'pedestrian confusion' and is typically found in a situation where no one gives a clear signal indicating which way they are going. This type is often found at Nytorv in spite of the large space which should make it easy to avoid each other. Type D is termed 'both giving in' and illustrates when both pedestrians give in a little, and pass each other by moving a little to the side. Type E is the 'zigzag turner' and is exemplary of the pedestrian in a hurry zigzagging through the site (like the cyclist at high speed). To reach their goal faster, they zigzag in and out between other pedestrians, and often turn the upper body sideways, in order to fit between people walking closely together. Finally I found Type F, which is 'stop to pass'. Type F is the situation where pedestrians simply stop for each other, to figure out which way to go and to pass.

The pedestrians have different ways of negotiating for space with the other road users. Those that choose to follow one of the designated lines of the street

148 *Practices of mobilities*

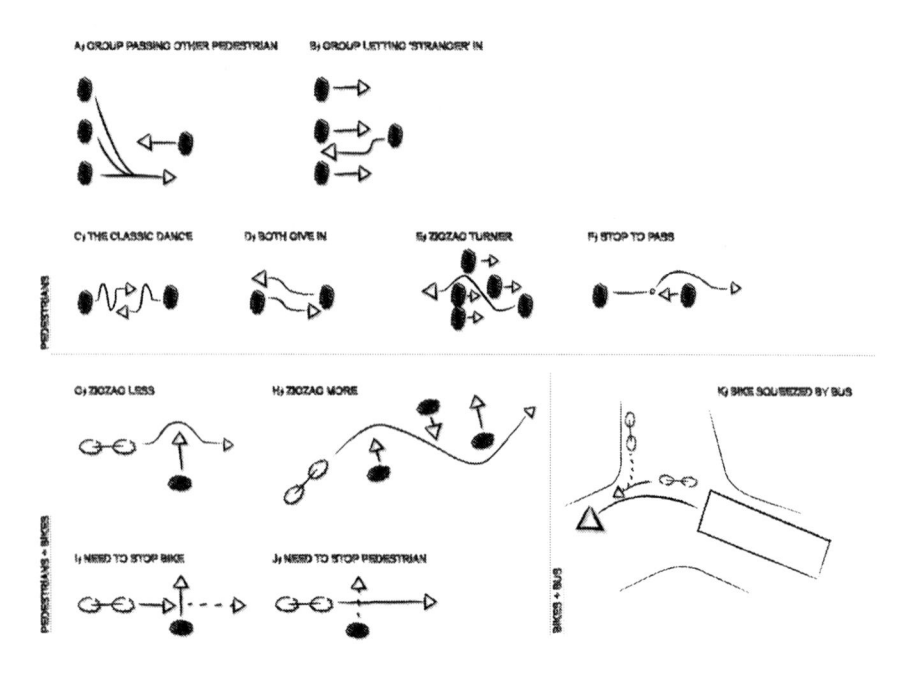

Figure 7.2 Techniques for 'negotiation in motion'.

in order to cross in a sense negotiate with the other road users by sending the signal that here they feel safe, as if they communicated: 'I need to cross the road. Here I feel safe. Here I do not expect to negotiate. I expect others to stand back.' In other situations the pedestrians express the same intention, but still end up negotiating. The pedestrians also negotiate with people cycling. The cyclists travel at a higher speed than the pedestrians, which affects the negotiation but still it seems to be a matter of negotiating. From the field observations it was found that some bicycles analyse the situation very carefully and observe the pedestrians in order to pass them without confrontation. This slows down the cyclist a little, but still he or she manages to avoid 'obstacles' by zigzagging more or less in between them. There are basically two ways of doing this. Either the bicycle follows the kerb and makes a small curve to get around the pedestrian. Alternatively cyclists move at high speed, making large curves to get around several pedestrians and moving faster through Nytorv without slowing down. If the cyclist does not analyse the situation there is a potential confrontation, maybe with eye contact and perhaps a need to stop to avoid an accident. In some cases no agreement is reached in the negotiation and the 'opponents' face each other head on.

Again I see two variations. The first is when the bicycle stops – this is mostly seen at zebra crossings where pedestrians often do not want to negotiate. Danish traffic legislation does not state that people waiting at a pedestrian crossing automatically have the right to walk and that cars and other vehicles must stop at all times. However, as soon as the pedestrian is in the crossing zone the burden of responsibility shifts to the other road users. This makes the negotiation situation just before entering the crossing zone highly dynamic and exemplary of 'negotiation in motion' and the interface between the sidewalk and the zebra crossing becomes a 'critical point of contact'. The second is when a pedestrian stops carefully and stands back either at the sidewalk or on the road, not wanting to negotiate either (but in contrast to the former situation, merely waits for free passage). The question is whether bicycles always perform a meticulous dynamic interaction with other people moving across Nytorv. This seems not always to be the case. In fact I did see bicycles totally ignore other vehicles and therefore pass Nytorv without any confrontation at high speed! Judged by observation these cyclists did in fact not see the other potential 'collision parties' and thus did not apply the 'I pretend not to have seen you' tactics but simply took a risk (however, this is an interpretation based on observations only).

Between the pedestrians and the cars at Nytorv no extensive negotiation was observed. The pedestrians seem to accept the rather small number of cars and therefore cross the street when it is free of cars. If we turn to the pedestrians' interaction with the buses at Nytorv there is an altogether different picture. This is mainly due to the fact that the buses are larger, take up more space and drive more slowly through Nytorv. This makes more buses stop for the pedestrians at the pedestrian crossings, but on the rest of the road pedestrians carefully evaluate the situation and the speed of the buses. Buses rarely hold back and wait for people to cross outside the zebra crossings, but hold back if someone is in the middle of crossing the street. From the observations I find that people turn their heads to try to catch the eye of the bus driver and thereby tell them to stop for passage. When we study the cycles in negotiation there are three different kinds of mobile interactions. Either they avoid, stop or continue. This might seem banal, but in the different categories there are differences and elaborations. Here speed has a lot to say. A cyclist moving quickly will for the most part either avoid or simply continue. In the avoidance situation speed is again a vital factor. At high speed the cyclist will make large curves around the pedestrians, at lower speed the curves will be smaller and run very close to the pedestrian and the kerb. From the observation it is estimated that the cyclists are the ones that negotiate the most. Pedestrians are not as 'afraid' of cyclists as they are of the buses and cars, and the buses and cars are not forced to stop or hold back for cyclists in the same way as they are for the pedestrians. This puts cyclists in a rather vulnerable position. The relatively large number of buses causes a negotiation between them and cyclists. From the observation the negotiation is primarily a matter of cyclists evaluating the situation, and sometimes risk getting squeezed.

The negotiation between the buses, on how to hold back and when to turn, is definitely an internal communication system between the bus drivers. They have an internal system concerning how to navigate at Nytorv. The negotiation between the cars is not really relevant at Nytorv, since there is so little car traffic. As a general rule the trucks do not negotiate. In the morning they drive where they need to drive and 'interact' only in that they sound the warning alert when they are reversing, telling people to beware (and move out of harm's way). In their most interesting moment, when they are parked alongside the kerb and functioning like a 'stone in the stream', there is no negotiation between them and others as they become 'sediments'. For the mopeds, the case is as for cars where the number of passing mopeds is too insignificant to make any substantial conclusions.

The final dimensions to be considered are the ways of crossing the square. I will define four categories (needless to say, more might be relevant). The first type is the 'speed-up crosser' who is characterised by wanting to join a group of crossing people (an already-existing 'mobile with') before the cars/buses start to drive again. The speed-up crosser will, as the name suggests, speed up and maybe even run a little, or even jump to make it to the safe 'shore'. This is especially seen at the pedestrian crossings. Next I find the 'random crosser' who moves towards the road to cross, maybe even drifting towards the road, not paying much attention to the traffic. The random crosser might even reach the road before looking out for traffic. If there is traffic the person can take a step back and instead follow the edge of the sidewalk to cross. The practice of 'random crossing' is very prevalent at Nytorv and illustrative of how moving pedestrians read, interpret and negotiate the site and the mobile elements therein in a highly volatile and dynamic sense of 'negotiation-in-motion'. The third type is the 'shopping crosser' who generally moves from Algade to the right towards Bispensgade and crosses when the row of shops stops. The crossing line for the shopping crosser is very long and sloped (this type is defined by the contextual location of urban functions and thus becomes highly site-specific). The fourth and final type is the 'line crosser', which is a person that follows the lines in the pattern of the paving in the road to cross. There are two places in particular on the square where this type of crossing is invited. One is at Bispensgade close to the shopping centre Salling, and the other is between the hot-dog stand and Burger King and are as such an illustration of staging from above.

Concluding remarks

From the field study at Nytorv I have explored all three key dimensions of the *Staging Mobilities* framework. However, most emphasis has been put on the social interaction dimension, illustrating that movement is as much a cultural and communicative event as it is a question of moving from A to B. Needless to say, much deeper research efforts could have been displayed at Nytorv. Moreover, I would point to the need for further mobile ethnographic accounts within other types of urban spaces and transit locations. Having said this there are a number of theoretical and empirical claims that can be sustained on the background of the Nytorv study. Theoretically the main point has been to show the usefulness of rethinking the perspectives of scholars such as Goffman, and thus the value of the *Staging Mobilities* framework. This results in a redevelopment of the interaction perspective applied to phenomena such as mobile practices in the city. The outcome is a set of analytical concepts and a new vocabulary for understanding the meaning of mobilities in the contemporary city.

The point of departure was the mobile practices understood as meaningful actions, or what I termed 'mobile sense making'. A central concept is the notion of a 'mobile with' illustrating the interaction dynamics and collective dimension to everyday-life mobility. Furthermore, I saw that to capture the ephemeral quality of such interaction one may benefit from understanding these as 'temporary congregations'. By this is meant that people meet, team up and break up, in very rapidly changing social interactional patterns. But these are still sufficiently enduring to make us feel the collective (as when we share the experience of missing the bus). The unsettled and socially open character of urban mobility practices furthermore makes it clear that multiple decisions need to be made. Obviously we are aware of mode-of-transport and routing decisions. But also much more detailed and situational decisions, such as which way to pass a person approaching us, need conceptualisation. Here I argue for the usefulness of the notion of 'negotiation in motion' to capture the fact that the social interaction is made in a mobile space of norms, values and power. Some of these ways of encountering our mobile 'other' may be likened to an already-existing repertoire of actions, mobile negotiation techniques and mobile interaction tactics. These may range from the very physical embodied 'sliding and evasion techniques' that people apply to avoid collision to the more general (and culturally specific) norm of the personal distance accepted for either passing or co-presence in a mobile situation (e.g. bus riding). Also I find different levels of subtlety to the way power is displayed in mobile interactions. I saw the almost classic 'power of speed' and the more subtle 'I pretend not to have seen you' tactics. Here we are facing issues of 'situational and mobile power' that are highly unstable and volatile as the execution of such powers take place during motion, *in situ* and at times even at high speed. This is in relative terms, of course, as the speed and interactional dynamics in, for instance, a motorway armature is much different (this case will subject to analysis in the forthcoming *Designing Mobilities* book).

In this research I have identified a number of types relating to the meetings ('frontal', 'orthogonal' and 'parallel'). These are only emerging typologies. Also I found reason to look at the situation where people cross the main traffic arteries and thereby become interpreters of the situation and tactical in regard to how best to proceed. This is captured in the four types of crossings that I term the 'speed-up crosser', the 'random crosser', the 'shopping crosser' and the 'line crosser'. Again these may not be taken to be too general as, for example, the 'shopping crosser' category clearly is dependent on the actual site and the presence of shopping facilities. I saw the presence of different negotiation techniques. In particular I noticed six different negotiation techniques and typologies of passing that I termed 'group passing other pedestrian', 'group letting in stranger', the 'classic dance', 'both giving in', the 'zigzag turner' and the 'stop to pass' typologies. Needless to say, I might have come up with even more distinctions. Also these need to be verified by further research to become elevated to more robust action types. However, they bring to the forefront the complex dynamics surrounding the fact that people move in groups and perform mobilities with an eye to other groups in a situational field of multiple decisions about modes, routes and types of interactions. Finally, the research undertaken at Nytorv gave cause to coin the double metaphors of the 'river' and the 'ballet'. These metaphors obviously have blind spots, as have all metaphors. But seeing the transit space as a 'stream and a riverbed of sediments' makes it clear that at times we must look at every physical entity as an object (including people) whereas the knowledge of the ballet-like micro movements and interactions makes us see that urban mobility is about skilful interaction practices. To shift between these two analytical gazes our understanding of urban mobility increases and this furthermore is the key to the *Staging Mobilities* framework: to understand the dynamic interplay between staging from above and below.

There is often drawn a line of distinction between 'movement space' and 'staying space' in architecture and city planning (Gehl *et al.* 2006:108). However, such nice categorisation does not always hold. Such understandings seem to think that spaces can have only one purpose and one interpretation. In the case of Nytorv I find both types present at the same time. Clearly it is a 'movement space' as it includes road spaces and pavements. But equally people (predominantly youngsters) appropriate the space in front of McDonald's and turn the site into one of the main meeting points where they hang out after work, school and at weekends. Thus the phrase 'Let's meet in front of Mac D' is a very common saying amongst the local youth. We might start to think of Nytorv as not just a 'sociofugal space' forcing people apart due to its transit qualities but also as a 'sociopetal space' drawing people together (Lawson 2001:140). As I coined the notions in Chapter 3, Nytorv performs as a 'mobile sociofugal' and a 'mobile sociopetal' space simultaneously. In this sense Nytorv performs as both a transit space and an 'urban living room' where different social groups interact, mingle and meet to become a 'public domain' (Hajer and Reijndorp 2001).

The study at Nytorv has given reason to coin the following concepts to be incorporated into the *Staging Mobilities* framework. The first one being 'negotiation in motion': as people move in dense settings they are driven by multiple rationales and reasons. However, the act of avoiding physical contact is predominant in most mobile situations and the way to avoid such is by the many complex visual and embodied cues given by our bodily performances of mobilities whether within vehicles or as pedestrians. To understand situational mobilities as they are staged and acted out is to understand the cultural and social complexities of the negations taking place in motion. Second, I speak about 'temporary congregations': in the mundane and ordinary everyday life we make multiple 'temporary congregations' as we slip in and out of different 'mobile withs'. So the 'mobile with' comes into being very quickly and can be dissolved equally swiftly. The everyday-life experience with 'mobile withs' thus carries a certain ephemeral quality to it. The short-lived and fast small-group interactions are seen as temporary congregations in multiple networks and sites of mobility infrastructures. The notion of the 'river' helps us see how the material objects in the mobile situation (the actual layout of the site with kerbs, basins and urban furniture) create a 'riverbed' shaping the flows of people as water in a stream. By looking at people 'as a river', a simplification and act of homogenisation is made as if they were all equal and alike. In addition to this perspective the concept of the 'ballet' takes us to eye-level with the mobile subjects. Here we see the gestures, gazes and embodied negotiations and interactions that take place ever so swiftly. Studying the 'ballet' it becomes clear that there are certain patterns and types of moving (tactics) just as there are individuals with different motives, interests and intentions.

Even though Nytorv seems marked by random interactions on the move, I observe the presence of normative codes of mobile action regulation. These range from the formal traffic regulatory frameworks that lead most people to pass on the right-hand side and drive on the right side of the road. But also informal and situational norms become visible as I start to explore this site of flow and stasis. Much more is taking place than just people moving, and a significant proportion of this has to do with the production of social norms, cultures of interaction and identity. We are slowly beginning to understand the complexity of such apparently simple and mundane activities. And with the *Staging Mobilities* framework we are in the process of articulating new theoretical vocabularies for enhancing this understanding of 'negotiation in motion'.

The third chapter in this section will continue to explore the empirical field studies as I now move on to the study of mobilities within urban metro systems in Chapter 8.

8 Metro mobilities

The production of lived mobility in urban metro systems

> A metro system is an excellent demonstration of how the built environment influences the quality of our lives. The building of tunnels for trains is usually seen in isolation from the provision of spaces for people – even though they are part of a continuous experience for the traveller, starting and ending at street level.
>
> Norman Foster, *Norman Foster Works 3*, 2007, p. 484

> It is thus quite obvious that if everyone has his or her 'life to live' in the metro, that life cannot be lived in a total freedom, not simply because no freedom could ever be totally lived in society at large, but more precisely because the coded and ordered character of subway traffic imposes on each and every person codes of conduct that cannot be transgressed without running the risk of sanction, either by authorities, or by the more or less effective disavowal of other users.
>
> Marc Augé, *In the Metro*, 2002, p. 29

Introduction

In this chapter I will engage with a particular setting for the staging of mobilities, namely two cases of urban mass transit and metro infrastructure. The cases of the Copenhagen Metro (Jensen 2008b, 2012a) and the Bangkok Sky Train (Jensen 2007a) will be the pivotal examples, but en route there will be shorter discussions of the Métro in Paris and the 'Tube' in London. The chapter is structured so that after the presentation of the key concept of 'metroscape', I present the Copenhagen case and then the Bangkok case. The chapter ends with a few concluding remarks.

The staging of mobilities in 'metroscapes'

I shall look at two key concepts underpinning the *Staging Mobilities* perspective which describe the Copenhagen Metro and the Bangkok Sky Train, as well as many other examples of everyday mobilities. The first one is the 'mobile with', which I have already defined and used in previous chapters. What is interesting in this context, though, is how groups coordinate and organise their mobile movements through urban space. From previous studies I have found that it makes a difference whether it is a family with children as a 'mobile with' or a group of girlfriends out shopping. Likewise, the negotiation and staging of mobilities will play out differently if we are looking at a group of young men coming into town. Whilst some 'mobile withs' strive to attract as little attention and interaction as possible, it will often be reversed with the latter group. We are thus down to the bodily micro level studying how various 'mobile withs' deal with and stage themselves in everyday mobility practices. This will be the case at the front of the queue at the ticket machine, at the entrance of subway trains, when identifying a seating position and for the various interaction types associated with the use of mobile media (GPS, mobile phones, PC, etc.). As an aside, I may report on a train ride from Gatwick Airport to London. In my compartment sat three young men in their mid-twenties. The first thing they did after sitting down was to put their smart phones on the table (Blackberry was the favourite model here). A couple of them had both smart phones and regular phones and this whole impressive 'set-up' was a manifestation of the 'mobile with' where technology as an identity marker was an effective mechanism. But it was also illustrative of how a 'mobile with' acquires and territorialises an urban mobility space. The 'mobile withs' may vary with the dynamic and volatile movements in and out of such 'teams'.

We become part of such a 'mobile with' when we sit in the same compartment or train carriage irrespective of whether we think we have anything in common or not. In case of a dramatic collapse of systems such as in the event of technological failures or terrorist attacks the common experience of being a 'mobile with' suddenly becomes conspicuous. This I experienced during the global travel disruption caused by the eruption of the Icelandic volcano Eyjafjallajökull whilst I was in the United States in 2010 (see Jensen 2011). Another example would be if you are stuck in an elevator with strangers. We may say that we can both be in the 'mobile with' in advance as when family or friends are out around town and slide in and out of multiple 'mobile withs' during our physical movements through the city. This rapid and often temporary slipping in and out of 'mobile withs' and the fleeting and temporary group formations we get included in is what I term 'temporary congregations'. An example could be groups of passengers waiting to board the metro or passengers occupying a Sky Train compartment. Mobility staging happens here through 'negotiations in motion' and represents a mediation of the infrastructural, technical and regulatory systems staging from above as well as numerous face-to-face interactions and negotiations from below. As already mentioned, Goffman's optics are seen to be innovative for mobilities research and are very sensitive to the actual micro-interactions that social life consists of. However, it must be noted that *Staging Mobilities* as an analytical perspective requires more interfaces to mobilities theory. This is expressed in the second key concept of 'metroscapes' presented here as an umbrella term for the network structures and socio-technical systems that must be in place in order to orchestrate mobilities in the metro. A 'metroscape' is thus to be understood as a mobility 'landscape' consisting of everything from rails and (driverless) train cars to ticket machines and security cameras. The theories behind this perspective are captured largely by Latour

(1996, 2009), Farias and Bender (2010), DeLanda (2006), Valderrama (2010), Valderrama and Jørgensen (2008) and Graham and Marvin (2001). This perspective defines urban metroscapes as physical mobility landscapes as well as the codes, rules and cultural norms that create the active joining of technologies, infrastructures and social practice.

If we connect the notion of 'metroscape' to Goffman's perspective we will find a new analytical model that provides a range of options. Seeing the situation 'as drama' is an interaction context where the person might be seen as 'playing a role', but the role definition and 'script' are most often created by others in a process of staging from above and below (e.g. timetables governing when to catch the bus or the payment requirement which leads one to the ticket machine at the metro station). Moreover, Goffman's analysis illustrates that the 'order' that keeps the situation and interaction together is fragile and unpredictable. There is ample opportunity to 'collapse' norms and embarrassment in Goffman's interaction model. From previous comparisons of the metro systems in London, Paris and Copenhagen I concluded that lived mobility in these metro systems are afforded by the assembling of trains, tracks, stations, platforms, elevators, subway personnel, travellers, signs, advertisements, musicians, homeless, police, tickets, ticket machines, power supplies, newsagents, coffee bars, customers and so on in a complex socio-technical system that creates the lived metro mobility in these cities (Jensen 2008b:22).

CPH Metro

The Copenhagen Metro is nothing less than one of the most profound physical transformations of the Danish capital since King Christian IV (1577–1648). It is a huge socio-technical experiment in 1:1 scale. The chapter will show how the Copenhagen Metro system provides a significant framework for everyday contemporary urbanism. With the Copenhagen Metro project we not only find a new and almost frictionless mobility machine; we also find a specific configuration of the technology, infrastructure and sociality that are based on a particular rationality and understanding of mobility. Through field studies I have accumulated a thorough empirical knowledge of the Copenhagen Metro as well as two distinctly different metros: namely those of Paris and London. The analysis shows what is unique to Copenhagen, and especially what notions of mobility and urbanism this socio-technical mobility configuration is based on. The Copenhagen Metro is an almost 100 per cent 'pure' motion machine whose opportunities for public activities and urban programmes seem deliberately and intentionally limited (as opposed to the metros in London and Paris). The empirical data was collected during annual field trips to London, Paris and Copenhagen in September/October of 2006, 2007, 2008, 2009 and 2010 (and is reported in Jensen 2008b, 2012a).

Copenhagen is a historical centre and a European capital city often known abroad for its 'landmarks' (from Christiansborg Parliament to the travelling 'Little Mermaid'). But Copenhagen cannot be comprehended as a city and urban phenomenon without including its connections externally (e.g. motorways, Internet, air and water traffic) and internally (e.g. ring roads, bike paths, S-train network and Metro) as major characteristics of the city's physical function as well as its urban culture. We saw Dahl point out in an earlier chapter that the 'trivial' actions undertaken in 'Transport Denmark' lack what he terms 'meta treatment' (Dahl 2008). This notion of lack of 'meta treatments' in daily mobility fits this chapter's analytical aim: to help us understand the importance of urban metro systems as more than just a transport system and more than just a large investment whose budgets, decision-making procedures etc. one may want to discuss. We need an analytical frame that enables us to grasp what the metro is and how it changes both everyday practices and cultures almost imperceptibly. This is precisely where the *Staging Mobilities* framework becomes relevant. In our movement through public spaces, whether on foot or by bike, car or subway we are effectively in social interaction even though it might look as though we are oblivious to one another. *Staging Mobilities* is about the codes, norms and cultural patterns of interaction that take place often imperceptibly and with a high degree of complexity due to the speed of movement, the density of crowds and the complex networks of signs and codes we use to navigate through modern cities. The 'civil inattention' is fundamental to coordinating our 'mobile interaction order' and can be seen, for example, in the ordinary practice of embarking on a metro journey across town. This practice is 'staged' from above through signage, station design, ticket systems, traffic rules and so on, but can only be understood in depth if we also comprehend that there is a 'staging' from below amongst mobile subjects as they either push or hold back in their negotiation process during metro embarking and disembarking.

Metro 1.0: between generic circulation machine and lived urbanism

Staging Mobilities thus takes place in the Copenhagen Metro in a socio-technical system and an everyday spatiality which I term 'CPH metroscape' and which I will now take a closer look at. The Copenhagen Metro began operation in 2002 and currently has two lines serving 22 stations. The full length of the system is 16.8 km and the Metro has an estimated weekly occupancy rate of approximately 1.2 million travellers (see www.m.dk). The trains are driverless and monitored by advanced communications and surveillance systems. According to the Metro Company itself, they have a 'timeless' and generic design for all stations and trains. The fact that many of the stations are designed with natural daylight is said to help give passengers a greater feeling of security as the daylight effect counteracts the feeling of being 20–30 m below ground. Besides this the Metro Company highlights the presence of daylight as a character trait that makes the subway perform as an urban space. The Metro's station design system is termed a 'cut and cover' system. In popular terms this means that a hole is dug out and a 'box' is submerged and covered. This has the obvious advantage that the Metro Company can operate with highly standardised and thus cost-effective solutions since custom-made solutions would be much more expensive. This is also related

158 *Practices of mobilities*

to another general design principle, which is termed 'more of the same'. This means that all trains, stations and platforms are identical in their construction, materials and designs (Figure 8.1).

This leads to both a very tight and clear aesthetic code and a rational management of resources (and is also a point of criticism in connection with the discussion of identity-free and generic designs).

To capture the diverging forms of representing metro mobilities from above well as from below, the Internet site 'YouTube' is an interesting window onto these differences. One of the most widely used passenger representations are movies filmed through the windscreen. The front seat is a hit and thanks to the train being driverless it is possible to sit absolutely at the front. But there is also the Metro Company's own self-representation where 'YouTube' is used for self-dramatisation, for example in the film about a Metro steward's everyday life, or another film titled *Metro 24/7* intended to illustrate how the Metro is part of a vibrant and never-sleeping city that is active 24 hours a day, 7 days a week. These two levels of representation reflect different 'logics of representation' and refer to the two basic perspectives of *Staging Mobilities* where passenger films express their own experiences (staging from below) while the Metro Company films express a 'staging from above' in a deliberate and strategic attempt to control, brand and stage a positive image of the Metro.

Figure 8.1 Generic circulation machine.

Welcome to flow space: towards the seamless travel

The design of the Copenhagen Metro is modernist and keeps to an aesthetic code that has no forms of ornamentation. The materials used are concrete, steel and glass, and adhere to a strict design code for the trains, station platforms, signs and ticket machines. The aesthetic and visual staging in the Copenhagen metroscape is thus in almost 100 per cent compliance with the underlying rationale: to circulate locals and visitors in as frictionless a manner as possible. However, this is simultaneously also where the Metro is under-utilising some potential. As mentioned earlier, I have studied the Paris and London metro systems and these are characterised by a variety of functions and activities associated with a metro station. Thus newspaper kiosks, restaurants, bars and shops are in close association with several of these stations. Likewise, the users in London and Paris are also people who are not necessarily on their way to any particular place or, for that matter, being 'ideal passengers'. In several places you find beggars, buskers and people who simply use the metro system as an urban space in line with squares, streets and public spaces (however, many of the entertaining musicians are working under formal contracts with the operators, who thus exercise some control over them). The Copenhagen experience is special and does not work in favour of 'down-and-out' existences in the city or even just the coffee drinkers and chess-playing people who 'hang out' in the metros of London and Paris. In this way, the CPH metroscape is the staging of a 'seamless journey' where an unobstructed flow of passengers is the key. There is nothing wrong with this while it is the stated goal of the Metro Company. But when the company claims to have created 'new urban spaces' with its system, it is a stretch.

Moreover, unlike in Paris and London, the CPH metroscape is a system where the only geographic place reference you will get whilst in transit is the sign that informs you of the name of the station. There are no geographical or thematic references that provide details about where you are relative to geography 'above'. The mobile subject whom the Metro Company wants to cater to has a social profile as the 'ideal passenger' who is interested in fast and reliable transport only. Admittedly the Metro affords 'temporary congregations' but these are characterised by a minimum of social interaction as it is the instrumental journey from A to B which is paramount. You buy a ticket from a machine because there are no humans at the stations. There are so-called Train Stewards who get on trains to ensure that tickets are bought and stamped but on the whole it is a 'non-humanised staging' that the Metro Company has established. There are, of course, one's fellow passengers, but the lack of 'authorised persons' in the Metro is noticeable and together with one's awareness of being in a driverless train system this creates an interesting trust-dependent relationship. In London's 'Tube' there are a few driverless trains where they had to put inspectors into the driver's compartment pretending to drive the train in order to reassure passengers. This element of trust created by the presence of human actors has been omitted in Copenhagen, and from my field observations this seems to bother no one amongst the passengers. There is, in other words, complete trust in the passenger-processing assemblage of the CPH metroscape.

Flow machine or urban space?

The design code is strict and is reflected in the fact that the Metro Company has attempted to keep the amount of commercials to a minimum (at least compared to the metros in London and Paris). There is obviously a huge commercial pressure to increase their quantity, as this will mean revenue for the company. Here a balance is constantly being struck between the Metro Company's own design philosophy and the relentless market pressures. There are a number of screens that can display advertisements in the train 'tubes' at the stations as well as on the glass doors on the platforms but they have kept the stairwells and other larger spaces free of permanent advertising as well, as it is only occasionally that we see large commercial banners (typically hung in connection to a launch of cosmetic products). Here we find some ambivalence in the Metro Company's staging of the transit space as a commercial space. At present it offers passengers an experience of more 'calm' aesthetics without the semiotic 'pollution' that we find in the other metro systems. But the Metro is also a site of diversity. However, the social mix of user groups is much higher in London and Paris. One thus starts to understand that the Copenhagen Metro is staged on a deliberate strategy of exclusion of the homeless, drug addicts and so-called 'unruly elements' and is thus an illustration of the 'dark side' of mobilities related to power and social exclusion. Interestingly, this is done not only by means of traditional power techniques such as closed-circuit television (CCTV) and personally surveying the Metro but also by the more subtle strategy of staging a space where mobility is the only practised activity. There is a minimum of friction in relation to this mobility staging, but there is also a minimum of social interaction. The social agent's own 'staging' from below is thus limited to a small reservoir of interaction types. Obviously, the metros of London and Paris are also made to afford instrumental flows of commuters with minimal friction. But unlike the Copenhagen Metro the systems of Paris and London contain the opportunity to 'step out of circulation' and engage in social, cultural and commercial interactions whose effect is urban in a much more diversified way than in the Copenhagen metroscape. There is most certainly also a time factor at play since the Metro in Copenhagen is so new that various counter-practices and 'other ways' of using it have not been able to coalesce. This is a process of collective appropriation that may take some time and which will determine how a technology like the Metro is 'translated' and diffused into the wider urban fabric and amongst the citizens.

The actual train ride is characterised by a physically effortless and smooth bodily sensation, where train compartment design and furnishing provide the classic opportunities to interact with one's fellow 'mobile with' or to 'keep to oneself'. The 'temporary congregations' of 'mobile withs' are seen when groups of passengers move around the system. But in the rush hours when most passengers must stand in very close physical proximity we find the traditional 'tools' for creating and managing a 'mobile front stage' and 'mobile back stage' missing. It is, for example, possible outside the rush hour to put one's bag on a vacant seat, entrench oneself behind a newspaper or talk on the mobile phone in the electronically mediated spaces that transcend the body's simultaneous presence. These techniques are to some extent also present during the rush hour, but they are used significantly less and it is mainly the closed body language and 'eyes turned towards the floor' we see as the way to organise a 'mobile front stage' towards the other passengers. If we move into the larger spatial areas such as platforms and stair areas we see pretty much the same type of territorialisation techniques we can observe at bus stops and the like. Passengers who travel individually seek to position their bodies in as sheltered a manner as possible (often using the escalators to create an object that they can stand with their back to) while the 'mobile withs' taking up the space apply more extroverted and dominant techniques. Here one must distinguish between groups of youths who 'run' around the metro and whose presence often seems intimidating or threatening and, for example, families with prams and small children that make up an altogether different type of 'mobile with'. Tourists in groups constitute a third form of 'mobile with' seeking to read Metro's geographic references to the city 'above' as well as possible.

Metro 2.0

As mentioned there are alternative metro design practices elsewhere that use conscious design and decoration in such a manner that stations acquire a unique identity and that passengers may use this to navigate and orient themselves in the system. Furthermore, such diverse design practices may promote aesthetic and artistic experiences that go beyond simply using public transportation. However, the Metro Company is very conscious about their specific staging of mobility which deliberately is based on generic and place-independent tools. But there may be a change in this design philosophy on the way with the design of the new 'City Ring'. One significant point about the generic design code is that it is not only very cost-effective to keep everything 'the same'. It also means that the Metro Company has succeeded in staging and orchestrating a system that rejects certain behaviours. Thus there are no benches in the Copenhagen Metro so that neither the destitute nor other 'undesirable elements' will feel tempted to 'hang out' there. Actually, no one is 'hanging out' in these spaces and when senior citizens complain about the lack of proper benches and argue that the 'leaning devices' on the platform are inadequate to rest on, the laconic reply has been that you do not have to sit anywhere since a train will arrive within a very few minutes! So we find a mobility and transit experience being staged from above with a very clear restriction on how passengers may stage themselves. They cannot 'hang out' and use the Metro as the 'city's living room', which is a distinct possibility in other metro systems. In Copenhagen the design of the Metro is a design that appeals to motion, and will not foster or afford any staying or other alternative ways of occupying its space. It is, in other words, a clearly monitored and controllable space. The next expansion phase of the Metro is termed the 'City Ring' and contains 17 new stations expected to be completed in

2018. Already some focus is on the critique of the existing design principles. The Metro Company is, for example, experimenting with new colours and even different colours for different train stations based on the new design dictum of 'local identity' in order to connect more clearly to the physical geography of the city. However, the basic construction principles and the 'cut-and-cover' principle will not be abandoned. Likewise, the next generation of the 'Copenhagen metroscape' will be based on the technology of driverless trains and very high arrival and departure frequencies. Whether this helps in dealing with the issues presented in this chapter concerning under-utilisation of urban potentials and the missing of cultural experiences remains to be seen.

From this example I turn now to the Sky Train in Bangkok where I have previously carried out research (Jensen 2007a). The Sky Train story supplements the Copenhagen Metro as it puts even more focus on social geography and the potential for segregation as a function of infrastructural design and is as such an even more clear example of the 'dark side' of mobilities design.

City of layers: Bangkok's Sky Train and how it works in socially segregating mobility patterns

The second case in this chapter concerns the construction of the Bangkok Sky Train (BTS) in central Bangkok. The research explores the socially segregating effect of the BTS on Bangkok mobility patterns. The approach to this particular case has been a combination of qualitative research interviews with experts and informants, document studies and field studies (for more details, see Jensen 2007a). In relation to the latter, the author has attempted to understand the mobile ethnography of Bangkok by walking and riding the different means of transportation during the field study (Figure 8.2).

Setting the scene: getting to know the context

The political culture of Thailand is made up of a complex relationship between monarchy, democracy and Buddhism. Infrastructure plays a vital role in the Bangkok/Thai culture – not just as systems of mobilities; rather they carry an important symbolic meaning. Thus most main infrastructures are symbolically blessed by the king in person before being put into use. Furthermore, the naming of large infrastructure armatures indicates the monarchy's symbolic importance. During the field work in April 2006 there was political unrest in Thailand, which culminated in the so-called 'Silk Coup' of 19 November 2006 in which the military took over the government. In other words, the political culture of Thai governance carries the hallmark of a distinct mixture of religious beliefs, monarchy, democracy and 'rule of law', corruption and military intervention. This makes an interesting and very difficult to predict political context for urban intervention and transport investment (personal interview with former Bangkok traffic engineer). But it also goes to show the cultural background against which the Sky Train must be understood.

Figure 8.2 Bangkok Sky Train.

Some of the first things any visitor to central Bangkok will notice are the traffic jams and massive congestion as well as many signs of social segregation (Douglass 1998; Fryd 2005; HABITAT 2001; Hamilton 2000; Pacione 2005). The city is historically a 'water-based city', meaning that the many canals (*klongs* in Thai) were initially used as waterways in the urban transportation system. Bangkok has a long tradition of attracting foreign visitors and investors (Beek 2002:122). After the importance of water as the flow system for mobility decreased, asphalt took over, first in the form of collective transport and later in private-car use (Beek 2002:58–59).

The transport realities of everyday life in Bangkok

There are a number of different modes of transportation serving the population of Bangkok, and not all of them are equally safe or reliable. At the time of the field study (April 2006) the following modes were available to the mobile citizens of Bangkok. Walking and biking are here, as in any other Asian metropolis, widely used. The 'green minibuses' are at the inexpensive end of the spectrum. The advantages of this means of transportation are high frequency and low fares, whereas the disadvantage is the high risk, as they are mostly too full of passengers and often there are no doors! Next in the transport hierarchy are the 'red buses' with a 'fan' as the cooling technology. The 'blue aircons' are the air-conditioned buses (seen by many Bangkok residents as an essential feature) that charge depending on the distance travelled. The 'orange aircons' are newer buses all with air conditioning (in Thailand called 'European Buses' as the Thais find they resemble buses seen in Western movies). After this comes the 'purple minibus' where there is a seat guaranteed for all. Last in the bus hierarchy are the 'Toyota Hi-Ace minibuses' that run non-stop from point A to point B, and charge depending on distance. Leaving the collective means of transportation we find the taxis. Normally they carry up to four persons, but teenagers and less well-off families are able to cram 8–10 persons into a standard taxi. Next to the ordinary taxi we find the motorcycle taxis. These are mostly used to get from home to a bus station or a Sky Train station. The motorcycle taxi is indisputably the fastest mode of transportation – and by far the most dangerous as about 80 per cent of all traffic accidents in Thailand involve motorcycles. Closely related to the motorcycle taxi is the tourist icon of Bangkok, the 'tuk-tuk', which is a three-wheeled moped with a roofed passenger seat for 2–4 persons. They profit mainly from tourists who find them exotic and recognise them from the traveller's guide books. Finally we find the Subway and the Sky Train as the newest modes of transportation in the mobility portfolio of Bangkok. Next to these modes of mobilities, the private car obviously has taken the lion's share of public space and traffic infrastructure here as in many other cities.

Rot-Fai-Fah: *the 'car with fire up in the air'*

When the local population of Bangkok speaks of the BTS they term it *Rot-Fai-Fah*, literally meaning 'the car with fire up in the air'. The first real steps towards realising the Sky Train came in April 1992 when BMA (Bangkok Metropolitan Authority) awarded the BTSC (Bangkok Mass Transit System Plc) a 30-year concession to build and operate the system. At that time the goal was to create a mass-transit system that was safe, comfortable, fast, convenient, reliable and affordable (Hoskins 2000:47). However, the first contract, with Siemens and ITD, was not signed until July 1995. Further delays made the first day of operation 1 January 2000 (Hoskins 2000:49). Operating on the two lines, the 'Sukhumwit Line' (the longest line with the most stations) and the 'Silom Line', the Sky Train (with a total track length of 55 km) has made it possible to travel at triple the average car speed in the city by operating at 35 km/h. Thus, one can make a cross-town trip from Chatuchak Market to Sukhumwit Soi in less than 30 minutes, compared to the 90 minutes it took before the Sky Train (Hoskins 2000:45). Running across town and above other infrastructures of the city at 12 m above the ground it forms a massive elevated concrete band with 2.5 m in diameter support columns touching down at 32 stations.

In the beginning the BTS could not meet the break-even point. The fare was relatively expensive and the Bangkok population did not relate the new situation to its 'time value' (personal interview with Dr Nopanant Tapananont). This has since changed due to many factors such as rising oil prices and a transformation of the price ratio between bus and BTS in favour of the latter. But what seems to be the most illustrative lesson from this is the notion of 'time value' as a culture-specific mobility norm that was not present at the beginning of BTS operation but that has now become a well-established calculus of the Bangkok middle class and business people. The BTS is cited as the main reason that business people now de facto are able to make time-specific appointments across town – and keep them. The Sky Train (within its limited radius) contributes to a new 'culture of punctuality' in Bangkok; a culture that for a very long time has been the norm in many Western cities, as for example noticed by Georg Simmel in Berlin in the 1880s (Simmel 1903/50). This suggests that the rationalities for coping with daily mobilities in Bangkok have changed (for some) as a more profound way of relating to time and space gets inserted into a new way of comprehending urban flows and mobilities.

City of edges and layers

Bangkok is a city of edges and layers in physical as well as in socio-spatial terms. Physically Bangkok is very much marked by its mobility layers. Some observers say the Sky Train has introduced a new sense of order in Bangkok as it is 'clean, cool and quiet' (Hoskins 2000:54) – the antithesis to much else of Bangkok's urban fabric. However, one could also say that the BTS spreads generic designs as it scatters more or less soulless concrete train platforms along its route. Moreover, the Sky Train creates dark tunnels below which the congestion fumes and the heat become unbearable (Beek 2002:121). According to a study by Vichiensan and Miyamoto (2006:6), there is a very clear connection between property prices and the BTS. This is also recognised by one of the leading Bangkok real-estate agencies:

> The Government's decision to invest in mega projects over the next few years is good news in the property market, particularly those mass transit and road network projects. Those projects will open new corridors for new property development opportunities. Many areas that now have no property development potential will benefit from their better accessibility. This means developers can develop new projects outside the downtown area and offer them at lower costs thanks to lesser expensive land prices in those areas. Once those projects are developed, Jones Lang LaSalle expects a growth in real estate, beginning with the residential sector, followed by retail and the office sector in certain locations.
>
> (Jones Lang LaSalle 2006)

As Jones Lang LaSalle argues, there is reason for investors to look with great expectation at the new infrastructure link to the shopping centre at Siam Paragon since it is going to be the 'hottest retail development project planned for completion this year' (2006). Academic analysts also find reason to expect a positive relationship between property prices and Sky Train infrastructure:

> In close proximity to the city's Sky Train system condominiums offer tremendous luxury at premium prices and most of the residents are well off business-men and expatriates. Away from the nodes the glitter and glamour is exchanged by bare concrete and residents are more likely to be factory workers and taxi drivers.
>
> (Wissink *et al.* 2005:8)

According to other real-estate agents in Bangkok, the market seems slowly to be adjusting to the new conditions created by the BTS. Not in the sense of making accessibility more evenly distributed, but in the sense that the Sky Train can be seen as taking of some of the 'heat' from the centrally located areas. New zones of high-end development are following the track of the Sky Train, and thus re-allocating investments along these armatures. In this way the Sky Train facilitates a segregated geography transcending the 'traditional' horizontal divide between rich and poor urban enclaves. The BTS is over-layering Bangkok with a new vertical geography of segregation. The Sky Train not only facilitates easy access to buildings by means of direct sky-bridges; it also facilitates a development of the Thai version of the 'gated communities' known throughout the Western world. Together with the private car and the sealed-off enclave, the Sky Train adds a layer of secure, fast and comfortable mobility potential to the well-off:

> a first view does clearly indicate that the daily networks of high-end mubahnchatsan [gated communities] inhabitants are very extensive, the car in combination with the sky train being the main means of transportation. Alternatively, the networks of the inhabitants of informal settlements and low-end mubahnchatsan are small, with most activities being restricted to the vicinity of the neighbourhood.
>
> (Wissink *et al.* 2005:15)

The informal settlement structure and squatter settlements are often the next zone of development. The settlement occupies or rents land and attracts services. The process then gets accelerated with the advent of infrastructure projects: 'With the upgrading of infrastructure, an urban site becomes more attractive and the residents of these settlements come under pressure to be evicted' (Ribeiro 2001:118). In summary the chairman of the Real Estate Association, RICS, Simon Landy explained that the Sky Train has impacted demand patterns in the city to some extent. First, in the office market, tenants are showing a growing preference for office buildings within easy reach of a Sky Train or underground station. Second, in the residential market, buyers and tenants are similarly drawn to properties in the vicinity of Sky Train stations. This preference has become even more marked since the rapid escalation in oil prices. Some developers are switching to building more inner-city condominiums because they are finding that buyers are more reluctant to buy houses on suburban estates, at least partly because of the increased commuting costs (personal communication with Simon Landy).

An icon of modernity

Politicians are keen to think of the BTS as a symbol of progress set against the bleaker image of a car-congested city. As such the BTS might be said to fulfil a larger role as a branding object and imaginary icon. To estimate the total effect of the Sky Train on everything from traffic to economic activity is not an easy task, but some consider the main effect of the Sky Train to be its symbolic branding value (Suwanarit 2005:48). Many commentators explain that there was an initial resistance to the Sky Train, but that this mostly was expressed in terms of environment and aesthetics (Hoskins 2000; personal interviews with Dr Tapananont and B. Mekvichai, deputy governor of Bangkok). Accordingly, the voices against the concrete pillar construction quietened as time passed and the public 'got used to it':

> Nonetheless, as people become used to the Sky Train, it emphatically alters the way in which they experience Bangkok. It is as if time and space in the city have become new dimensions and, for example, a shopping excursion between business appointments in Silom to the Emporium on Sukhumwit Road is now not an impossibility ... Moreover, the City is viewed differently. Seen from the vantage point of 12 meters above the streets, Bangkok reveals itself as a far greener city than imagined with gardens normally hidden behind compound walls suddenly exposed.
>
> (Hoskins 2000:52)

However, the gaze to the sky from below has been even further segregated since the Sky Train effectively creates congested tunnels of car emissions: 'Roofed by the tracks above, many city streets have become tunnels of noise and smog. To most people below, the sky is almost invisible, yet this has somehow developed into an accepted landscape' (Suwanarit 2005:47).

Clearly the Sky Train is more than a machine for shifting people from A to B. The fact that an increasing number of 'modern', Western-inspired music videos by Thai rock and pop artists are filmed on Sky Train platforms indicates that this is a space of particularly strong iconic connotations. In this way the Sky Train facilitates the illusion of a 'first-world urban aesthetics' bracketed off by deliberate and meticulous selected camera angles. Furthermore, tourists are taking pictures of the BTS as much as the Royal Castle, illustrating the point that Bangkok has a global mobility icon in its urban landscape. But the BTS is more than a media-made icon of Modernity as the 'ordinary Thai' seems to understand it as symbolising the transition of Thailand towards being a global player in the networked world of global capitalism: 'For Thai people the BTS is a symbol of progress and modernisation' (personal interview with Dr Nopanant Tapananont).

Sky Train and below: parallel worlds and new public domains

Interestingly, the practice of policing the privatised spaces of the walkways, platforms and connections to the Sky Train has changed dramatically. At the beginning of the existence of the Sky Train all types of vendor activities where strongly prohibited and strictly enforced (B.B. Jensen 2004:88). However, today the wide gangways and semi-plazas connecting the Siam Square station with the MBK shopping mall are filled with street vendors selling everything from designer clothes copies to Thai souvenirs. Here we see a process of appropriation and diffusion that has not yet started to materialise in the Copenhagen Metro as hinted at earlier. Evidently such practices are creating new forms of 'public domains' (Hajer and Reijndorp 2001) within the city. The BTS thus plays a trick on fixed notions of private and public spaces. New hybrid forms of public–private domains are the result thereof. In this sense the BTS (unintentionally) supports the economic culture of the street side-by-side with the huge shopping malls that the Sky Train connects, thereby adding to the complexity of Bangkok's transit flows and urban geography. To the Western tourist the street vendors on the BTS platform add 'exotic experiences' to urban transport. Obviously the private owners of these facilities have opened up access to this type of activity because it adds to the commercial attractiveness of the Sky Train as it may capture more high-spending tourists. However, not all analysts are so positive. The situation on the Sukhumwit Line below and around the On Nat station offers grounds for another interpretation, as Marling suggests:

> On Nat is the terminal station of the Sky Train. Due to the creation of the Sky Train it has become a transferral, which today is the main identity of the area. The image of the area is dominated by fences which increase when experienced at eye-level. By mapping functions around the station, it was discovered that all the sites in the area were private and turned into gated communities. This is clearly an area with high disparity between poor and rich persons and poor exchange between different social classes. This means that the only place where you are allowed to stay and wait for the bus is on the sidewalk of the very busy 6-laned roads.
>
> (Marling 2005:198)

So to some social groups the Sky Train has realised a very profound change in mobility patterns and cultures, segregating the city into poorer residents and immigrant workers on the one hand and business people and tourists on the other. Though senior government officials seem to think of the Sky Train as socially inclusive and open to all classes (personal interview with B. Mekvichai, deputy governor of Bangkok), the train is adding another layer to a city already marked by social segregation (Andersen *et al.* 2002:33):

> The upper middle classes and the rich people transport themselves and live generally speaking, from 3rd floor and up. They work in buildings with air condition; they shop in air conditioned shopping malls; go to cinemas and train in cool fitness centres. They even transport themselves in air conditioned cars on elevated high ways or in sky trains.
>
> (Marling 2005:34)

The Sky Train connects to the upper layer of the city that has already been taken over by the rich in high-rise buildings. This is reminiscent of the remarks by Koolhaas who, in his essay on 'The Generic City' (1995), notices the ground being possessed by the poor and the sky by the rich. To the question of whether the BTS has socially segregating effects, some analysts would say that it was the case at the start due to the expensive fares, but also that more people are now using it (personal interview with Dr Nopanant Tapananont). Higher up the hierarchy the assessment of the BTS is even more positive, as here in the words of the deputy governor: 'Personally, I think ... everyone uses the Sky Train ... that is a new perception ... This is convenient and you know exactly when you get somewhere' (personal interview with B. Mekvichai, deputy governor of Bangkok). On the other hand, even the deputy governor acknowledges that 'Bus and BTS accommodate different people'.

Circulating shoppers and capital

Some argue that the BTS has become a new symbol and icon of Bangkok's entry into the realm of super-modern or perhaps post-modern metropolises:

> Six years on, it [the BTS] has attained a unique status as the icon of contemporary Bangkok. Its overwhelming presence is featured in every conceivable media – new music videos, movies or advertisements. The Sky Train is an indispensable symbol of the new generation. Its new mode of movement, floating high above the ground, allows the commercial buildings that exists along its 13-kilometre distance to 'plug-in' to their nearest stations, sucking commuters to engage in shopping activities, forming a new type of hyper-shopping experience – a central shopping district. The Sky Train functions as an organ of capital flow.
>
> (Ayuthaya 2005:16)

Aside from being seen as the new icon of the city, the BTS facilitates two major circuits and flows: shoppers and capital. However, the BTS facilitates shoppers and tourists more than, for example, everyday commuters. There is a huge part of the population that is cut off from the 'cathedrals of consumption' (Ritzer 2005) that the new middle and upper classes enjoy in the contemporary city. Sky-bridges convert the flows of passengers into flows of power-shoppers. In the early life of the BTS the pecuniary tentacles were few and unnoticed, but during the last few years the mushrooming shopping malls and luxury condominiums increasingly latch on to the armature in order to profit from the spending masses. Although it could be argued that the BTS does not have any identifying central node, the Siam station marks the centre of tourist commercial gravity – in particular linking to the huge MBK shopping centre. What strikes one as a passenger of the BTS is the seamless experience of travel one gets when first embarking on the journey above the busy and smoggy streetscapes of 'Bangkok below'. Sensing the cool breeze of the air-conditioned environment is probably the most obvious difference in terms of bodily sensation that makes one feel that this is not a municipal bus. The design and layout of train stations, ticket machines and the interior of the carriages is cool, functional and aesthetically held in an international/generic style leaving you with no clues whatsoever as to whether you are in Asia, North America or Europe.

Reassembling the metros: concluding remarks

From the cases of the Metro in Copenhagen and the Sky Train in Bangkok there are important lessons to be learned. The two cases are both understood in the light of the *Staging Mobilities* framework, but with very different perspectives. The Copenhagen case is conceptualised around the way this generic flow space sets the scene for an everyday staging of mobilities where order and staging from above are key. Obviously the Bangkok Sky Train is also very much staged from above, but what emerges in this case is the mobility technologies' impact and mediation effects on the social geography and mobility powers of the city. The uneven time–space geographies facilitated by the Sky Train in Bangkok sets the scene for an altogether more segregated urban mobilities model.

Here I will first draw some general conclusion on the Copenhagen case. This brief chapter is obviously not able to do justice to the empirical field study of the Metro (see Jensen 2012a). Within the concept of *Staging Mobilities* we have seen how both the system and the actors create mobile front stages and back stages in diverse attempts to exercise conspicuous (self-)control. The Copenhagen Metro is a living space in the city that is slowly being 'appropriated' by locals and visitors. This is seen in the dynamics creating multiple 'mobile withs' and 'temporary congregations' in the Metro. The new circulation machine is simultaneously a cultural and social space where human interaction (face-to-face as well as mediated through various mobile technologies) creates a unique assemblage of systems, actors, bodies, technologies and social norms that collectively provide what I have termed the 'Copenhagen metroscape'. It should be noted that changes may be about to happen. For instance, I noticed on 10 March 2011 both a saxophonist and a major cosmetics advertising banner at Kongens Nytorv station. The banner was of the type often seen in singular ad hoc promotional events. But the saxophonist was undeniably a new feature. I subsequently wrote to the Metro Company's information department and asked if they had changed their policy and signed a contract with a musician, or whether this was just a single 'free agent' plying his trade to earn some pennies. Responses have not been received, but it leaves the impression that the Metro is under pressure, both commercially and in relation to the unused interaction potential illustrated by musicians and other 'performers'. The broader perspective on this study of the project I grandly termed 'the greatest transformation of the nation's capital since King Christian IV' is to unfold the analytical perspective of *Staging Mobilities* to the Copenhagen Metro. The new extension is a project that, together with the existing Metro, changes Copenhagen's physical geography, as well as its cultural and mental geography. The project has received daily press attention and will have historians' attention for many years to come.

Next I conclude on the Bangkok Sky Train case. The BTS does not shift large enough volumes of passengers to seriously affect the congestion in Bangkok. Nevertheless, the environmental effect of the BTS is considered to be positive (Perera 2006). The socio-spatial effects of the BTS are quite a different story though. Research into the BTS illustrates how the new networked geographies of Bangkok configure a relational set of infrastructure nodes facilitating 'critical points of contacts' (Jensen and Morelli 2011) in the city (e.g. expensive high-rise accommodation or shopping centres). This research suggests that the mobile elite of Bangkok (being business people and well-off tourists) not only increase their 'speed potential' in motility terms but they also in fact use this potential for fast, safe and reliable movement within the city. Seen as illustrative of the 'dark side' of mobilities, the BTS re-produces urban segregation as the mobility practices related to the train are nested within social hierarchies and systems of resource allocation that makes mobility a value-laden phenomenon. In Bangkok there is a problem of 'double segregation'. First, the BTS contributes physically and geographically to segregation as the clean-aired infrastructure over-layers the smog-filled streetscape below. Second, the BTS contributes to a socio-economic segregation as it separates its users along the lines of economic income and thus limits the relative motility of the less well-off inhabitants while it caters to the rich, the middle class and the many international tourists riding the BTS.

As the BTS spreads its tentacles in the form of sky-bridges into the enclaves of capital to be found in high-end condominiums or shopping centres along the route it becomes increasingly clear that the BTS works in a socially segregating way, creating socio-spatial inequality in both relative and absolute terms. However, it also spurs effects that transform the more subtle expressions of the mobilities culture in Bangkok. This is most predominantly seen in the way the BTS reconfigures the rationality behind urban travel as social agents start understanding the concept of 'time value'. The BTS facilitates the system of punctuality in the city as business people now start to make reliable meeting appointments. Sociologically speaking the BTS therefore cannot be understood as socially 'neutral' to the mobility patterns of Bangkok. It may carry great advantages for business people, tourists and the middle classes but in relative terms the less well-off inhabitants clearly face worse conditions as they are condemned to the dark and heavily congested tubes of infrastructure created below the armatures of the Sky Train. Furthermore there is evidence of a positive relationship between Sky Train stations and increasing property prices near the sites (this correlation is obviously also found in Copenhagen near the Metro stations, but in a much less segregated context). As the main stations operate in the inner-city areas there is no reason to believe that this increase in property values will not benefit the well-off property owners in the Central Business District. Moreover, the construction of sky-bridges to shopping centres such as the Siam Paragon (where Italian luxury cars are on display at the entrance level) clearly demonstrates that the BTS has an effect on the socio-economic geography of

Bangkok that favours capital-intensive developers and investors. In the networked urban geographies of Bangkok's transportation system new mobilities practices are played out in a relational space where the potential for movement is shifted in favour of the elite and tourists. The BTS reconfigures the mobility patterns of the inner city of Bangkok in ways that are much more than just planning policies to overcome congestion and traffic jams. They are also expressions of power, social exclusion and ultimately of the 'dark sides' of mobilities. In the 'city of layers' the Sky Train facilitates socially segregating mobility patterns.

The key terms to draw from this chapter to add to the *Staging Mobilities* vocabulary are 'metroscapes' and 'segregated mobilities practices'. A 'metroscape' is to be understood as a mobility 'landscape' consisting of everything from rails and driverless train cars to ticket machines and security cameras. This perspective defines urban metroscapes as physical mobility landscapes as well as the codes, rules and cultural norms that create the active joining of technologies, infrastructures and social practice. 'Segregated mobilities practices' are the mobility patterns segregated along the lines of income and social hierarchy often complexly wedded to the infrastructure systems of the city in respect both to 'switched-off areas' and to the more general social strata of the city. Both cases are examples of the 'dark sides' of 'segregated mobilities practices' but in very different contexts and utilising different technologies of separation and exclusion. These concepts point towards understanding the *Staging of Mobilities* as related to both complex socio-technical assemblages and mobile power-geometries.

From this part of the book with its empirically focused chapters I shall now move to the fourth and final part in which more general issues and conclusions will be addressed.

Part IV
Towards a sociology of staging mobilities

9 Materialities of mobilities
Learning from the design fields

> It is difficult to design an urban space so maladroitly that people will not use it, but there are many such spaces.
>
> William H. Whyte, *City: Rediscovering the Centre*, 1988, p. 1

> A bee puts to shame many an architect in the construction of her cells but what distinguishes the worst of architects from the best of bees is this, that the architect raises the structure in imagination before he erects it in reality.
>
> Karl Marx, *Capital*, 1887/1972, p. 233

> Few spaces are designed exclusively for interaction at just one of the distances identified here [intimate, personal, social and public distance]. In most of the settings we might imagine, people move around, and in many cases different relationships might well exist between various people within the same space.
>
> Bryan Lawson, *The Language of Space*, 2001, p. 120

Introduction

In this chapter I return to what has been claimed to be a key feature of the *Staging Mobilities* framework, namely its focus on the material sites and physical dimension of mobilities. In particular I am concerned with the ideas, activities and practices staging and shaping the environments of mobilities (here understood very broadly as 'design' of mobilities). One of the key aims of focusing on the materialities of mobilities in this chapter is to put emphasis on the very tangible but, within the 'mobilities turn', still under-explored sensitivity to how things actually work, look and come into being. One of the main contributions from the *Staging Mobilities* perspective to the 'mobilities turn' is to bring attention to the work done by 'designers' of mobilities. Here 'designers' must be understood in a very broad sense, including planners, urban designers, architects, engineers etc. These are all representative of disciplines and 'communities of practice' engaged in 'intervention' rather than 'analysis' (or at least with intervention as a necessary outcome of analysis). In being occupied within the 'interventionist' fields of practice the 'designers of mobilities' are instrumental in the actual shaping of the sites and 'scenes' of practised mobilities. Thus there is a strong need for adding this dimension to the research agenda of the 'mobilities turn'.

Even though this can only be done here on a preliminary basis within the confines of a book chapter, the opening up towards the design of sites, technologies and infrastructures of mobilities must be engaged with. As I move towards articulating a sociology of *Staging Mobilities* in the final chapter, this chapter points to the potentials and gains to be found in opening up the 'mobilities turn' much more to material- and design-oriented perspectives. I am interested in establishing the first set of issues and questions for a research agenda and perspective that has been neglected in the mobilities research so far. This theme will be followed up in more detail in the *Designing Mobilities* book to be published as a companion to this book. Here I believe in the value of introducing the 'mobilities turn' audience to a less familiar literature. However, the 'interventionist' disciplines mentioned very often lack a theoretical underpinning to their existing practices and in particular they are unreceptive to the potentials of the 'mobilities turn' with its new transdisciplinary insights. Moreover, innovative and creative theory building not only has the task of providing a field of reflection for existing practices. 'Interventionist' fields of practices might also 'use' theory to explore new fields and create new practices. As I shall return to in the final chapter I am strongly convinced that there is potential for a fruitful two-way relationship between the 'analytical' disciplines within mobilities research (e.g. sociology, human geography, transport studies) and the 'interventionist' disciplines. From my own work based in the field of intervention (urban design) and with a background in the 'analytical' disciplines (sociology), I think it is safe to say that just as the 'interventionist' may profit from theoretical reflection and research so can the 'analytical' disciplines be enriched by getting a deeper understanding of the more pragmatic and practical issues related to getting mobility systems 'up and running' and to the design of the sites of mobilities etc. There is not the space to engage here in a debate about the epistemological common ground of the 'mobilities turn' and the 'interventionist' fields, but some element of pragmatism does seem to be of relevance (Cuthbert 2006; Moudon 1992).

A final word of caution in this context: of course making a distinction between the 'analytical' and 'interventionist' disciplines in such a crude way as I have just done is too simplistic. This is so partly because practices and reflections in professional disciplines are inseparable (Jensen 2004), and partly because there are differences internally within these two crude categories that would need to be accounted for in all fairness. But for now, the distinction must be taken for what it is: a heuristic tool.

The structure of the chapter is the following: after the introduction section, two sections explore in more detail the fields of practice related to the shaping and designing of mobilities as we may find them within architecture, planning and urban design. As presented in Chapter 2, the notion of 'critical mobilities thinking' entails both an insight into the 'dark sides' of mobilities as well as an openness to new and innovative 'potentials' within mobilities. After this section I move towards positions that in very explicit terms find potentials for positive social interaction and culture in mobilities rather than simply seeing these as necessary evils. I am, however, not simply advocating a happy and positive design doctrine here. Therefore I will use the fourth section of this chapter to address one of the key challenges to future mobilities: the situation of post-carbon mobilities as an expression of crisis in the prevailing mobility systems. The chapter ends in the fifth section with some concluding remarks pointing towards the general conclusion of the final chapter.

Designing materialities of mobilities

As explained in more detail elsewhere (Jensen 2010d), the notion of 'design' is by no means straightforward and simple. Here I only touch upon this in very general terms (and more will be said about this in *Designing Mobilities*). As a starting point I consult Webster's Dictionary only to learn that the notion of 'design' comes from the Latin word 'designare', which means to 'mark out or designate'. Likewise the Oxford English Dictionary defines 'design' as a verb meaning 'to set something apart for someone, to intend, to make an imaginary sketch' (Shane 2005:104). Coming closer to the field of cities and mobilities we may take our point of departure in Norman's definition of design as 'the deliberate shaping of the environment in ways that satisfy individual and societal needs' (2007:171), or the definition of Monö who argues that design is 'the conscious process to develop physical objects with functional, ergonomic, economic and aesthetic concern' (Rune Monö, quoted in Molotch 2005:263). Also, the point made by Gänshirt is worth including as he argues that 'designing means devising a form for an object without having that actual object in front of you' (2007:57). However, there is no need to confine the word to physical objects and spaces alone: institutions, processes, software and all other sorts of 'things' may be designed. The definition I personally have found most useful in relation to cities and mobilities is that made by Lynch as he argues that

> Design is the playful creation and strict evaluation of the possible forms of something, including how it is to be made. That something need not be a physical object, nor is design expressed only in drawings. Although attempts have been made to reduce design to completely explicit systems of search and synthesis, it remains an art, a peculiar mix of rationality and irrationality. Design deals with qualities, with complex connections, and also with ambiguities.
>
> (Lynch 1981:290)

Indeed, the 'peculiar mix of rationality and irrationality' means that we are in cross-disciplinary territory and furthermore that we are facing a creative field of solutions to practical problems in the world. Some of these even have a strong ethical dimension to them as the discussion about the political and normative dimension to design stems from socially concerned projects like 'Design Like You Give a Damn' (see http://architectureforhumanity.org) to explorations of the meaning of design to the public good in general (Erlhoff *et al.* 2008). Much more is obviously to be said on the concepts and disciplines related to design. As already mentioned the key field that I shall be relating to is that of urban design. Here I cannot enter the discussion of definitions and boundaries but instead refer to the key literature that I find of relevance in this regard (e.g. Bacon 1967; Carmona *et al.* 2010; Cullen 1996; Gehl 2010; Halprin 1963; Krieger and Saunders 2009; Lang 2005; Lawson 2001; Lynch 1981; Madanipour 2003; Shane 2005, 2011; Whyte 1988). Regardless of what sort of 'designer' (urban designer, city planner, road engineer etc.) one is thinking of, it all boils down to the crucial fact that 'design decisions are largely based upon models in the head of the designer' (Lynch 1981:277). The obvious relation to mobilities has to do with the fact that urban design is concerned with the physical, material and socio-cultural practices afforded by the public spaces of cities in general. Mobilities are key elements in this, even though there is a debate to be had and a line of demarcation to be drawn concerning city planning, architecture, landscape architecture and engineering (Lang 2005:393). One might want to think of urban design as city planning with a focus on three-dimensional forms and material sites as well as the social practices afforded by these (Figure 9.1). That there is a connection between mobilities and urban design should not require explanation. However, there is a deeper connection than simply having to afford movement and securing access. As shown in Chapters 1 and 2 we are looking at practices that are much more than just movement from A to B. This theoretical claim connects with a very practical understanding of what streets, for example, are for:

Figure 9.1 Designing materialities of mobilities.

'The concern in urban design in the Western world is today increasingly focused on the quality of streets as seams for life and not simply as channels for vehicular traffic' (Lang 2005:366). Here the materialities of mobilities are linked to the staging of physical movements as well as the staging of social interaction, territorial identities and relations to places.

It is important, however, not to think that 'designers' have got it all perfect and that theorists are the ones looking for answers that can only come out of the pragmatic everyday solutions to mobilities design. As Lawson rightly points out: 'the idea that people will walk where the hard landscape goes is so silly that one wonders how designers can become so detached from reality' (2001:218). So looking at design of mobilities and sites thereof may just as well be indicative and enlightening due to the fact that they are not working well, or that they are inscribed with rationales and norms that supposedly are neutral to their users but after more thorough scrutiny in fact are shown to be acts of dominance and power – or even ignorance! The key insight to be gained from design is therefore not to be established by looking at it without any theoretical backdrop, so to speak. Rather, by looking at material design through the framework of *Staging Mobilities* we come to see how it actually works by staging practices of mobilities. Moreover, the critical and more reflective part of the design literature is most certainly no simple apology for design. Jane Jacobs' seminal text, *The Death and Life of Great American Cities* (1961), was one persistent act of critique targeted at design, planning and architectural practices of the day, as is Jan Gehl's (2010) work on the design of public spaces that has taken place over several decades now. In a similar vein, Kevin Lynch targets bad solutions to real-life planning and design issues. Moreover, he also sees potentials in mobilities since he perceives mobilities as more than A to B. Thus he speaks of the 'road experience' (1990:268) and to understand a given area as a set of journeys: 'a community is also seen while passing through it, whether as a tourist or on habitual trips. This may be the principal way of experiencing larger areas' (1990:274). In the essay 'Sensuous Criteria for Highway Design' from 1966 (co-authored with Donald Appleyard in Lynch 1990:563–578) Lynch describes some of the basic assumptions that were behind the seminal *View from the Road* published a few years earlier (Appleyard *et al.* 1964). One such assumption concerns the more positive potential of infrastructures:

> To the bystander, the city expressway is a threat or at least a nuisance, and from his [*sic*] standpoint avoidance of problems should be the basis of many of the basic sensuous criteria. We will try to show, however, that highways might also play a more positive role for him, although concrete examples are rare.
>
> (Lynch 1990:563)

The discussion of sensuous criteria circles around the notions of legibility, visibility and coherence of design that were pertinent to Lynch. But also the experiential dimension is given consideration:

> The expressway should offer the traveler a stimulating, coherent, and developing experience. Motion, spatial enclosure, the view, goal attainment, activity, signs, surface character, and light are primary components; continuity and contrast, rhythm and progression are organizing factors ... finally, the expressway should be designed as a meaningful and informative experience. What the traveler sees should be worth looking at.
>
> (Lynch 1990:573–574)

Needless to say, we still perform multiple instrumental and less inspiring travels every day. Lynch was concerned with the way armatures were designed so that they could provide experiences beyond the instrumental movement. This is clear in his use of the notion of a 'melodic organisation' of the path:

> There is a final way of organizing a path or a set of paths, which will become of increasing importance in a world of great distances and speeds. It might be called 'melodic' in analogy to music. The events and characteristics along the path-landmarks, space changes, dynamic sensations – might be organized as a melodic line, perceived and imaged as a form which is experienced over a substantial time interval.
>
> (Lynch 1960:99)

Such 'melodic' organisation suggests a particularly playful and creative attitude to the staging of mobilities, an idea I return to later in this chapter.

Lawson reminds us that design is a quite different matter from scientific experiment or philosophical thought. Despite many years of design research Lawson admits to not having come to a full understanding of its true nature. However, he does claim that design is prescriptive rather than descriptive, and that it requires action and active decisions even though the underpinning levels of knowledge and information may not be as well consolidated as one might wish (Lawson 2001:247). Elsewhere Lawson discusses in more detail what the design process in general is about (2006) and how this ties in to particular frames of knowledge (2004). As mentioned, there is a very direct link between the urban design field and mobilities issues. One way of thinking about this is by making a distinction between movement space and social space: 'Public space can be considered in terms of movement space and social space. A crucial difference is that movement space for pedestrians is also social space, but movement space for vehicles often annihilates its potential as social space' (Carmona *et al.* 2010:84). Such a distinction has the advantage of illustrating one of the key conflicts in urban design and city planning, namely who to design for: the slow or the fast? Unfortunately such a simple distinction also clouds the fact that to move and to interact are not necessarily each other's antithesis. Needless to say, this may be the case when a city prioritises the car at the expense of the pedestrians. In fact, the notion of a 'street hierarchy' was developed by the German planner and architect Ludwig Hilberseimer, accommodating the dual concern of increased traffic speeds with safer routes for children (Carmona *et al.* 2010:87). However, if we start exploring how interaction is being remodelled and reconfigured in light of, for example, networked technologies (as shown in Chapter 7) the picture is less monochrome. At least we should acknowledge that 'the qualities of streets, squares and other urban places and the links between them, as behaviour settings and as aesthetic displays, are amongst the core concerns of urban design' (Lang 2005:60). Halprin goes even further in his argument for how intertwined urban design and mobilities are:

> We need a system to program movement carefully and analyze it, a system which will allow us to schedule it on a quantitative as well as qualitative basis. Since movement and the complex interrelations which it generates are an essential part of the life of a city, urban design should have a choice of starting from movement as the core – the essential element of the plan. Only after programming the movement and graphically expressing it, should the environment – an envelope within which movement takes place – be designed. The environment exists for the purpose of movement.
> (Halprin 1963:209)

Even though the language here is permeated with one of the key weaknesses of design thinking, that of being able to 'program' activities and thus the illusion of omnipotent power and control in planning and design, Halprin's acknowledgement of the importance of mobilities to urban design is crucial. Also the influential urban designer and city planner Ed Bacon realised that catering to different speeds of movement was crucial for good city design (Bacon 1967:35). Very much in parallel to the notion of 'critical points of contacts' I introduced in Chapter 2, Bacon (albeit in a more artful manner) saw the connections between movement systems as a particular design task:

> The trunk of the tree, which establishes the path of movement of thousands of tubes, diverging in the branches and delivering the chemicals necessary for growth to the leaves, can be linked to a city's movement systems. Water acts as the vehicle to propel the chemicals to the leaves, and in turn it evaporates into the air. The point of change from water for vapor is the place where the flowers and fruit develop. So in cities the points of connection between systems should be places of special emphasis and design enrichment.
> (Bacon 1967:35)

As the discussion of design for mobilities is rather comprehensive I will only look into one dimension and mode of mobility here, which is the automobile and its relationship to urban mobilities design.

Streets for cars: spaces for life?

In discussing design and mobilities for cities the issue of cars and streetscapes are unavoidable. Much has been written about the hegemony of the car and its destructive impact on the city (e.g. Jacobs 1961; Gehl 2010; Halprin 1966; Mumford 1938). Having noticed this (and to a certain extent become almost too familiar with these arguments) the parts of the design literature that actually are looking for more balanced interpretations of the city–car relationship may offer more and new insights. As I discussed in Chapter 2 the tendency to articulate a moral geography that may cloud insights of unforeseen or under-utilised potentials has prevailed throughout the history of urban thought. However, if we start elsewhere (but by no means ignoring the critical voices on the car) we see another point in the design literature. Namely, that contrary to the 'analytical' and academic disciplines, the design fields are often rather open-minded in looking for new potentials, unrealised opportunities or creative ways of using existing technologies, objects and spaces. At the risk of contributing yet another simplistic division we may say that the 'analytical' disciplines are expert at detecting problems, whereas the 'interventionist' disciplines are much more alert to detecting potentials (and leaving aside that quite a few 'interventionist' disciplines do not deliver on this variable). In the social sciences the role of research and its potential for influencing society has long been a sensitive debate. This I cannot engage with in philosophical terms here, but instead take note of the many challenges that contemporary societies are facing (from global warming and climate change to energy shortages to dramatically shifting demographics). A new role for a social science like the 'mobilities turn' may well be to add the competence of detecting potentials to the well-established one of identifying problems. Halprin for one starts by acknowledging that mobilities are crucial to the city, and that the settings where mobilities are being staged is a vital aspect:

> the city comes alive through movement and its rhythmic structure. The elements are no longer merely inanimate. They play a vital role, they become modulators of activity and are seen in juxtaposition with other moving objects. Within the spaces, movement flows, the paving and ramps become platforms for action, the street furniture is used, the sculpture in the street is seen and enjoyed. And the whole city landscape comes alive through movement as a total environment for the creative process of living. We call this chapter the *choreography of the city* because its implication of movement and participation – movement of people, of cars, of flying kites, of clouds and pigeons, and even the change of season.
>
> (Halprin 1963:9; emphasis added)

Obviously some of these moving elements (e.g. pigeons) are beyond the direct reach of human design! But it is safe to say that the built environment and the way it hosts and affords mobilities is related to the capacities for design and equally importantly to the values related thereto (Halprin 1963:199). This is similar to the concerns voiced by Appleyard *et al.* in their seminal study of the highway experience (1964). Moreover, Halprin was concerned to keep the design principle for the 'scenic highway' strictly separate from that of the 'urban highway' as these were to be seen to be two very different mobilities environments: where the scenic highway gently follows the curvatures of pastoral rural landscapes, the urban highway by its nature needs to be integral to the city's fabric with narrow rights of way, linear qualities and multiple levels (Halprin 1963:202). To Halprin (1966) the design of freeways was just as much a form of art in a slightly similar fashion as it is to Ingersoll, to whom I will return below. Here is praise of the freeway in the characteristic techno-optimist language of the 1960s:

> These vast and beautiful works of engineering [the highways] speak to us in the language of a new scale, a new attitude in which high-speed motion and the qualities of change are not mere abstract conceptions but a vital part of our everyday experiences.
> (Halprin 1966:16)

This language actually does an injustice to Halprin's more balanced analysis of the pros and cons of auto-mobilities and the critical understanding of the role of the car and its infrastructures. He states that 'freeways have done terrible things to cities in the past decade' (1966:23). To Halprin the issue was not whether there should be cars or not, but rather how the design philosophy underpinning the mobilities design was articulated and implemented. Thinking much in line with a pragmatic design field Halprin identified both the good and the bad (the 'potential' versus the 'dark side' of mobilities), and ended up asking if 'it is possible to maintain beautiful cities and yet move traffic through them on freeways?' (1966:26) This being a rhetorical question Halprin calls for transportation to take its place as a 'form-giving rather than destructive element' (1966:54). A number of rather technical design solutions to urban freeways are discussed in Halprin's book that I cannot engage with here. However, the point is to change the perception of instrumental sites of mobilities as here in the example of the interchange where it is said that 'we need once again to conceive of these great interchanges as places' (1966:97). Rather the interchanges have, according to Halprin, been ignored as 'form-giving events'. After a long analysis of different design principles Halprin voices his most general point, namely that freeways (as well as other transportation infrastructures) must be integral to the process of rebuilding cities (1966:113). This is the case in successful urban armatures as far back as the Grand Canal of Venice or the Ponte Veccio in Florence. The analysis of Halprin is of its time and place (1960s America) so the call for highway design to become a partner in urban design rather than a master (Halprin 1966:149) must of course be seen against the background of increasing sprawl, out-of-town shopping development and increasing car traffic as hallmarks of post-war American society. The solutions of Halprin may not have been that effective and his imprint on the actual mobilities design modest, but interestingly his analysis points towards some of the key insights discussed in earlier chapters. Halprin thus had a quite futuristic vision of the city that seems to coincide well with the relational geographies of networked places in socio-technical assemblages I discussed in Chapters 3 and 7:

> The city of the future must be conceived of as an enormous megastructure in which the landscape with its recreational and life-giving qualities becomes a part of the immense urban environment. The green open spaces will be within a structured complex. But the city of the future need not imply any diminution of the amenities of urban living – if we can only recognize its potentials as well as it problems.
>
> (Halprin 1966:154)

Here Halprin both connected to the interpretative model that later became known as 'Landscape Urbanism' (to which I return below) and highlighted the dynamic tension between potentials and problems I started out discussing in this chapter. Quite opposite to this interpretation is the analysis of Gehl who is concerned with the 'human scale' and the crowding out of social and cultural activities due to the amount of space and awareness the car receives (Gehl 2010) and Jacobs who already in the 1960s argued that 'everyone who values cities is disturbed by automobiles' (1961:338). This, of course, makes sense as one looks at the 'mobility battles' waged across almost all post-war societies. However, for the purpose of getting closer to understanding the meaning of mobilities we should keep a distance from the moral arguments and try to focus on some of the interpretations of mobilities and sites of mobilities that are illustrative of the cultural significance they also may embed.

From the discussion of how to design and stage for auto-mobilities in the city I have highlighted that (some) designers and design thinkers are interesting and inspirational due to their resistance to thinking in terms of pre-set moral geographies as they explore creative and innovative solutions to problems with the mobility technologies at hand. This perspective of seeing opportunities and new solutions is a key feature that the 'mobilities turn' may learn to incorporate much better. Therefore I will look a little deeper into what I term 'mobilities potential thinking'. As mentioned this is the one side of 'critical mobilities thinking' (the other related to the 'dark sides' will be discussed afterwards).

Mobilities potential thinking

In the following section of this chapter I engage with a number of designers and urban scholars who have interpreted the spaces and sites of mobilities in accordance with a more open-minded and potential-seeking framework. Obviously this is not an argument for not being critical of mobilities design and practices that are, for example, polluting, socially excluding or otherwise problematic. But it is a dimension that lies within what I in Chapter 1 termed 'critical mobilities thinking'. In this context, being critical thus relates to new ways of interpreting the existing practices and sites of mobilities as potentially interesting and enriching rather than simply mono-dimensional and instrumental. Seen this way, this is yet another dimension to the *Staging Mobilities* credo of investigating 'more than A to B'.

Jump-cut urbanism

Ingersoll refers to the 'new sensations' of auto-mobility which is closely based on the legacy of Appleyard *et al.*'s seminal 1964 study, *The View from the Road*. Accordingly, car driving transgresses instrumental wishes to go from point A to point B. Ingersoll claims that 'driving a car is somewhat like editing a film' (2006:vii):

> For a driver, buildings, signs, and background perspectives are arranged much like a sequence of shots assembled for a film, and when the driver uses the rear-view mirror, the extraordinary phenomena of seeing forward and backward simultaneously occurs just like the montage of a cinematic jump cut ... With the advent of the automobile, the theatrical order of the urban street was converted into a cinematic one, composed of long shots, close-ups, pans, tracking shots, and above all, the accelerated montage of jump cuts.
>
> (Ingersoll 2006:75)

To Ingersoll the driver resembles the film director, assembling bits of disconnected shots (2006:80). With a reference to the Soviet cinema icon Dziga Vertov's notion of *Kinopravda*, Ingersoll points to the fact that montage and 'jump-cut urbanism' may be seen as a modern liberation from human immobility (2006:84). Seen from the perspective of Vertov, jump-cut urbanism and the fragmentation by way of the montage is a new code of perception surpassing the norms of the perspectival code (Ingersoll 2006:85). Jump-cut urbanism is an argument in favour of a mobile perception that does not understand mobility as pathology. However, Ingersoll does not advocate a mindless urbanism without regulation and intervention, but rather advocates a 'coordinated montage' where the 'cuts' are related by planning and design narratives (2006:89). This comes out of recognising that 'movement becomes the most reliable point of reference' (2006:95). Ingersoll is advocating that we should go beyond a simple notion of movement from point A to point B. However, Ingersoll's argument comes from a special direction as he argues for seeing infrastructure 'as art'. The point of departure is the question: can infrastructures be understood and comprehended within the realm of aesthetic pleasure? This was also illustrated when Lynch and Hack suggested that 'exposed pipes can be handsome' (1984:206). It seems worth noticing that Ingersoll is also aware of the destructive potentials of contemporary infrastructure to the environment as well as to the social fabric: 'works of infrastructure have an underlying utility: they do the dirty work that tends to distance them from the aesthetic realm' (2006:101). In exploring whether one dares to see beauty in these armatures, Ingersoll follows the route of the modern futurists (e.g. Marinetti 1909) that focused on the enjoyment of mobility but finds that Le Corbusier (much inspired by the Futurists) took it too far, leading him into 'antisocial urban models' like La Ville Radieuse (Ingersoll 2006:103). Ingersoll's position is somewhere between the Futurists' uncritical hailing of the uninhibited flow and the moral dismissal of infrastructure seen purely as instrumental and utilitarian artefacts. With a reference to the avant-garde art of Marcel Duchamp, Ingersoll argues for a new way of seeing infrastructures: 'dams, highways and airports become readymades at a scale of 1:20.000' (2006:109). What it means for infrastructure to become readymades indicates that they are awaiting a new form of understanding or a reinterpretation based upon decontextualisation:

> Transportation infrastructures continue to be designed with the positivist ethos of government institutions and thus elicit a certain inevitable determinism that corresponds to the economics of increased mobility. Despite their potential consensus: these interventions are often upsetting and alienating ... citizens and designers could demand more of infrastructure than just its primary functions ... Infrastructure as utilitarian responses to the pressing problems of mobility invariably cause environmental and social problems. To approach infrastructure as art can provide a way of dealing with the violence it interjects into the urban system and become a means of creating civic meaning.
> (Ingersoll 2006:123–124)

Creating 'civic meaning' means to take stock of both the meaningfulness of mobilities and the fact that subjectivity is being created on these stages. Seeing infrastructure 'as art' may be enlarged from looking at the infrastructures in isolation to cover the multiple mobilities practices carried out at various scales. We need to 'see more' than instrumental and utilitarian goal satisfaction in the hardware of mobilities as well as in the fluid practices themselves.

Landscape urbanism

The knowledge of urban mobilities as an important and potentially enjoyable experience has also been addressed within the approach to urban design and planning termed 'Landscape Urbanism'. Accordingly, the 'horizontal field of urbanisation' has found new relevance (Waldheim 2006a:15). Shane argues that there is a direct link from the works of Lynch to the 1990s notion of 'Landscape Urbanism' (Shane 2005:69). This approach has grown out of dissatisfaction with the established notions of cities as single-nucleus and bounded sites. It is a critique of the city as a bounded enclave and thus opens up to the understanding of cities as integral to their flow systems and armatures:

> The design and integration of new transportation infrastructure is central to the functioning of urban space. The importance of mobility and access in the contemporary metropolis brings to infrastructure the character of collective space. Transportation infrastructure is less a self-sufficient service element than an extremely visible and effective instrument in creating new networks and relationships. Whereas the railroad station and the airport

offer a centralized infrastructural condition – a density that almost resembles the city, in terms of services and programs – the more amorphous connective web of roads have rarely been recognized as a collective space unto itself.

(Wall 1999:238–239)

The central point is the attempt to revalorise the 'amorphous connective web' as a new collective space. Urban designers within the realm of landscape urbanism have thus argued for a positive value of infrastructure. Wall offers two examples of how urban design can contribute to a positive valorisation of infrastructure and how these may become a collective space. One is the second beltway of Barcelona completed for the 1992 Olympics. The other case in point is the 1995 trolley line running between St Denis and Bobigny in Paris (Wall 1999). However, 'the real challenge to urban design is to accept that infrastructure is as important to the vitality and experience of the contemporary metropolis as the town hall or square once was' (Wall 1999:246). Some theorists within 'Landscape Urbanism' thus see urban infrastructures as urban development drivers (Waldheim 2006b:39). Furthermore, there are clear elements within the 'Landscape Urbanism' perspective that opens up for an interpretation of urban mobility landscapes as (potential) new public domains: 'Across a diverse spectrum of cultural positions landscape has emerged as the most relevant medium through which to construct a meaningful and viable public realm in North American cities' (Waldheim 2006b:41). Evaluating the many 'Landscape Urbanism' projects, Waldheim argues that one of the key strategies of 'Landscape Urbanism' is the integration of transportation infrastructures into public space (2006b:45).

There is in other words a movement within some areas of the design fields themselves to open up the understanding of mobilities towards seeing its potential for creating both physical and social stages for interaction. One such attempt to rethink mobilities is reported in the 2003 book *Mobility: A Room with a View*, to which I now turn.

A Room with a View

The Dutch-led *A Room with a View* project is interesting as a contemporary reading of urban mobilities that runs parallel to the *Staging Mobilities* perspective. From the framing of the project we get a clear sense of this:

Mobility is part of modern society; it is a daily pursuit, just like housing work and recreation. Mobility is not just about traffic jams, asphalt, delays and tollgates, but also about people deriving a sensory experience from their everyday life mobility. Every day, travelling along roads and railways, millions of people experience the changes of the city and countryside. For them, the train and the car are also 'A Room With a View'.

(Houben 2003:26)

In the conclusion of the project, Calabrese summarises the findings of the many case studies and emphasises this notion of non-instrumental mobilities thinking which is closely related to the *Staging Mobilities* framework:

> Today's spaces of mobility are 'rooms' which users and participants can identify with and even take psychological possession of without the need for legal ownership. Spaces of mobility need to go beyond the boundaries of standard democratic formality. They could become sites of the city's contested spaces of heterotopias. To empower the grassroots communities [and] to nurture the capability of reflection ... In the final analysis, it is about pluralism. It is about the tolerance of difference, about creative rebelliousness. This is the essence of those spaces.
>
> (Calabrese 2003:349)

The general project contains a number of individual cases of which I will only present a few. The Los Angeles freeway system is one case where the traditional interpretation of freeways as instrumental structures is challenged (a point made by Banham 30 years before; see Banham 1971/2009):

> Perhaps more than anywhere else, the freeway system in LA is not simply a neutral infrastructure, but exists as a dynamic landscape and disciplining institution, a site of spectacle and media events, a moving scene of collective imagination and desire, and is arguably the one great public space of the city.
>
> (Arrigadan *et al.* 2003:137)

The Pearl River Delta freeway is another case in point. Here in the shadow of the highway lies the world's biggest market; a market that is partly a commercialised zone of enterprise, partly an important public realm (Gutierrez and Portefaix 2003:227). The paths and transportation infrastructures of the Tokyo Ring Line add a further dimension to this discussion of a mobile public domain:

> The easiest (and cheapest) way of spending time in the train is appreciating the ads which are pasted everywhere ... TV screens are being installed in the latest models, showing commercials, news, weather forecasts, and last but not least, train information ... Railway lines seem to have become the most appropriate spatial reference frame for this huge city. In Tokyo the train system is more than mere transportation infrastructure. It provides a communicative framework for the geographical space. Train lines can be seen as boulevards in contemporary Tokyo life ... The railway system allows the Tokyoites to skip the hierarchical territory structure completely. Amazingly, the system is open to everyone, and it can be accessed from almost any point in Tokyo. Its rhizomatic structure allows routes to be travelled in an infinite number of combinations.
>
> (Ohno 2003: 168, 170–178)

Materialities of mobilities 189

The book also contain a case of Beijing's Ring Road and the way billboards may afford both commercial communication and political slogans (Yan *et al.* 2003:197) that might qualify as contribution to the general point of seeing infrastructure as spaces of potentials rather than problems.

The 'dark sides' of mobilities

As mentioned in Chapter 2, 'critical mobilities thinking' should lead both to criticism of the taken-for-granted assumptions related to mobilities and to the exploration of the 'dark sides' of mobilities. As shown in Chapter 8, the 'dark side' dimension of 'critical mobilities thinking' in a rather classic way may facilitate a deeper understanding of the relationship between social exclusion, power and urban mobilities. This dimension is very important, but the 'dark side' also reaches into more design-oriented and technical discussions of failure, breakdown, risk and vulnerability (which obviously all may connect to the social exclusion dimension of mobilities). Therefore I will discuss this dimension in relation to the scenarios and analysis made by Dennis and Urry (2009) on how life 'after the car' might be envisioned.

Reflections upon a possible post-carbon future

The presented interest in innovative and creative mobilities solutions is not an uncritical and socially detached happy design philosophy. So I end this chapter with some reflections on a very real challenge to the future of mobilities design, namely that of imagining a post-carbon mobility future. According to Dennis and Urry in their stimulating and thought-provoking book *After The Car* (2009), some of the elements in dealing with the mobility challenges may be achieved simply by means of negative sanctioning (e.g. new transport policies) but most of the other elements invite a creative rethinking of what a 'post-car system' might look like and of how to dissolve the path dependency interlocking the car system (Figure 9.2). The analysis of the car system with all its complexities and mutual interdependencies is illustrative of the challenge. The notion of places as relationally and mobility defined in networks and socio-technical assemblages presented in earlier chapters now become very tangible with this simple model illustrating how things are affected across what we normally perceive to be separate domains (e.g. living, work and leisure practices and materials for a post-car system). There are huge challenges both to each theme in this model and to unlock the determinations 'locked-in' as a consequence of the path dependencies of the areas. In light of the *Staging Mobilities* framework I have focused most on the theme that in the model is termed 'new living, work and leisure practices'. But the very fact that this theme is an integral part of the car or the post-car system is evidence of the fact that what might look like purely technical and instrumental questions (e.g. fuels systems or new materials) actually point at issues of culture, identity and social communities. The discussion of how to imagine a post-car system is illustrative of the claim in *Staging Mobilities* that

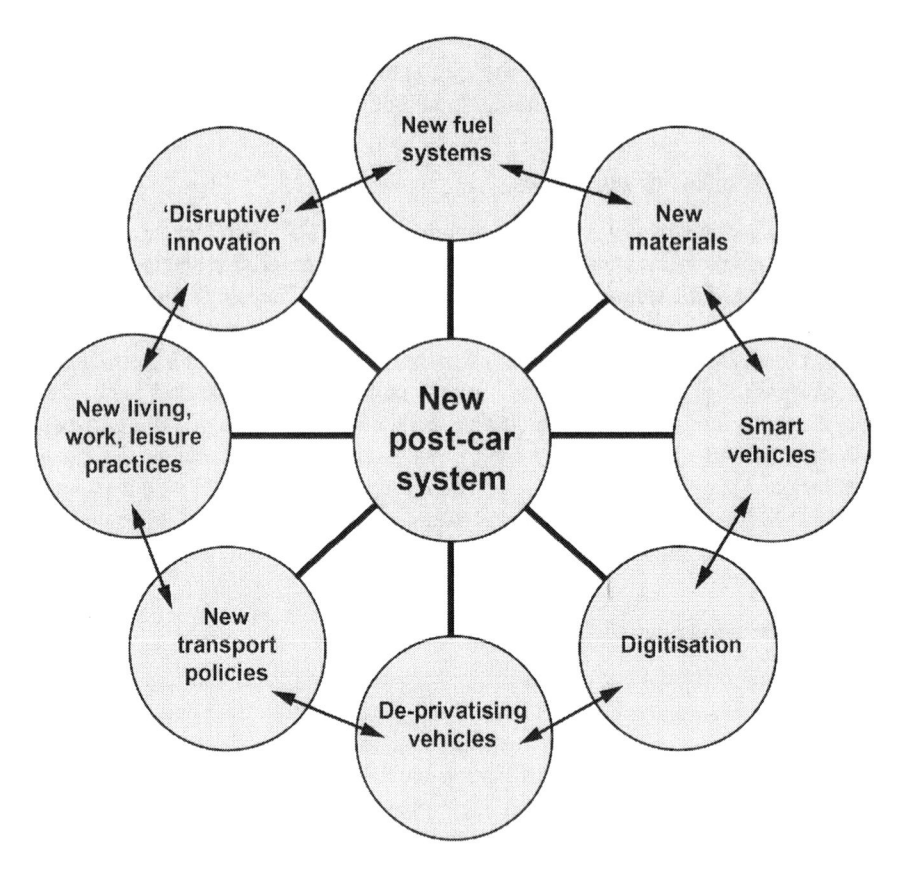

Figure 9.2 Post-car system (source: Dennis and Urry, *After the Car*, 2009:65. By permission of Polity Press).

we are dealing with much more than A to B movements. As mobilities are being assembled in complex networks of social actors and technical systems we come to see that the staging of mobilities is as much a sociological and cultural issue as anything else.

Clearly this simple model illustrates only some of the design challenges if the staging of a future post-car mobilities system is to become operative. Here there is not space for getting to grips with the complexity of this huge task but from the analysis of Dennis and Urry it seems quite obvious that we may have to mobilise some serious 'potential thinking' within the 'mobilities turn' if the staging of future mobilities is to move beyond restrictions due to lack of resources, systems breakdowns and more or less apocalyptic scenarios of dystopia and 'dark sides' of mobilities. This is a delicate line of balancing since uncritical beliefs in 'technical fixes' and playful imaginings obviously do not meet the grand challenges of future mobilities. On the other hand I do believe that undogmatic and open-minded thinking about how to innovate and make creative solutions to the staging of future mobilities needs to tap into the human capacity to break free from habitual ways of doing. In his book *Climate Change and Society* (2011), John Urry argues that in order for future policies and interventions to succeed there must be a level of social acceptance and even playful interest in order for humans to engage with these new challenges. Of course a 'happy mind' will not make it alone, but the challenge to the staging of future mobilities hinges on a creative ability to envision systems, technologies and practices that people may even engage with 'for fun' or at least consider to be more inviting than those initiated by prohibitions and failures. There is a link from the 'potential thinking' within the design fields to some of these new challenges that needs to be explored. Urry points at a minimum condition: 'It [the post-car scenario] has to be a system that is fashionable and faddish, that wins the hearts and minds, that is better and more fun' (2011:132). As argued elsewhere the solutions to these challenges will have to engage with some level of utopian thinking (Jensen and Freudendal-Pedersen 2012). Not in the sense of far-fetched and unrealistic futuristic dreams, but in the sense that the challenges for staging future mobilities may involve a phase of critique as well as one of creative re-imagining. In the words of planning scholar John Friedman:

> Utopian thinking, the capacity to imagine a future that is radically different from what we know to be the prevailing order of things, is a way of breaking through the barriers of convention into a sphere of the imagination where many things beyond our everyday experience become possible.
> (Friedman 2002:103)

Part of such utopian re-imagining of a prevailing mobilities system 'after the car' will stand a much better chance of being embraced if there are elements of fun, playfulness and creative engagement to attach to. The link is tied to the discussions I made in earlier chapters on the very important point of seeing mobilities as much more than instrumental movements from A to B. If we engage the rethinking of mobilities through the perspective of *Staging Mobilities* with its understanding of mobilities as cultural and identity-forming practices we will see that looking for potentials as well as problems and thinking about the playful and the ludic in relation to mobilities might be a path that needs to be explored if the staging of future mobilities is to move beyond restrictions, scarcity and havoc (which obviously are still possible scenarios that may end up influencing the design solutions and policies of the future).

Concluding remarks

In this chapter I have been concerned with opening up a path of dialogue between the 'mobilities turn' and thinkers within the design fields (a rather general and imprecise descriptor which nevertheless serves the practical purpose). First of all, when we are interested in the actual and practical issues related to the staging of mobilities it does make quite some sense to seek inspiration amongst those who are occupied with either designing these or at least reflecting upon the design of mobilities. Second, there is some value to the rather simple distinction between 'analysis' and 'intervention'. Needless to say there are overlaps and most intervening practitioners within design may claim to perform analysis as well. However, there are surely differences in the self-perception as well as practices between, for example, a sociologist analysing mobilities and an urban designer or a city planner drawing up plans and schemes for urban mobilities. Incorporating the insights from the latter group is part of the *Staging Mobilities* approach to mobilities research and this is done only in a preliminary fashion with this book. Much more interaction and dialogue must take place in the future along this axis. A third point that has been coming out of this consulting of the design fields is a confirmation of the theoretical claim advanced earlier, namely that mobilities as a social and spatial practice is about much more than instrumental acts of moving from point A to point B. As we gain insights into the staging of mobilities from the perspective of the design fields we understand that whether we are staging mobilities from above through design and planning or from below in social interaction with fellow mobile subjects we are engaging a field of cultural practices, social norms and identity construction.

There is an important argument springing from this notion of 'more than A to B' which ties in with the fourth point in this chapter. This has to do with the ability to see mobilities practices and sites as carrying potentials for more than just transport. And equally importantly that such 'potential thinking' may be the route to solving some of the grand challenges that ties mobilities into issues of global climate change, resource scarcity and massive demographic shifts. What I termed 'mobilities potential thinking' is thus a radical way of thinking about mobilities in a much less predetermined way. Related to 'critical mobilities thinking', the notion of 'mobilities potential thinking' is about exploring how sites of mobilities and practices of mobilities may be under-utilised and may carry potentials for new types of practices, cultures and forms of interactions that may provide people with new and positive experiences. I realise that the many 'mays' are indicative of the uncertainty as well as the very different perspective of *Staging Mobilities* compared to 'mainstream' social analysis. If there is one thing to learn from the design fields it is that every intervention (regardless of how well-informed and recurrent) in principle is an open and non-determined act within a field of emergent properties. People may do this and they may do that, but we cannot know with 100 per cent certainty. The designers like to think of this as part of the creative stimulus to their work – knowing that they are not designing for machines and objects, but for humans in complex settings of social interaction. I believe there is yet another point to derive from this uncertainty and lack of predetermination which is the point about 'potential thinking' as a function of this uncertainty. If the future is uncertain and outcomes are contingent this may be challenging to both analysis and intervention. But it could equally inspire more imaginative and creative thoughts about things taken for granted – like ordinary acts of everyday-life mobilities and what these mean to social life. This connects to the other dimension of 'critical mobilities thinking' which I have termed the 'dark sides' of mobilities. To some 'analytical' disciplines the uncovering of the 'dark sides', whether these are related to social conflict, power and exclusion or to issues of crisis, failure and breakdown, is understood to be the key focus (most 'critical' social research, in fact). However, there is scope for more exploratory and deeper understandings if these 'dark side' issues are related to key questions in the 'interventionist' fields with their focus on how to actually create systems, to deliver services, to connect people etc.

The materialities of mobilities are surely staged by many diverse sets of professions and disciplines. However, in this chapter I have argued for a close and fruitful link between 'designers' and the 'mobilities turn'. As stated earlier: exploring the nature and the potential of this link is only in its infancy and should be examined much more carefully. The research agenda for the future of studying the materialities of mobilities thus connects to how a creative dialogue between the design fields and the 'mobilities turn' may become established. I return to this theme at the very end of this book as I move into the final and concluding chapter.

10 *Staging Mobilities*
Conclusion

> Innovation results from academic mobility across disciplinary borders, a mobility that generates ... 'creative marginality'.
> John Urry, *Sociology beyond Societies*, 2000, p. 210

> The slippery and intangible nature of mobility makes it an elusive object of study. Yet study it we must for mobility is central to what it is to be human.
> Tim Cresswell, *On the Move*, 2006, p. 1

> As the most quintessential expression of life, movement – both human and non-human, technologically-aided or unaided, imagined or actualised, loved or dreaded, of long or short duration, fast or slow, hardly or easily accessible, ritualized or improvised, failed or successfully performed, individual or collective – marks what it means to be alive. And different ways of moving mark, well, different ways of life.
> Phillip Vannini, *Ferry Tales*, 2012, p. 11 (emphasis original)

Introduction

The concluding chapter returns to the overall research questions and lays out the further implications for mobilities research within the social sciences, the ambition being to contribute to the sociological understanding of contemporary urban mobilities with the new perspective of *Staging Mobilities*. The chapter is structured in two parts. The first is a summary of the conclusions made during the book, relating these to each other. During this section the new concepts and words will be presented in a joint context. The second part becomes more general as I move towards some statements on mobilities research and future challenges within the field of the 'mobilities turn' in general and to the perspective of *Staging Mobilities* in particular.

Staging Mobilities: summary

I started out in Chapter 1 by raising this general research question: *What are the physical, social, technical, and cultural conditions to the staging of contemporary urban mobilities?* By this stage we should hopefully have gained insights that will allow us to answer this question and the set of sub-questions that was also presented in Chapter 1:

1. What are the implications of the physical form and material design of sites and spaces hosting mobilities for the sociality of contemporary urban life?
2. How are social interactions and their dynamic interrelations produced by and re-producing mobilities and cultures of contemporary urban life?
3. How does it feel to be a social agent on the move within the contemporary network city, and what normative and social ties are created between social agents, places and objects in the network?
4. How are mobilities being shaped and given meaning by semiotic systems of communication, circulation and mobilities processing?
5. How are networked technologies facilitating and underpinning mobilities of contemporary urban life?
6. How are infrastructures of the network city creating new cultural practices and ways of using the city, and how are they creating mechanisms of social exclusion and power?

The answer to these questions must be given on the basis of the *Staging Mobilities* framework that includes the three dimensions of physical settings, material spaces and design; embodied performances; and social interactions with a particular focus on situational mobilities and everyday-life practices (Figure 1.1). Furthermore, I argued for seeing the staging of such situational mobilities as both a staging process from above by planning, design, regulations and institutions and from below by consociates in interaction and individual performances of mobile self-presentation. It is within this framework that novel insights into contemporary mobilities are shaped. I started out by arguing for 'critical mobilities thinking' that had a focus on the critical issues related to social phenomena like power, social exclusion, mobile justices and other dimensions of the 'dark sides' of mobilities. But it also means to be critical about the taken-for-granted understanding of mobility, as for example a cost-full and rational minimisation of travel distance from point A to point B. 'Critical mobilities thinking' means that we have come to see that our lives are what happens not just in static enclaves, but also in all the interstices and the circulation in-between places and thus to realise 'potential thinking' as an equally important dimension.

Staging Mobilities obviously takes place in physical settings and material spaces that are designed and practised. Seen this way the staging from above as well as the staging from below becomes material and realised in the physical geographies of multiple mobilities systems and practices. Within this theme I spoke of 'mobile biotopes' as a way to articulate that mobilities must be understood as meaningful social and cultural practices creating identities and cultures as well as material movement of bodies, goods and vehicles taking place within human-made systems. Moreover, I distinguished between 'mobile sociopetals' and 'mobile sociofugals' as a way of capturing how some sites and settings are particularly well-functioning in getting people to go there and undertake their activities, whereas others tend 'push' people away or distribute them from their centre of gravity. Under the theme of the physical realm I paid particular attention to the signs and semiotic systems of the city and discussed 'mobile semiotics' as an illustration of how signs (in their broadest possible sense) afford, process and coordinate (or obstruct) the physical circulation and movement of people, vehicles and goods in more or less codified systems of infrastructure (Figure 10.1).

Linking this notion to the theories of geosemiotics I talk about 'mobile geosemiotics' as a way to think about material locations as signs as well as the fact that signs are interpreted in motion and that moving makes different interpretations possible. This basically touches upon one of the key issues behind the *Staging Mobilities* framework, namely to reflect upon the meaning of movement, or put differently 'mobile sense making' as a defining process where signs and meanings are materially situated in the world and the moving human body creates particular challenges and complexities for making sense of the world. Along the way I argued that none of the empirical cases described in this book can be understood if we do not gaze at them from the perspective of a theory of assemblages. In a more specific way I proposed that the systems and sociotechnical networks that 'host' contemporary mobilities are complex and large material environments where technologies, humans, software, codes, semiotic

Figure 10.1 The staging of mobilities in codified systems.

Conclusion 197

and communicative systems, objects and artefacts are assembled in a specific combination facilitating and affording certain practices and restricting or preventing others. 'Mobile assemblages' specific to particular modes of transport mix and relate to the material design and manifestation of contemporary mobilities in ways that must be understood relationally. The key issue is how systems and networks assemble humans and non-humans in an attempt to 'stage' mobilities. The semiotic systems modify and interact with the human body and sensations as the subject moves and thus afford particular motions, directions, speeds, modes and routes. This led me to speak of an increasing number of semiotic techniques, designs, media, symbols and signs coming together in an emerging 'mobile semiotic grammar'.

Staging Mobilities argues for taking the vantage point of the 'little practices' of everyday-life mobility, seeing how contemporary social agents 'perform mobility' as a significant cultural practice of everyday life. This amounts to understanding mobilities as performative actions. By this is meant actions producing and re-producing significant elements of the individual's self-understanding, perceptions of the material environment and the social networks within which the actor engages. To understand this process I introduced the notion of the 'mobile with' and the 'networked self'. From the former notion we saw that our movement in the city is a dynamic and socially complex affair that has more repercussions than 'just being traffic'. Humans make sense of their environment as they move and this means important things for the way we engage with our consociates whether we know these or not. In the midst of such complexity we find processes of 'negotiation in motion' as illustrations of how things often have to be decided swiftly and 'on the fly', as well as in social interactions that are of an ephemeral nature and thus deserve the nomenclature of 'temporary congregations'. In relation to the notion of a 'networked self' I am not trying to contribute to a general theory of identity, but rather to focus on how urban everyday-life mobility is deeply embedded in all sorts of networks (from 'hard' infrastructure to 'soft' digital communication systems). Some of these are the 'channels in which we move', so to speak. Others are pass-the-time communication and entertainment systems (e.g. commercials or digital gaming). And, finally, it seems that more and more of the networking in digital systems becomes mobile, meaning that the social agent to a large extent is becoming what he or she is whilst being on the move. As we are 'linked in motion', the ways this plays out in socio-technical systems, sorting software and new interactive practices need investigation. The notion of the 'networked self' is a first beginning at providing a theoretical concept for such investigation.

It should now be clear that there are a number of well-defined modes of mobilities that all have repercussions for life in the contemporary city: walking, skateboarding, cycling, motorcycling, car driving, bus riding, train riding and aeroplanes and boats (as inter-urban mobility forms). Each of these mobility domains involves a set of practices and normative regulating principles that one needs to either master for practical reasons or deliberately contest by counter-practices (e.g. skateboarding on park benches or in busy streets). So there are 'walking codes', 'cycling codes' etc. Clearly, these are ways of acting that we can see as more or less explicitly articulated cultures. Such 'mobility cultures' are linked to official and legal sanctions and mobility regulations. However, they are also embedded in the body as tacit mobility cultures. Some are more globally generic mobility codes, whilst others are locally anchored and as such are expressions of local norms and customs. Beyond understanding these mobility practices as embedded in legal and cultural contexts, they express particular 'ways of knowing'. In other words, there is 'cycling knowledge' and 'aeroplane knowledge' etc. to be accumulated. Such continuous learning processes of practical mobility coping will in all likelihood continue for the rest of our 'mobile lives'. I have developed an understanding of how contemporary material flows, symbolic orders and meanings are produced and re-produced at different spatial scales. By maintaining these urban flows, social agents are also reproducing the social order of the fluid network-based contemporary city. Moreover, the individual is negotiating and constructing her/his identity whilst taking into account how the movement patterns are configured and in relation to the types of interactions and meetings these flows facilitate.

In the analysis I found that embodied cultures of mobilities and their relationships to the infrastructures, spaces, technologies and artefacts affording these is a complex but important discussion. The 'staging' from above of mobile bodies and the way these mobile bodies 'stage' themselves have repercussions for experiences and cultures. Setting the body at the centre is a consequence of the situational perspective of *Staging Mobilities*. Along this route I talked about a new 'mobility aesthetics'. The realm of aesthetics becomes highly relevant as we engage with the wider production of subjectivity and the meaning of movement to perception. We are looking at 'experience in motion' and the body plays the pivotal role in creating the situational touch points for the creation of cultures and practices related to mobilities. From understanding the moving body in its many different subject–space–object configurations (walking, running, cycling etc.), I found that two essential outcomes are created. First, the mobile body produces and re-produces a mobile aesthetics that creates new subjectivities and new ways of perceiving the world. This is the case regardless of whether the embodied mobility practice we study is walking or driving. Following from this comes the second point. This has to do with the way that new mobile embodied perceptions are creating systems, patterns and models of moving and being moved. That is to say, embodied mobilities afford particular normative and social interactions that aggregate into cultural patterns of 'mobilities meaning'. Such embodied 'cultures of mobilities' are at one and the same time very different for particular modes of mobility (cars afford different experiences than walking shoes) and identical (our body and senses interact with systems, technologies and artefacts that have the same 'body interface' regardless of whether we are driving, sailing or flying). The self–world relation is enacted differently as our bodies are either fixed or moving through spaces that may be familiar or unknown, local or global, generic or specific and much of this is increasingly being mediated, afforded and created by technologies, artefacts and complex systems of mobilities. The mobile body is the entry point to understanding the individual's engagement with the world and is the key to seeing the way meaning and norms are created in embodied 'cultures of mobilities'. To this is linked a notion of 'mobile sensations' meaning that the human body senses the world visually and corporeally by moving in it. The physical and almost 'mechanical' part of this relates to a 'mobile kinaesthetic' by which the human body experiences the world as it moves and by the way heat and cold are sensed and by the effort and 'work' the body has to perform to become mobile. These come together under the notion of 'mobile embodied performances' focusing on the fact that humans experience the world in bodily motion and, equally importantly, that they act in the world by their mobile embodied practices. Such practices may be thought of as performative in the sense that we stage and act in front of 'others' but also in the sense that the mobile body enacts and creates identities and relationships by its movement.

Embodied mobility has performative capacities. The material sites and the technologies that our bodies negotiate in mobile practices may then be thought of as 'mobility affordances'. By this is meant how the specific relation between the moving body and its material environment opens up to particular modes of mobility, different speeds, trajectories, temporalities etc. 'Mobility affordances' illustrate the very specific and material dimensions to mobile situations. As the body in motion is working hard to orient itself, make complex decisions and interpret the motives and intentions of other bodies what is taking place is 'coordination in motion'. This relates to the more instrumental feature of continuous monitoring and more or less self-conscious work by mobile bodies aiming at preventing physical contact with fellow mobile subjects as well as avoiding collision with physical obstacles or 'dangerous' mobile objects (e.g. cars, trains). Across all cases of mobilities research the moving and perceiving body is crucial. However, what becomes even more interesting under the notion of a 'mobile body semiotics' is that not only do human bodies move and sense the material and semiotic environment, the body on its own also becomes a 'sign vehicle' communicating intentions and norms targeted at orchestrating mobilities. Therefore the codified regulatory principles governing the gestures of the mobile bodies as they move in traffic become an interesting and illustrative case of a 'mobile body semiotics'. In almost direct connection to the 'mobile body semiotics' is therefore the idea of a 'mobilities choreography'. This is reflected in the orchestration and the notations capturing both the intentions from above as well as the signifying practices from below. As we look at how the environment's semiotic layer instructs and affords particular mobile practices it makes sense (to a certain extent) to think of these in terms of the self's 'choreography', such as when we study a busy street crossing or an airport space processing passengers.

The staged mobile situations of everyday life relate to networked technologies of different sorts. In relation to such technologies issues of 'mobilities divides' are socially stratifying practices that relate to mobility differentials that either come about as a function of economic resources, intellectual and knowledge capabilities, practical skills, geographical location or cultural frames, all of which contribute to the fact that some people know how to, can and will be mobile whilst this is out of range for others (or even fully constrained, as in immobile citizens in either jails or nursing homes). The sorting and filtering that goes on within the complex networked technologies are staged by software, or what I term 'mobility code'. 'Mobility codes' may, as may all other situational mobility, be considered from above as when code stages movement through the city by means of ITS systems as well as from below when we stage our movement by means of personalised technologies such as location-aware smart phones etc. The outcome of 'mobility code' is protocols for organising mobile practices. The working of such protocols is due to the stretching of technologies taking place across time and space thereby facilitating a new dimension to the 'proximity–connectivity nexus'. By this is meant a new dialectical and dynamic relationship between physical co-presence and mediated connections across time and space and how this effects the mobile situations. Connections and distances have been influencing each other for a long time, but now the networked technologies described here create a new and dynamic interface and mediation, or what I term a 'nexus'. The distinction refers to that between topography (proximity) and topology (connectivity). The multiple mobility practices that are being organised and orchestrated by 'mobility code' across a vast landscape of scales and technologies mean that knowing what to do and how in terms of making connectivity work as facilitator for mobilities becomes a quite complex endeavour. Ultimately this potentially contributes to social stratification, mobility segregation and new 'mobility divides'. As these technologies are part of the complex assemblages we call cities, practising situated mobilities in everyday life may be seen as a constant juggling of material spaces, social interactions, embodied performances and networked technologies.

As we move across time and space we may find ourselves on different rungs of the 'mobility skills ladder'. At times struggling with opening a gate or finding our way, at other times having difficulty paying or entering certain spaces. Not rare of course are social actors with social, economic and cultural capital who are capable of organising the mobile situations in very close accordance with their imagined trajectories or their 'will to connection'. But there is no formal logic at work here. The unemployed or the homeless may navigate as seamlessly and smoothly across town as any Young Urban Professional. Moreover, both ends of the social spectrum might fall victim to failure, breakdown and fragilities of the 'systems' that facilitate the movements in everyday life. This is not to suggest that the networked technologies are contributing to a more equal or just distribution of mobility skills and options per se. Rather I want to point to the complexities of situated mobilities and warn against automatic interpretations.

Seen in the light of networked technologies the city has become a 'sentient' space collecting and distributing data and information in complex systems either to the immediate user (e.g. real-time travel information or location-based services on a mobile phone) or to some level of systems surveillance and monitoring (e.g. the traffic regulation system or the police tracking suspects). This means that the virtual/digital and the physical/material realms need to be reconnected in our conceptual frameworks and theories. The advantage of taking our point of departure in the *Staging Mobilities* framework thus becomes one of setting the practical situation at the centre and then exploring how material/non-material, human/non-human and digital/physical realms constantly are being enacted in complex processes of mobilities. Regardless of how much scholarly research within disciplinary boundaries we may consult, and regardless of the many different government bodies and departments at work, the single mobile subject does not experience life (and thus mobilities) in either scientific disciplines or municipal jurisdictions. Rather we move more or less effortlessly through our everyday life practising mobilities and experiencing them in concrete and complex situations. *Staging Mobilities* offers a clear gaze at the 'situational mobilities' of the everyday-life practices by foregrounding analytically distinct themes (material space, embodied performance and social interaction) and helping to understand how networked technologies are staging mobilities and thus ultimately affecting our will to connection.

From the empirical cases studied in this book I have taken my point of departure from mobile practices understood as meaningful actions or 'mobile sense making'. A central concept is the notion of a 'mobile with' that illustrates the interaction dynamics and collective dimension to everyday-life mobility. Furthermore, we saw the ephemeral quality of such interaction as 'temporary congregations'. By this is meant that people meet, team up and break up, in very volatile social interactional patterns. But these are still sufficiently enduring to make us feel part of the collective (as when we share the experience of missing the bus). The unsettled and socially open character of urban mobility practices furthermore makes it clear that multiple decisions need to be made. Obviously we are aware of mode of transport and routing decisions. But also much more detailed and situational decisions, such as which way to pass a person coming towards us needs conceptualisation. Here I argued for the usefulness of the notion of 'negotiation in motion' to capture the fact that the social interaction is made in a mobile space of norms, values and power. Some of these ways of encountering our 'mobile other' may be likened to an already-existing repertoire of actions, mobile negotiation techniques and mobile interaction tactics. These may range from the very physically embodied 'sliding and evasion techniques' that people apply to avoid collision to the more general (and culture-specific) one of the personal distance accepted for either passing or co-presence in a mobile situation (e.g. bus riding). Also there are different levels of subtlety to the way power is being displayed in mobile interactions.

From the field studies we saw the almost classical 'power of speed' and the more subtle 'I pretend not to have seen you' tactics. Here we are facing issues of situational and mobile power that are highly unstable and volatile as the execution of such powers take place during motion, *in situ* and at times even at high speed. As people move in dense settings they are driven by multiple rationales and reasons. However, the act of avoiding physical contact is predominant in most mobile situations and the way to avoid this is by the many complex visual and embodied cues given by our bodily performances of mobility whether within vehicles or as pedestrians. To understand situational mobilities as they are staged and acted out is to understand the cultural and social complexities of 'negotiations in motion'. The short-lived and fast small-group interactions are seen as 'temporary congregations' in multiple networks and sites of mobility infrastructures. Moreover, we saw how material objects in the mobile situation (the actual layout of the site with kerbs, basins and urban furniture) might create a 'riverbed' shaping the flows of people as water in a 'river'. At eye level with the mobile subjects we found the 'ballet' and saw the gestures, gazes and embodied negotiations and interactions that take place ever so swiftly.

With the concept of *Staging Mobilities* we have seen how both the system and the actors create mobilised front stages and back stages in diverse attempts to exercise conspicuous (self-)control. As I analysed complex socio-technical assemblages of urban metros and city dwellers we came to see that there is such a thing as a 'metroscape'. By this I understand a mobility 'landscape' consisting of everything from rails and driverless trains to ticket machines and security cameras. This perspective defines urban metroscapes as physical metro mobility landscapes and as the codes, rules and cultural norms that create the active joining of technologies, infrastructures and social practices. 'Segregated mobilities practices' are the mobility patterns segregated along the lines of income and social hierarchy often complexly wedded to the infrastructure systems of the city both in respect to 'switched-off areas' and to the more general social strata of the city. Together these two concepts point towards understanding the *Staging of Mobilities* as at one and the same time complex socio-technical assemblages and mobile power-geometries.

As we furthermore gain insights into the staging of mobilities from the perspective of the design fields we come to see that regardless of whether we are staging mobilities from above through design and planning or from below in social interaction with fellow mobile subjects, we are engaging with a field of cultural practices, social norms and identity construction. What I termed 'mobilities potential thinking' is thus a new way of thinking about mobilities in a much less predetermined way. Related to 'critical mobilities thinking' the notion of 'mobilities potential thinking' is about exploring how sites of mobilities and practices of mobilities may be under-utilised and may carry potentials to new types of practices, cultures and forms of interactions that may provide people with new and positive experiences. Equally important is the awareness of the manifold expressions of the 'dark sides' of mobilities ranging from social exclusion and power to systems breakdown, failure and crisis. The materialities of mobilities are surely staged by many diverse sets of professions and disciplines. However, I have argued for a close and fruitful link between 'designers' and the 'mobilities turn'. Exploring the nature and the potential of this link is only in its infancy and should be examined much more carefully in the immediate future. The research agenda for the future of studying the materialities of mobilities thus connects to how a creative dialogue between the design fields and the 'mobilities turn' may become established.

After this general summary I will now propose a manifesto-like set of statements that might be perceived as slightly provocative in all their simplicity but that should be thought to point towards the future of mobilities research.

Ten pointers for future mobilities research

1 Mobilities must be thought of in the plural

The phenomenon of mobilities is empirically diverse, and thus calls for theoretical and methodological diversity.

2 There is no singular discipline for understanding mobilities

As a consequence of the ontological and epistemological pluralism of mobilities there is no singular discipline with a patent on how to make sense of contemporary mobilities.

3 Thinking mobilities does NOT turn everything into flows

Thinking mobilities is not a threat to classical social science issues of power, territory and identity that are left floating in abstract space. Rather, thinking critically about mobilities means to foreground mobilities to better understand contemporary social dynamics.

4 Think relationally about place

Contemporary mobilities need to be framed within a notion of a relational geography seeing places as networked and relational entities within complex sociotechnical assemblages.

5 Rehabilitate and politicise the armature

Armatures may be 'rehabilitated' as sites that are more than a necessary evil in getting from point A to point B. Sites hosting mobilities are (potentially) meaningful spaces of social interaction and therefore also the potential new public agoras and sites of political voice.

6 Encourage mobilities potential thinking

As part of 'critical mobilities thinking' the 'analytical' disciplines might benefit from identifying not only problems but also potentials. Actually this may be the hallmark of critical social analysis if it is at all to contribute to solving the grand challenges of climate change, demographic shifts and resource scarcity.

7 Understand the 'dark sides' of mobilities

Next to the innovative dimension of potentials 'critical mobilities thinking' must also pay attention to the 'dark sides' of mobilities as they manifest themselves in issues of social exclusion, power, segregation, systems failure, crisis, breakdown and disruption.

8 Explore 'mobilities design'

The analysis so far suggests that in order to get a deeper understanding of the meaning of mobilities the 'mobilities turn' should start working on questions related to the material design of sites, spaces and systems of mobilities. Exploring the materialities of mobilities means establishing a dedicated field of 'mobilities design'.

9 Mobile pragmatics

Mobilities research is theoretical and conceptual as well as empirical. But at the end of the day it will benefit from being understood in pragmatic terms. This means that mobilities research will profit from setting the question of 'what might the practical effects be?' at the centre of investigation.

10 It all comes together 'in situ'

From the explorations of the analysis in both theoretical and empirical terms it should now be clear that the situational focus of the *Staging Mobilities* framework carries a large potential for future mobilities research. Mobilities are staged 'from above' by planning, regulation and design and 'from below' in social interaction. The most fruitful place to study this complexity is in everyday practices and lived situations.

From the research perspective of *Staging Mobilities* I have already pointed to a need for more design- and material-oriented research. As announced, this will be the case in the companion volume to this book titled *Designing Mobilities*. The perspective coming out of this is the emergence of a new research field or dimension of mobilities research clearly focused on what I term 'mobilities design' (Figure 10.2).

Figure 10.2 Mobilities design.

Thus far I have shown the usefulness of a situational and very concrete model of analysis that I term *Staging Mobilities*. With its focus on concrete and material situations of mobilities and how these are constantly negotiated and played out between design and planning from above and social interaction from below I have aimed to contribute to the theoretical vocabulary within the 'mobilities turn'. This is obviously not finished, nor is it fully coherent. However, as it is said: any journey starts with the first step. Quite a few are bound to follow those explored here.

Bibliography

Adey, P. (2006) 'If mobility is everything then it is nothing: towards a relational politics of (im)mobility', *Mobilities*, 1(1): 75–94.
Adey, P. (2010) *Mobility*, London: Routledge.
Adey, P. and Bissell, D. (2010) 'Mobilities, meetings, and futures: an interview with John Urry', *Environment and Planning D: Society and Space*, 28: 1–16.
Allen, J. (2000) 'On Georg Simmel: proximity, distance and movement', in M. Crang and N. Thrift (eds) *Thinking Space*, London: Routledge, pp. 54–70.
Allen, J. (2003) *Lost Geographies of Power*, Oxford: Blackwell.
Alred, R. (2010) '"On the outside": constructing cycling citizenship', *Social & Cultural Geography*, 11(1), February: 35–52.
Amin, A. and Thrift, N. (2002) *Cities: Reimagining the Urban*, Oxford: Polity Press.
Andersen, L.L., Fryd, O., Poulsen, L.R. and Sauvé, S.N. (2002) *Bangkok Byways*, Aalborg: Study Board of Architecture and Design.
Andersson, B. and Harrison, P. (eds) (2010) *Taking-Place: Non-Representational Theories and Geography*, Farnham: Ashgate.
Andrade, V., Harder, H., Jensen, O.B. and Madsen, J.O. (2010) *Bike Infrastructures*, Department Working Paper, Aalborg University: Department of Architecture, Design and Media Technology, vol. 37.
Appleyard, D., Lynch, K. and Myer, J.R. (1964) *The View from the Road*, Cambridge, MA: MIT Press.
Archigram (1994) *A Guide to Archigram 1961–74*, London: Academy Group.
Arrigadan, D., Buck, B., Dean, P., Diaz-Granados, R., Huljich, G., Loew, A., Nguyen, D., Olsen, C., Siegl, B. and Somol, R. (2003) 'Los Angeles: manifest mobility', in F. Houben and L.M. Calabrese (eds) *Mobility: A Room with a View*, Rotterdam: NAi Publishers, pp. 130–157.
Augé, M. (1995) *Non-Places: Introduction to an Anthropology of Supermodernity*, London: Verso.
Augé, M. (2002) *In the Metro*, Chicago: University of Minnesota Press.
Augoyard, J.-F. (1979/2007) *Step by Step: Everyday Walks in a French Urban Housing Project*, Minnesota: University of Minnesota Press.
Austin, J.L. (1962) *How to Do Things with Words*, Oxford: Oxford University Press.
Ayuthaya, M.I. (2005) 'Intense multiplicity: Bangkok', *Architectural Design*, 75(6): 16–17.
Bacon, E.N. (1967) *Design of Cities*, London: Penguin.
Bale, J. (2011) 'Running: running as work', in Cresswell, T. and P. Merriman (eds) *Geographies of Mobilities: Practices, Spaces, Subjects*, Farnham: Ashgate, pp. 35–49.

Banham, R. (1971/2009) *Los Angeles: The Architecture of Four Ecologies*, Berkeley: University of California Press.
Bauman, Z. (1998) *Globalization: The Human Consequences*, Oxford: Polity Press.
Bauman, Z. (2000) *Liquid Modernity*, Oxford: Polity Press.
Beck, U. (1986/96) *Risk Society: Towards a New Modernity*, London: Sage Publications.
Beckmann, J. (2001) 'Risky mobility: the filtering of automobility's unintended consequences', PhD thesis, Copenhagen: Department of Sociology.
Beek, S.V. (2002) *Bangkok: Then and Now*, Nonthaburi: AB Publications.
Benjamin, W. (2002) *The Arcades Project*, Cambridge, MA: Harvard University Press.
Birenbaum, A. and Sagarin, E. (eds) (1973) *People in Places: The Sociology of the Familiar*, New York: Praeger Publishers.
Bissell, D. and Fuller, G. (eds) (2011) *Stillness in a Mobile World*, London: Routledge.
Bissell, D. (2012) 'Pointilist mobilities: rethinking proximity through the loops of neighbourhood', *Mobilities*, DOI: 10.1080/17450101.2012.696343.
Borja, J. and Castells, M. (1997) *Local & Global: Management of Cities in the Information Age*, London: Earthscan Publications Ltd.
Bouchet, D. (1998) 'Information technology, the social bond and the city: Georg Simmel', updated, *Built Environment*, 24(2/3): 104–133.
Brenner, N. (2004) *New State Spaces: Urban Governance and the Rescaling of Statehood*, Oxford: Oxford University Press.
Bryant, C.G. and Jary, D. (eds) (1991) *Gidden's Theory of Structuration: A Critical Appreciation*, London: Routledge.
Büscher, M., Urry, J. and Witchger, K. (eds) (2011) *Mobile Methods*, Abingdon: Routledge.
Buscher, M., Boyko, C., More, K. and Dant, T. (2010) 'New IO? Interaction in the networked city', paper for the 'Futureeverything Conference', Manchester, 14 April 2010.
Calabrese, L.M. (2003) 'Fine tuning: notes from the project', in F. Houben and L.M. Calabrese (eds) *Mobility: A Room with a View*, Rotterdam: NAi Publishers, pp. 343–362.
Carmona, M., Tiesdell, S., Heath, T. and Oc, T. (2010) *Public Places, Urban Spaces: The Dimensions of Urban Design*, 2nd edn, Oxford: Architectural Press.
Casey, E.S. (1997) *The Fate of Place: A Philosophical History*, Berkeley: University of California Press.
Casey, E.S. (2001) 'Body, self and landscape', in P. C. Adams, S. Hielscher and K. E. Till (eds) *Textures of Place: Exploring Humanist Geographies*, Minneapolis: University of Minnesota Press, pp. 403–425.
Castells, M. (1996) *The Information Age: Economy, Society and Culture, vol. I: The Rise of the Network Society*, Oxford: Blackwell Publishers.
Castells, M. (1997) *The Information Age: Economy, Society and Culture, vol. II: The Power of Identity*, Oxford: Blackwell Publishers.
Castells, M. (2002) 'Urban sociology in the twenty-first century', in I. Susser (ed.) *The Castells Reader on Cities and Social Theory*, Oxford: Blackwell, pp. 390–406.
Castells, M. (2005) 'Space of flows, space of places: materials for a theory of urbanism in the information age', in B. Sanyal (ed.) *Comparative Planning Cultures*, London: Routledge, pp. 45–63.
Chang, H. and Chang, H. (2009) 'Exploring recreational cyclists' environmental preferences and satisfaction: experimental study in Hsinchu technopolis', *Environment and Planning B: Planning and Design*, 36: 319–335.
Conley, J. (2012) 'A sociology of traffic: driving, cycling, walking', in P. Vannini, L.

Budd, O.B. Jensen, C. Fisker and P. Jirón (eds) *Technologies of Mobility of the Americas*, New York: Peter Lang, pp. 219–236.
Corner, J. (1999) 'The agency of mapping: speculation, critique and invention', in D. Cosgrove (ed.) *Mappings*, London: Reaktion Books Ltd., pp. 213–252.
Crang, M. and Graham, S. (2007) 'Sentient cities: ambient intelligence and the politics of urban space', *Information, Communication & Society*, 10(6): 789–817.
Cresswell, T. (2004) *Place: A Short Introduction*, Oxford: Blackwell.
Cresswell, T. (2006) *On the Move: Mobility in the Modern Western World*, London: Routledge.
Cresswell, T. (2010a) 'Towards a politics of mobility', *Environment and Planning D: Society & Space*, 28: 17–31.
Cresswell, T. (2010b) 'Mobilities I: catching up', *Progress in Human Geography*, 2010, DOI: 10.1177/0309132510383348.
Cresswell, T. and Merriman, P. (eds) (2011) *Geographies of Mobilities: Practices, Spaces, Subjects*, Farnham: Ashgate.
Cullen, G. (1996) *The Concise Townscape*, Oxford: Architectural Press.
Cuthbert, A.R. (2006) *The Form of Cities: Political Economy and Urban Design*, Oxford: Blackwell.
Cwerner, S., Kesselring, S. and Urry, J. (eds) (2009) *Aeromobilities*, London: Routledge.
Czarniawska, B. (2004) *Narratives in Social Research*, London: Sage.
Dahl, H. (2008) *Den usynlige verden*, Copenhagen: Gyldendal.
Dahlen, E.R. Martin, R.C., Regan, K. and Kuhlman, M.M. (2005) 'Driving anger, sensation, impulsiveness and boredom proneness in the prediction of unsafe driving', *Accident Analysis and Preservation*, 37: 341–348.
Danish Road Directorate (DRD) (2006) *Rapport nr. 315*, Copenhagen: Vejdirektoratet.
Dant, T. (2004) 'The driver-car', *Theory, Culture and Society*, 24(4/5): 61–79.
Dear, M.J. (2000) *The Postmodern Urban Condition*, Oxford: Blackwell.
De Botton, A. (2002) *The Art of Travel*, London: Hamish Hamilton.
DeCauter, L. (2004) *The Capsular Civilization: On the City in the Age of Fear*, Rotterdam: NAi Publishers.
DeCerteau, M. (1984) *The Practice of Everyday Life*, Berkeley: University of California Press.
DeLanda, M. (2006) *A New Philosophy of Society: Assemblage Theory and Social Complexity*, New York: Continuum.
Deleuze, G. (1992) 'Postscript to the societies of control', in N. Leach (ed.) (1997) *Rethinking Architecture: A Reader in Cultural Theory*, London: Routledge, pp. 309–313.
Deleuze, G. and Guattari, F. (1987/2003) *A Thousand Plateaus: Capitalism and Schizophrenia*, London: Continuum.
Deleuze, G. and Guattari, F. (1997) 'City/State', in N. Leach (ed.) *Rethinking Architecture: A Reader in Cultural Theory*, London: Routledge, pp. 313–316.
Dennis, K. and Urry, J. (2009) *After the Car*, Cambridge: Polity.
Douglass, M. (1998) 'World city formation on the Asia-Pacific Rim: poverty, "everyday" forms of civil society and environmental management', in N. Brenner and R. Keil (eds) (2006) *The Global Cities Reader*, London: Routledge, pp. 268–274.
Dovey, K. (2010) *Becoming Places: Urbanism/Architecture/Identity/Power*, London: Routledge.
Duff, C. (2010) 'On the role of affect and practice in the production of place', *Environment and Planning D: Society & Space*, online, DOI: 10.1068/d16209.

Durkheim, E. (1982) *The Rules of Sociological Method*, Houndmills: Macmillan.
Easterling, K. (2011) 'Fresh field', in N. Bhatia, M. Przybylski, L. Shepard and M. White (eds) *Coupling: Strategies for Infrastructural Opportunism*, New York: Princeton Architectural Press, pp. 10–13.
Ek, R. (2012) 'Topologies of human-mobile assemblages', in R. Wilken and G. Goggin (eds) *Mobile Technology and Place*, London: Routledge, pp. 39–54.
Ellin, N. (1999) *Postmodern Urbanism*, 2nd edn, New York: Princeton Architectural Press.
Elliott, A. and Urry, J. (2010) *Mobile Lives*, London: Routledge.
Erlhoff, M., Heidkamp, P. and Utikal, I. (eds) (2008) *Designing Public: Perspectives for the Public*, Basel: Birkhäuser.
Farias, I. (2010) 'Introduction: decentering the object of urban studies', in I. Farias and T. Bender (eds) *Urban Assemblages: How Actor Network Theory Changes Urban Studies*, London: Routledge, pp. 1–24.
Farias, I. and Bender, T. (eds) (2010) *Urban Assemblages: How Actor-Network Theory Changes Urban Studies*, London: Routledge.
Featherstone, M. (2004) 'Automobilities', *Theory, Culture & Society*, 21(4/5): 1–24.
Fincham, B., McGuinness, M. and Murray, L. (eds) (2010) *Mobile Methodologies*, Basingstoke: Palgrave Macmillan.
Fiske, R. (1989) *Introduction to Communication Studies*, London: Routledge.
Fisker, C.E. (2011) 'End of the road? Loss of (auto)mobility among seniors and their altered mobilities and networks – a case study of a car-centred Canadian city and a Danish city', PhD thesis, Aalborg University.
Fjellstrom, K. (2003) 'Transit reform in Bangkok', *SMART Urban Transport*, November: 6–8.
Flyvbjerg, B. (1996) 'The dark side of planning: rationality and "Realrationalität"', in S.J. Mandelbaum, L. Mazza and R.W. Burchell (eds) *Explorations in Planning Theory*, New Brunswick, NJ: Rutgers, The State University of New Jersey, pp. 383–394.
Foster, N. (2007) *Norman Foster Works 3*, Munich: Prestel.
Foucault, M. (1997) 'Of other spaces: utopias and heterotopias', in N. Leach (ed.) *Rethinking Architecture: A Reader in Cultural Theory*, London: Routledge, pp. 350–356.
Freudendal-Pedersen, M. (2009) *Mobility in Daily Life: Between Freedom and Unfreedom*, Farnham: Ashgate.
Freund, P. (1993) *The Ecology of the Automobile*, New York: Black Rose Books.
Friedman, J. (2002) *The Prospects of Cities*, Minneapolis: University of Minnesota Press.
Frisby, S. and Featherstone, M. (eds) (1997) *Simmel on Culture: Selected Writings*, London: Sage.
Fryd, O. (2005) *Metropica*, Aalborg University: Department of Architecture and Design, MA Thesis.
Fuller, G. (2002) 'The arrow: directional semiotics – wayfinding in transit', *Social Semiotics*, 12(3): 231–244.
Fuller, G. and Harley, R. (2004) *Aviopolis: A Book about Airports*, London: Black Dog Publishing.
Fuller, R.B. (1963) *Ideas and Integrities: A Spontaneous Autobiographical Disclosure*, ed. by Robert W. Marks, Toronto: Collier Books.
Furness, Z. (2010) *One Less Car: Bicycling and the Politics of Automobility*, Philadelphia: Temple University Press.
Galis, V. (2006) *From Shrieks to Technical Reports: Technology, Disability and Political*

Bibliography

Processes in Building Athens Metro, Lindköping: Lindköping University, Studies in Arts and Science no. 374.

Game, A. (1991) *Undoing the Social: Towards a Deconstructive Sociology*, Milton Keynes: Open University Press.

Gänshirt, C. (2007) *Tools for Ideas: An Introduction to Architectural Design*, Basel: Birkhäuser.

Gartman, D. (2004) 'Three ages of the automobile: the cultural logics of the car', *Theory, Culture & Society*, 21(4/5): 169–195.

Gehl, J. (1971/96) *Livet mellem husene: Udeaktiviteter og udemiljøer*, Copenhagen: Arkitektens Forlag.

Gehl, J. (2010) *Cities for People*, Washington, DC: Island Press.

Gehl, J., Gemzøe, L., Kirknæs, S. and Søndergaard, B.S. (2006) *New City Life*, Copenhagen: The Danish Architectural Press.

Gibson, J.J. (1986) *The Ecological Approach to Visual Perception*, New York: Psychology Press.

Giddens, A. (1976) *New Rules of Sociological Method*, Berkeley: University of California Press.

Giddens, A. (1984) *The Constitution of Society*, Oxford: Polity Press.

Giddens, A. (1990) *The Consequences of Modernity*, Oxford: Polity Press.

Giddens, A. (1991) *Modernity and Self-Identity: Self and Society in the Late Modern Age*, Cambridge: Polity Press.

Girot, C. (2006) 'Vision in motion: representing landscape in time', in C. Waldheim (ed.) *The Landscape Urbanism Reader*, New York: Princeton Architectural Press, pp. 87–103.

Goffman, E. (1949) 'Some characteristics of response to depicted experience', unpublished master's dissertation, Department of Sociology, University of Chicago.

Goffman, E. (1953) 'Communication conduct in an island community', unpublished PhD thesis, Department of Sociology, University of Chicago.

Goffman, E. (1959) *The Presentation of Self in Everyday Life*, New York: Doubleday.

Goffman, E. (1961) *Encounters: Two Studies in the Sociology of Interaction*, New York: The Boddy-Merril Company Inc.

Goffman, E. (1963) *Behaviour in Public Places: Notes on the Social Organisation of Gatherings*, New York: The Free Press.

Goffman, E. (1967/82) *Interaction Ritual: Essays on Face-to-Face Behaviour*, New York: Pantheon Books.

Goffman, E. (1972) *Relations in Public: Micro Studies of the Public Order*, New York: Harper & Row.

Goffman, E. (1974/86) *Frame Analysis: An Essay on the Organization of Experience*, Boston: North Eastern University.

Goffman, E. (1979) *Gender Advertisements*, New York: Harper & Row.

Goffman, E. (1981) *Forms of Talk*, Oxford: Basil Blackwell.

Goffman, E. (1983) 'The interaction order', *American Sociological Review*, 48, February: 1–17.

Gordon, E. and Silva, A.S. (2011) *Net Locality: Why Location Matters in a Networked World*, Chichester: Wiley-Blackwell.

Gottdeiner, M. (1995) *Postmodern Semiotics: Material Culture and the Form of Postmodern Life*, Oxford: Blackwell.

Graham, S. (2010) 'When infrastructures fail', in S. Graham (ed.) *Disrupted Cities: When Infrastructure Fails*, London: Routledge, pp. 1–26.

Graham, S. (2011) *Cities under Siege: The New Military Urbanism*, London: Verso.
Graham, S. and Marvin, S. (2001) *Splintering Urbanism: Networked Infrastructures, Technological Mobilities and the Urban Condition*, London: Routledge.
Gutierrez, L. and Portefaix, V. (2003) 'Pearl River Delta', in F. Houben and L.M. Calabrese (eds) *Mobility: A Room with a View*, Rotterdam: NAi Publishers, pp. 212–237.
Guy, S., Marvin, S. and Moss, T. (eds) (2001) *Urban Infrastructure in Transition: Networks, Buildings, Plans*, London: Earthscan.
HABITAT (2001) *Cities in a Globalizing World: A Global Report on Human Settlements 2001*, London: Earthscan.
Hajer, M. and Reijndorp, A. (2001) *In Search of New Public Domain*, Rotterdam: NAi Publishers.
Hall, E.T. (1966) *The Hidden Dimension*, New York: Anchor Books Doubleday.
Halprin, L. (1963) *Cities*, New York: Reinhold Publishing Corporation.
Halprin, L. (1966) *Freeways*, New York: Reinhold Publishing Corporation.
Hamilton, A. (2000) 'Wonderful, terrible: everyday life in Bangkok', in G. Bridge and S. Watson (eds) *A Companion to the City*, Oxford: Blackwell, pp. 460–471.
Hansen, N.G. (1991) *Sansernes Sociologi: Om Georg Simmel og det Moderne*, Copenhagen: Tiderne Skifter.
Hård, M. and Misa, T.J. (eds) (2008) *Urban Machinery: Inside Modern European Cities*, Cambridge, MA: MIT Press.
Harvey, D. (1996) *Justice, Nature and the Geography of Difference*, Oxford: Blackwell.
Healey, P. (2000) 'Planning in relational space and time: responding to new urban realities', in G. Bridge and S. Watson (eds) *A Companion to the City*, Oxford: Blackwell, pp. 517–530.
Heidegger, M. (1927/62) *Being and Time*, Oxford: Blackwell.
Held, D. and Thompson, J.B. (eds) (1989) *Social Theory of Modern Societies: Anthony Giddens and His Critics*, Cambridge: Cambridge University Press.
Highway Code (2008) *The Original Highway Code: Reproductions of Highway Code Booklets from the Thirties, Forties, and Fifties*, London: Michael O'Mara Books Ltd.
Hommels, A. (2006) *Unbuilding Cities: Obduracy in Urban Socio-Technical Change*, Cambridge, MA: MIT Press.
Hoskins, J. (2000) *Bangkok: Subways, Sky Trains and a City Redefined*, Bangkok: CURIOSA Publishers.
Houben, F. (2003) 'A room with a view', in F. Houben and L.M. Calabrese (eds) *Mobility: A Room with a View*, Rotterdam: NAi Publishers, pp. 22–77.
Houben, F. and Calabrese, L.M. (eds) (2003) *Mobility: A Room with a View*, Rotterdam: NAi Publishers.
Ihde, D. (1990) *Technology and the Lifeworld: From Garden to Earth*, Bloomington and Indianapolis: Indiana University Press.
Ihde, D. (1993) *Postphenomenology: Essays in the Postmodern Context*, Evanston, Illinois: Northwestern University.
Ihde, D. (2002) *Bodies in Technology*, Minneapolis: University of Minnesota Press.
Ingersoll, R. (2006) *Sprawltown: Looking for the City on Its Edge*, New York: Princeton Architectural Press.
Ingold, T and Vergunst, J.L. (eds) (2008) *Ways of Walking: Ethnography and Practice on Foot*, Farnham: Ashgate.
Jacobs, J. (1961) *The Death and Life of Great American Cities*, New York: Vintage Books.
Jacobsen, M.H. and Kristiansen, S. (2002) *Erving Goffman: Sociologien om det elementære livssociale former*, Copenhagen: Hans Reitzels Forlag.

212 Bibliography

Jacobsen, M.H. and Kristiansen, S. (2006) 'Goffmans metaforer: om den genbeskrivende og rekontekstualiserende metode hos Erving Goffman', *Sosiologi i dag*, 36(1): 7–35.

Jencks, C. (1969) 'Semiology and architecture', in C. Jencks and K. Korpf (eds) (2006) *Theories and Manifestos of Contemporary Architecture*, Chichester: Wiley, pp. 43–46.

Jenkins, R. (2010) 'The 21st-century interaction order', in M.H. Jacobsen (ed.) *The Contemporary Goffman*, London: Routledge, pp. 257–274.

Jensen, B.B. (2004) 'Case study Sukhumwit Line: or learning from Bangkok', in T. Nielsen, N. Albertsen and P. Hemmersham (eds) *Urban Mutations: Periodization, Scale and Mobility*, Aarhus: Arkitektskolens Forlag, pp. 184–218.

Jensen, A. and Richardson, T. (2007) 'New region, new story: imagining mobile subjects in transnational space', *Space & Polity*, 11(2): 137–150.

Jensen, C.B., Lauritsen, P. and Olesen, F. (eds) (2007) *Introduktion til STS: Science, Technology, Society*, Copenhagen: Hans Reitzels Forlag.

Jensen, M. (2011) *Mobilitetsmani: Det mobile liv og rejsers betydning for moderne mennesker*, Aarhus: Aarhus Universitetsforlag.

Jensen, O.B. (2004) 'There is nothing as practical as a good theory', *Planning, Theory and Practice*, 5(2): 254–255.

Jensen, O.B. (2006) 'Facework, flow and the city: Simmel, Goffman and mobility in the contemporary city', *Mobilities*, 2(2): 143–165.

Jensen, O.B. (2007a) 'City of layers: Bangkok's Sky Train and how it works in socially segregating mobility patterns', *Swiss Journal of Sociology*, 33(3): 387–405.

Jensen, O.B. (2007b) 'Pleasure, fun and flow: urban travel in the works of Kevin Lynch', paper for the research seminar 'Contemporary Receptions of Kevin Lynch', Department of Architecture and Design, Aalborg University, 12 March 2007.

Jensen, O.B. (2007c) 'Biking in the land of the car: clashes of mobility cultures in the USA', paper for the conference 'Trafikdage', Aalborg, 27–28 August 2007.

Jensen, O.B. (2008a) 'Networked mobilities and new sites of mediated interaction', in K. Terzidis (ed.) *What Matter(s)? First International Conference on Critical Digital*, conference proceedings, Boston: Harvard Graduate School of Design, pp. 279–285.

Jensen, O.B. (2008b) 'European metroscapes: the production of lived mobilities within the socio-technical metro systems in Copenhagen, London, and Paris', paper for the 'Mobility, the City and STS' workshop, Technical University of Denmark, Copenhagen, 20–22 November 2008.

Jensen, O.B. (2009a) 'Flows of meaning, cultures of movements: urban mobility as meaningful everyday life practice', *Mobilities*, 4(1): 139–158.

Jensen, O.B. (2009b) 'Mobilities as culture', in P. Vannini (ed.) *The Cultures of Alternative Mobilities: Routes Less Travelled*, Farnham: Ashgate, pp. xv–xix.

Jensen, O.B. (2010a) 'Erving Goffman and everyday life mobility', in M. Hviid Jacobsen, (ed.) *The Contemporary Goffman*, New York: Routledge, pp. 333–351.

Jensen, O.B. (2010b) 'Negotiation in motion: unpacking a geography of mobility', *Space and Culture*, 13(4): 389–402.

Jensen, O.B. (2010c) 'Mobility charters and manifestos: exploring normative discourses and codes of "correct" mobility', paper for the 'Nordic Interdisciplinary Conference on Discourse and Interaction', Aalborg, 17–19 November 2010.

Jensen, O.B. (2010d) 'Design research and knowledge: introduction to *Design Research Epistemologies*', in O.B. Jensen (ed.) *Design Research Epistemologies I: Research in Architectural Design*, Aalborg: Department of Architecture, Design and Media Technology, pp. 7–20.

Jensen, O.B. (2010e) 'Embodied cultures of mobilities', paper for the 6th International

Cosmobilities Conference 'Cultures of Mobilities: Everyday Life, Communication, and Politics', Aalborg, 27–29 October 2010.
Jensen, O.B. (2011) 'Emotional eruptions, volcanic activity and global mobilities: a field account from a European in the US during the eruption of Eyjafjallajökull', *Mobilities*, 6(1): 67–75.
Jensen, O.B. (2012a) 'Metroens Arkitektur og Bevægelser', in J. Andersen, M. Freudendal-Pedersen, L. Koefoed and J. Larsen (eds) *Byen i Bevægelse: Mobilitet – Politik – Performativitet*, Frederiksberg: Roskilde Universitetsforlag, pp. 40–60.
Jensen, O.B. (2012b) 'If only it could speak: narrative explorations of mobility and place in Seattle', in P. Vannini, L. Budd, O. B. Jensen, C. Fisker and P. Jirón (eds) *Technologies of Mobility in the Americas*, New York: Peter Lang, pp. 59–77.
Jensen, O.B. and Freudendal-Pedersen, M. (2012) 'Utopias of mobility', in M.H. Jacobsen and K. Tester (eds) *Utopia: Social Theory and the Future*, Aldershot: Ashgate.
Jensen, O.B. and Morelli, N. (2011) 'Critical points of contact: exploring networked relations in urban mobility and service design', *Danish Journal of Geoinformatics and Land Management*, 46(1): 36–49.
Jensen, O.B. and Richardson, T. (2004) *Making European Space: Mobility, Power and Territorial Identity*, London: Routledge.
Jones Lang LaSalle (2006) *Market Wrap Up 2005: Thailand*, www.joneslanglasalle.co.th.
Jones, P. (2005) 'Performing the city: a body and a bicycle take on Birmingham, UK', *Social & Cultural Geography*, 6(6): 813–830.
Jørgensen, K.G. (1993) *Semiotik: En Introduktion*, Copenhagen: Samlerens Bogklub.
Jørgensen, K.M. (2011) 'Nye medier: nye steder', *Byplannyt*, 4: 18–19.
Katz, J. (1999) *How Emotions Work*, Chicago: University of Chicago Press.
Katz, J.E. and Aakhus, M. (eds) (2002) *Perpetual Contact: Mobile Communication, Private Talk and Public Performance*, Cambridge: Cambridge University Press.
Kaufmann, V. (2002) *Re-thinking Mobility: Contemporary Sociology*, Aldershot: Ashgate.
Kaufmann, V. (2010) 'Mobile social science: creating a dialogue among the sociologists', *British Journal of Sociology*, 61(1): 367–372.
Kellerman, A. (2006) *Personal Mobilities*, London: Routledge.
Kempf, P. (2009) *You Are the City: Observation, Organization and Transformation of Urban Settings*, Baden: Lars Müller Publishers.
Khaldûn, I. (2005) *The Muqaddimah: An Introduction to History*, Princeton: University of Princeton Press (originally published 1370).
Kingwall, M. (2008) *Concrete Reveries: Consciousness and the City*, New York: Viking.
Kitchin, R. and Dodge, M. (2011) *Code/Space: Software and Everyday Life*, Cambridge, MA: MIT Press.
Knowles, C. (2010) 'Mobile sociology', *British Journal of Sociology*, 61(1): 373–379.
Knudsen, A.-M.S., Harder, H., Simonsen, A.K. and Stigsen, T.K. (2011) 'Employing smart phones as a planning tool: the Vollsmose case', paper for the '4th Nordic Geographers Meeting', Roskilde, 24–27 May 2011.
Kolb, D. (2008) *Sprawling Places*, Athens, GA: The University of Georgia Press.
Koolhaas, R. (1995) 'The generic city', in R. Koolhaas and B. Mau (eds) *S, M, L, XL*, New York: The Monacelli Press, pp. 1239–1264.
Krieger, A. and Saunders, W.S. (eds) (2009) *Urban Design*, Minneapolis: University of Minnesota Press.
Kristiansen, S. (2001) 'Irving Goffman: Om Sociologisk mikroskopi og social orden mellem

tillid og Kynisme', in M. Carleheden *et al.* (ed.) *Tradition og fornyelse i sociologien: en problemorienteret teorihistorie*, Aalborg: Aalborg Universitetsforlag, pp. 351–367.
Lakoff, G. and Johnson, M. (1980) *Metaphors We Live By*, Chicago: Chicago University Press.
Lang, J. (2005) *Urban Design: A Typology of Procedures and Products*, Oxford: Architectural Press.
Larsen, J., Urry, J. and Axhausen, K. (2006) *Mobilities, Networks, Geographies*, Aldershot: Ashgate.
Latham, A. and McCormack, D.P. (2010) 'Globalization big and small: notes on urban studies, Actor-Network Theory, and geographical scale', in I. Farias and T. Bender (eds) *Urban Assemblages: How Actor Network Theory Changes Urban Studies*, London: Routledge, pp. 53–72.
Latham, A., McCormack, D., McNamara, K. and McNeill, D. (2009) *Key Concepts in Urban Geography*, London: Sage.
Latour, B. (1996) *Aramis or the Love of Technology*, Cambridge, MA: Harvard University Press.
Latour, B. (2005) *Reassembling the Social*, Oxford: Oxford University Press.
Latour, B. (2009) *En ny sociologi for et nyt samfund: Introduktion til Aktør-Netværk-Teori*, Copenhagen: Akademisk Forlag.
Lawson, B. (2001) *The Language of Space*, Oxford: Architectural Press.
Lawson, B. (2004) *What Designers Know*, Oxford: Architectural Press.
Lawson, B. (2006) *How Designers Think: The Design Process Demystified*, Oxford: Architectural Press.
Lechner, F.J. (1991) 'Simmel on social space', *Theory Culture Society*, 8: 195–201. DOI: 10.1177/026327691008003013.
Lefebvre, H. (1974/91) *The Production of Space*, Oxford: Blackwell.
Letherby, G. (2010) 'Have backpack will travel: auto/biography as a mobile methodology', in B. Fincham, M. McGuinness and L. Murray (eds) *Mobile Methodologies*, Basingstoke: Palgrave Macmillan, pp. 152–168.
Levine, J., Vinson, A. and Wood, D. (1973) 'Subway behaviour', in A. Birenbaum and E. Sagarin (eds) *People in Places: The Sociology of the Familiar*, New York: Praeger Publishers, pp. 208–216.
Ling, R. (2010) 'The "unboothed" phone', in M.H. Jacobsen (ed.) *The Contemporary Goffman*, London: Routledge, pp. 275–292.
Lonely Planet (2005) *Thailand*, London: Lonely Planet Publications.
Lorimer, H. (2011) 'Walking: new forms and spaces for studies of pedestrianism', in T. Cresswell and P. Merriman (eds) *Geographies of Mobilities: Practices, Spaces, Subjects*, Farnham: Ashgate, pp. 19–33.
Low, S.M. (2000) *On the Plaza: The Politics of Public Space and Culture*, Austin, TX: University of Texas Press.
Lynch, K. (1960) *The Image of the City*, Cambridge, MA: MIT Press.
Lynch, K. (1981) *Good City Form*, Cambridge, MA: MIT Press.
Lynch, K. (1990) *City Sense and City Design*, ed. by T. Banjeree and M. Southworth, Cambridge, MA: MIT Press.
Lynch, K. and Hack, G. (1984) *Site Planning*, Cambridge, MA: MIT Press.
McCullough, M. (2004) *Digital Ground: Architecture, Pervasive Computing, and Environmental Knowing*, Cambridge, MA: MIT Press.
McCullough, M. (2007) 'New media urbanism: grounding ambient information technology', *Environment and Planning B: Planning and Design*, 34: 383–395.

McCullough, M. (2008) 'Epigraphy and the public library', in A. Aurigi and F.D. Cindio (eds) *Augmented Urban Spaces: Articulating the Physical and Electronic City*, Aldershot: Ashgate, pp. 61–72.
McFarlane, C. (2011) 'The city as assemblage: dwelling and urban space', *Environment and Planning D: Society & Space*, DOI: 10.1068/d4710.
McIlvenny, P. (2010) 'Learning to be mobile: children in/on bikes in a pro-biking environment', paper for the Cosmobilities Conference, 'Cultures of Mobilities: Everyday Life, Communication, and Politics', Aalborg, 27–29 October 2010.
Mackenzie, A. (2006) 'From café to park bench: Wi-Fi® and technological overflows in the city', in M. Sheller and J. Urry (eds) *Mobile Technologies of the City*, London: Routledge, pp. 137–151.
McLuhan, M. (1964) *Understanding Media: The Extensions of Man*, London: Routledge.
Madanipour, A. (2003) *Public and Private Spaces of the City*, London: Routledge.
Manning, P. (1992) *Erving Goffman and Modern Sociology*, Cambridge: Polity Press.
Manovich, L. (2006) 'The poetics of augmented space', *Visual Communication*, 5(2): 219–240.
Marchetti, M.C. (2011) 'Space, mobility and new boundaries, the redefinition of social action', in G. Pellegrino (ed.) *The Politics of Proximity: Mobility and Immobility in Practice*, Aldershot: Ashgate, pp. 17–30.
Marinetti, F.T. (1909) 'Futurist-manifest', in G. Balling, M. Bogh, H. Reeh, M. Sandby and M. Zerlang (eds) (2006) *Den Moderne Kulturs Historie*, Copenhagen: GADs Forlag, pp. 159–163.
Marling, G. (2005) *Bangkok Songlines: Spaces, Territories, Mobility*, Aalborg University: Department of Architecture and Design.
Marshall, S. (2005) *Street Patterns*, London: SPON Press.
Marx, K. (1887/1972) 'Capital', in R.C. Tucker (ed.) (1972) *The Marx–Engels Reader*, New York: W.W. Norton & Company, pp. 191–318.
Massey, D. (1994) *Space, Place and Gender*, Oxford: Polity Press.
Massey, D. (1999) 'On space and the city', in D. Massey, J. Allen and S. Pile (eds) *City Worlds*, Milton Keynes: Open University Press, pp. 157–170.
Massey, D. (2005) *For Space*, London: Sage.
Massumi, B. (2002) *Parables for the Virtual: Movement, Affect, Sensation*, Durham, NC: Duke University Press.
Mayer, H. and Knox, P.L. (2006) 'Slow cities: sustainable places in a fast world', *Journal of Urban Affairs*, 28(4): 321–334.
Merleau-Ponty, M. (1945/94) *Kroppens fænomenologi*, Copenhagen: Det lille Forlag.
Merrifield, D. (1993) 'Place and space: a Lefebvrian reconciliation', *Transactions, British Institute of Geography*, N.S. 18: 516–531.
Merriman, P. (2007) *Driving Spaces: A Cultural-Historic Geography of England's M1 Motorway*, Oxford: Blackwell.
Meyrowitz, J. (1990) 'Redefining the situation: extending dramaturgy into a theory of social change and media effects', in S.H. Riggins (eds) *Beyond Goffman: Studies on Communication, Institution, and Social Interaction*, New York: Mouton de Gruyter, pp. 65–97.
Mikkelsen, J., Smith, S. and Jensen, O.B. (2011) 'Challenging the "King of the Road": exploring mobility battles between cars and bikes in the USA', paper for the 4th Nordic Geographers Meeting, Roskilde, 24–27 May 2011.
Mikoleit, A. and Pürckhauer, M. (2011) *Urban Code: 100 Lessons for Understanding the City*, Cambridge, MA: MIT Press.

Miller, D. (ed.) (2001) *Car Cultures*, Oxford: Berg.

Mitchell, W.J. (1999) *e-Topia: 'Urban Life, Jim, But Not as We Know It'*, Cambridge, MA: MIT Press.

Mitchell, W.J. (2003) *Me++: The Cyborg Self and the Networked City*, Cambridge, MA: MIT Press.

Mitchell, W.J., Borroni-Bird, C.E. and Burns, L.D. (2010) *Reinventing the Automobile: Personal Urban Mobility for the 21st Century*, Cambridge, MA: MIT Press.

Moles, K. (2008) 'A walk in thirdspace: place, methods and walking', *Sociological Research Online*, 13(4).

Molotch, H. (2005) *Where Stuff Comes From: How Toasters, Toilets, Cars, Computers, and Many Other Things Come to Be as They Are*, New York: Routledge.

Morley, D. (2000) *Home Territories: Media, Mobility and Identity*, London: Routledge.

Moudon, A.V. (1992) 'A catholic approach to organising what urban designers should know', in A.R. Cuthbert (ed.) (2003) *Designing Cities: Critical Readings in Urban Design*, Oxford: Blackwell, pp. 362–386.

Mumford, L. (1938) *The Culture of Cities*, New York: Harvest/HBJ Books.

Næss, P. and Jensen, O.B. (2005) *Bilringene og cykelnavet: Boliglokalisering, bilafhængighed og transportadfærd i Hovedstadsområde*t, Aalborg: Aalborg University Press.

Natter, W. and Jones III, J.P. (1997) 'Identity, space and other uncertainties', in G. Benko and U. Strohmayer (eds) *Space and Social Theory: Interpreting Modernity and Postmodernity*, Oxford: Blackwell, pp. 141–161.

Nesbitt, K. (ed.) (1996) *Theorizing a New Agenda for Architecture: An Anthology of Architectural Theory 1965–1995*, New York: Princeton University Press.

Nielsen, H.K. (2001) *Kritisk teori og Samtidsanalyse*, Aarhus: Aarhus Universitetsforlag.

Nielsen, J.B., Schultz, A.T., Nielsen, T.A.S. and Harder, H. (2005) *Byen, vejen og landskabet: Motorveje til fremtiden*, Frederiksberg: KVL, Center for Skov, Landskab og Planlægning.

Nold, C., Jensen, O.B. and Harder, H. (2008) *Mapping the City: Reflections on Urban Mapping Methodologies from GPS to Community Dialogue*, Aalborg: Department of Architecture and Design, Department Working Paper Series no. 25, December 2008.

Nordberg-Schulz, C. (1971) *Existence, Space and Architecture*, New York: Praeger.

Norman, D. (2007) *The Design of Future Things*, New York: Basic Books.

Ohno, H. (2003) 'Tokyo ring: mobility as a culture', in F. Houben and L.M. Calabrese (eds) *Mobility: A Room with a View*, Rotterdam: NAi Publishers, pp. 158–185.

Olesen, F. (2006) 'Technological mediation and embodied health-care practices', in E. Selinger (ed.) *Postphenomenology: A Critical Companion to Ihde*, Albany, NY: State University of New York Press, pp. 231–145.

Pacione, M. (2005) *Urban Geography: A Global Perspective*, London: Routledge.

Pae, K., Ahas, R. and Mark, Ü. (eds) (2006) *Joint Space: Open Source on Mobile Positioning and Urban Studies*, Tallin: Positium.

Park, R.E. and Burgess, E.W. (1925) *The City: Suggestions for Investigations of Human Behaviour in the Urban Environment*, Chicago: University of Chicago Press/Midway Reprint.

Patton, J.W. (2004) 'Transportation worlds: designing infrastructures and forms of urban life', PhD thesis, Rensselaer Polytechnic Institute, New York: Troy.

Peirce, C.S. (1994) *Semiotik og Pragmatisme*, Copenhagen: Gyldendal.

Pels, D., Heterington, K. and Vandenberke, F. (2002) 'The status of the object: performances, mediations and techniques', *Theory, Culture & Society*, 19(5/6): 1–21.

Perera, R. (2006) *Promoting Travel Demand Reduction in Transport Sector in Cities of*

Asian Developing Countries: Case of Bangkok, Pathumthani: Asian Institute of Technology.

Pesses, M.W. (2007) 'Do two wheels make it more authentic than four? Spaces of bicycle tourism', paper for the Annual Meeting of the Association of American Geographers, San Francisco, 17–21 April 2007.

Petersen, J. (2007) 'Pedaling hope', *Magazine on Urbanism*, 6: 36–39.

Pinder, D. (2005) *Visions of the City: Utopianism, Power and Politics in Twentieth-Century Urbanism*, Edinburgh: Edinburgh University Press.

Pine, B.J. and Gilmore, J.H. (1999) *The Experience Economy: Work Is Theatre and Every Business Is a Stage*, Boston: Harvard Business School Press.

Pinilla, C. (2007) 'Emergent urbanism', in W. Maas, A. Graafland, B. Batstra, A. Bilsen and C. Pinilla (eds) *Space Fighter: The Evolutionary City (Game:)*, Barcelona: Actar-D, pp. 80–93.

Poster, M. (1990) *The Mode of Information: Post-structuralism and Social Context*, Cambridge: Polity Press.

Price, C. (2003a) *Re:CP*, Basel: Birkhäuser.

Price, C. (2003b) *The Square Book*, Chichester: Wiley.

Pucher, J. and Buehler, R. (2008) 'Making cycling irresistible: lessons from the Netherlands, Denmark and Germany', *Transport Reviews*, 28(4): 495–528.

Putnam, R.D. (2000) *Bowling Alone: The Collapse and Revival of American Community*, New York: Touchstone Book.

Raban, J. (1974) *Soft City*, London: Picador.

Ribeiro, G. (2001) 'Bangkok: informal space', in P.D. Mortensen and H. Ovesen (eds) *Fields of Urban Research*, Copenhagen: The Royal Danish Academy of Fine Arts, School of Architecture, pp. 115–121.

Richardson, T. and Jensen, O.B. (2008) 'How mobility systems produce inequality: making mobile subject types on the Bangkok Sky Train', *Built Environment*, 34(2): 218–231.

Rigney, D. (2001) *The Metaphorical Society: An Invitation to Social Theory*, Lanham, MD: Rowman & Littlefield.

Ritzer, G. (1992) *Sociological Theory*, New York: McGraw-Hill.

Ritzer, G. (2005) *Enchanting a Disenchanting World: Revolutionizing the Means of Consumption*, Thousand Oaks, CA: Pine Forge Press.

Road Directorate (2002) *Beautiful Roads: A Handbook of Road Architecture*, Road Directorate, Ministry of Transport, Denmark.

Rosen, N. (2010) *Off the Grid: Inside the Movement for More Space, Less Governance and True Independence in Modern America*, New York: Penguin.

Sadler, S. (2005) *Archigram: Architecture without Architecture*, Cambridge, MA: MIT Press.

Sassen, S. (2000) 'New frontiers facing urban sociology at the millennium', *British Journal of Sociology*, 51(1): 143–159.

Savage, M. (2000) 'Walter Benjamin's urban thoughts: a critical analysis', in M. Crang and N. Thrift (eds) *Thinking Space*, London: Routledge, pp. 33–53.

Schaick, J. and Speek, S.v.d. (eds) (2008) *Urbanism on Track: Application of Tracking Technologies in Urbanism*, Delft: Delft University Press.

Schechner, R. (1988) *Performance Theory*, London: Routledge.

Schmitz, M. (2006) 'The strollogy of Lucius Burckhardt', *Topos*, 56: 79–83.

Schusterman, R. (2000) *Performing Live: Alternatives for the Ends of Arts*, Ithaca, NY: Cornell University Press.

Schusterman, R. (2008) *Body Consciousness: A Philosophy of Mindfulness and Somaesthetics*, Cambridge: Cambridge University Press.

Scollon, R. (2008) 'Geographies of discourse: action across layered spaces', paper for the 'Space Interaction Discourse' conference, Aalborg University, 12–14 November 2008.

Scollon, R. and Scollon, S. (2003) *Discourses in Place: Language in the Material World*, London: Routledge.

Scott, J.C. (1998) *Seeing Like a State: How Certain Schemes to Improve the Human Condition Have Failed*, New Haven, CT: Yale University Press.

Seiler, C. (2008) *Republic of Drivers: A Cultural History of Automobility in America*, Chicago: University of Chicago Press.

Sennett, R. (1994) *Flesh and Stone: The Body and the City in Western Civilization*, New York: W.W. Norton & Company.

Shane, D.G. (2002) 'The machine city', in P. Madsen and R. Plunz (eds) *The Urban Lifeworld: Formation, Perception, Representation*, London: Routledge, pp. 218–236.

Shane, D.G. (2005) *Recombinant Urbanism: Conceptual Modelling in Architecture, Urban Design, and City Theory*, Chichester: Wiley.

Shane, D.G. (2006) 'The emergence of landscape urbanism', in C. Waldheim (ed.) *The Landscape Urbanism Reader*, New York: Princeton Architectural Press, pp. 55–67.

Shane, D.G. (2011) *Urban Design since 1945: A Global Perspective*, Chichester: Wiley.

Shared Space (2005) *Shared Space: Plads til alle – en ny vision for det offentlige rum*, Leeuwarden: Interreg IIIB project Shared Space, Province Fryslân.

Sheller, M. (2004) 'Automotive emotions: feeling the car', *Theory, Culture & Society*, 21(4/5): 221–242.

Sheller, M. (2011) 'Mobility', *Sociopedia.isa*, 2011.

Sheller, M. and Urry, J. (eds) (2006) *Mobile Technologies of the City*, London: Routledge.

Shepard, M. (ed.) (2011) *Sentient City: Ubiquitous Computing, Architecture, and the Future of Urban Space*, Cambridge, MA: MIT Press.

Shields, R. (1991) *Places on the Margin: Alternative Geographies of Modernity*, London: Routledge.

Shields, R. (1997) 'Flow as a new paradigm', *Space and Culture*, 1: 1–4.

Sieverts, T. (2003) *Cities without Cities: An Interpretation of the Zwischenstadt*, London: Routledge.

Simmel, G. (1900/90) *The Philosophy of Money*, London: Routledge.

Simmel, G. (1903/50) 'The metropolis and mental life', in K.H. Wolff (ed.) (1950) *The Sociology of Georg Simmel*, New York: The Free Press, pp. 409–424.

Simmel, G. (1908/50) 'The stranger', in K.H. Wolff (ed.) (1950) *The Sociology of Georg Simmel*, New York: The Free Press, pp. 402–408.

Simmel, G. (1908/98) 'Sociologiens problem', in G. Simmel (1998) *Hvordan er samfundet muligt? Udvalgte sociologiske skrifter*, Copenhagen: Samlerens Bogklub, pp. 19–49.

Simmel, G. (1908/98) 'Ekskurs om Sansernes Sociologi', in G. Simmel (1998) *Hvordan er samfundet muligt? Udvalgte sociologiske skrifter*, Copenhagen: Samlerens Bogklub, pp. 73–94.

Simmel, G. (1909/97) 'Bridge and door', in N. Leach (ed.) (1997) *Rethinking Architecture: A Reader in Cultural Theory*, London: Routledge, pp. 66–69.

Simonsen, K. (2004) 'Spatiality, temporality and the construction of the city', in J.O. Bærenholdt and K. Simonsen (eds) *Space Odysseys: Spatiality and Social Relations in the 21st Century*, Aldershot: Ashgate, pp. 43–62.

Simonsen, K. (2005) *Byens mange ansigter: konstruktion af byen i praksis og fortælling*, Roskilde: Roskilde Universitetsforlag.
Simpson, D. (2006) 'RV urbanism: nomadic network urbanism of the senior Recreational Vehicle community in the U.S.', paper for the conference 'Media City – Media and Urban Space', Bauhaus Universität, Weimar, 10–12 November 2006.
Smith, S. (2010) 'Discovering urban voids and vertical spaces', in H. Kiib (ed.) *Performative Urban Design*, Aalborg: Aalborg University Press, pp. 146–153.
Soja, E.W. (2000) *Postmetropolis: Critical Studies of Cities and Regions*, Oxford: Blackwell.
Sommer, R. (2007) *Personal Space: The Behavorial Basis of Design*, Bristol: BOSKO.
Susteren, A.v. (ed.) (2005) *Metropolitan World Atlas*, Rotterdam: 010 Publishers.
Suwanarit, A. (2005) 'The Sky Train in Bangkok', *Topos*, 53: 45–48.
Thiessen, M. (2008) 'Uneven mobilities and urban theory: the power of fast and slow', in P. Steinberg and R. Shields (eds) *What Is a City? Rethinking the Urban after Hurricane Katrina*, Athens, GA: University of Georgia Press, pp. 112–123.
Thrift, N. (1996) *Spatial Formations*, London: Sage.
Thrift, N. (2004) 'Driving in the city', *Theory, Culture & Society*, 21(4/5): 41–59.
Thrift, N. (2008) *Non-representational Theory: Space. Politics. Affect*, London: Routledge.
Tonboe, J.C. (1993) *Rummets sociologi: Kritik af teoretiseringen af den materielle omverdens betydning i den sociologiske og kulturgeografiske tradition*, Copenhagen: Akademisk Forlag.
Tonboe, J.C. (2001) 'Georg Simmel: Det Sociales rummelighed', in M. Carleheden *et al.* (eds) *Tradition og fornyelse i sociologien: en problemorienteret teorihistorie*, Aalborg: Aalborg Universitetsforlag, pp. 133–153.
Tuan, Y. (1977) *Space and Place: The Perspective of Experience*, Minneapolis: University of Minnesota Press.
Turkle, S. (1984) *The Second Self: Computers and the Human Spirit*, New York: Simon & Schuster.
Turner, V. (1982) *From Ritual to Theatre: The Human Seriousness of Play*, New York: PAJ Publishers.
Urry, J. (2000a) *Sociology beyond Societies: Mobilities for the Twenty-first Century*, London: Routledge.
Urry, J. (2000b) *Inhabiting the Car*, published by the Department of Sociology, Lancaster University. Online: www.comp.lancs.ac.uk/sociology/papers/Urry-Inhabiting-the-car.pdf.
Urry, J. (2003) *Global Complexity*, Oxford: Polity.
Urry, J. (2004a) 'Connections', *Environment and Planning D: Society & Space*, 22: 27–37.
Urry, J. (2004b) 'The "system" of automobility', *Theory, Culture & Society*, 21(4/5): 25–39.
Urry, J. (2006) 'Inhabiting the car', in S. Böhm, C. Jones, C. Land and M. Paterson (eds) *Against Automobility*, Cambridge: Blackwell, pp. 17–32.
Urry, J. (2007) *Mobilities*, Cambridge: Polity.
Urry, J. (2010) 'Mobile sociology', *British Journal of Sociology*, 61(1): 347–366.
Urry, J. (2011) *Climate Change and Society*, Oxford: Polity.
Valderrama, A. (2010) 'The design of large technical systems: the cases of Transmilenio in Bogotá and Metro in Copenhagen', PhD thesis, Copenhagen: DTU.
Valderrama, A. and Jørgensen, U. (2008) 'Urban transport systems in Bogotá and Copenhagen: an approach from STS', *Built Environment*, 34(2): 200–217.

Vanderbilt, T. (2008) *Traffic: Why We Drive the Way We Do (and What It Says About Us)*, London: Allen Lane.

Vannini, P. (2008) 'A queen's drowning: material culture, drama and the performance of a technological accident', *Symbolic Interaction*, 31(2): 155–182.

Vannini, P. (ed.) (2009) *The Cultures of Alternative Mobilities: Routes Less Travelled*, Farnham: Ashgate.

Vannini, P. (2010) 'Mobile cultures: from the sociology of transportation to the study of mobilities', *Sociology Compass*, 4(2): 111–121.

Vannini, P. (2011) 'Mind the gap: the tempo rubato of dwelling in line ups', *Mobilities*, 6(2): 273–299.

Vannini, P. (2012) *Ferry Tales: Mobility, Place, and Time on Canada's West Coast*, London: Routledge.

Vannini, P., Budd, L., Jensen, O.B., Fisker, C. and Jirón, P. (2012) 'Technologies of mobility in the Americas: introduction', in P. Vannini, L. Budd, O.B. Jensen, C. Fisker and P. Jirón (eds) *Technologies of Mobility in the Americas*, New York: Peter Lang, pp. 1–20.

Van't Hof, C., Est, R. and Daemen, F. (eds) (2011) *Check In/Check Out: The Public Space as an Internet of Things*, Rotterdam: NAi Publishers.

Varnelis, K. (ed.) (2008) *The Infrastructural City: Networked Ecologies in Los Angeles*, Barcelona: Actar.

Venturi, R. and Scott Brown, D. (2004) *Architecture as Signs and Systems: For a Mannerist Time*, Cambridge, MA: The Belknap Press.

Venturi, R., Brown, D.S. and Izenour, S. (1972) *Learning from Las Vegas: The Forgotten Symbolism of Architectural Form*, Cambridge, MA: MIT Press.

Vichiensan, V. and Miyamoto, K. (2006) *Integrated Approach to Analyze Land-use Transport and Environment in Bangkok: Case Studies of Railway Impact and TRANUS Application*, Bangkok: Kasetsart University.

Virilio, P. (1991) 'The overexposed city', in N. Leach (ed.) (1997) *Rethinking Architecture: A Reader in Cultural Theory*, London: Routledge, pp. 382–390.

Virilio, P. (1977/2001) *Hastighed og politik*, Frederiksberg: Introite!

Wagner, A. (2006) 'The rules of the road, a universal visual semiotics', *International Journal for the Semiotics of Law*, 19: 311–324.

Waldheim, C. (2006a) 'A reference manifesto', in C. Waldheim (ed.) *The Landscape Urbanism Reader*, New York: Princeton Architectural Press, pp. 13–19.

Waldheim, C. (2006b) 'Landscape as urbanism', in C. Waldheim (ed.) *The Landscape Urbanism Reader*, New York: Princeton Architectural Press, pp. 35–53.

Wall, A. (1999) 'Programming the urban surface', in J. Corner (ed.) (1999) *Recovering Landscape: Essays in Contemporary Landscape Architecture*, New York: Princeton Architectural Press, pp. 232–249.

Wasiak, J. (2009) 'Being-in-the city: a phenomenological approach to technological experience', *Culture Unbound*, 1: 349–366.

Weber, M. (1968) *Economy and Society*, vols I and II, Los Angeles: University of California Press.

Whyte, W.H. (1988) *City: Rediscovering the Centre*, Philadelphia: University of Pennsylvania Press.

Wilken, R. and Goggin, G. (eds) (2012) *Mobile Technology and Place*, London: Routledge.

Willis, K.S. (2008) 'Places, situations and connections', in A. Aurigi and F.D. Cindio (eds) *Augmented Urban Spaces: Articulating the Physical and Electronic City*, Aldershot: Ashgate, pp. 9–26.

Wilson, E. (1991) *The Sphinx in the City: Urban Life, the Control of Disorder, and Women*, Berkeley: University of California Press.

Wissink, B., Dijkwel, R. and Meijer, R. (2005) 'Bangkok living: social networks in a gated urban field', paper for the conference 'Doing, Thinking, Feeling Home: The Mental Geography of Residential Environments', 14–15 October 2005, OTB, Delft.

Wolff, M. (1973) 'Notes on the behaviour of pedestrians', in A. Birenbaum and E. Sagarin (eds) *People in Places: The Sociology of the Familiar*, New York: Praeger Publishers, pp. 35–48.

Wolff, K.H. (ed.) (1950) *The Sociology of Georg Simmel*, New York: The Free Press.

Wood, D.M. (2008) 'Towards spatial protocol: the topologies of the pervasive surveillance society', in A. Aurigi and F.D. Cindio (eds) *Augmented Urban Spaces: Articulating the Physical and Electronic City*, Aldershot: Ashgate, pp. 93–105.

Yan, H., Yi, H. and Pang, Z. (2003) 'Beijing ring roads', in F. Houben and L.M. Calabrese (eds) *Mobility: A Room with a View*, Rotterdam: NAi Publishers, pp. 186–211.

Zachary, G.P. (2000) *The Global Me: New Cosmopolitans and the Competitive Edge*, London: Nicolas Brealey Publishing.

Index

Aalborg Stiftstidende 140
accessibility 8
actor-network theory (ANT) 32, 76–7, 93
Adey, P. 25, 34, 94
aesthetics 119, 198; of car spaces 113–15
affect *see* emotions/affects
affordances 94–5, 120, 199
airports 90; code/spaces of 131; signs 57
Allen, J. 69–70, 133
Alred, R. 109
ambient environments 85, 124
Amin, A. 21, 22, 133
analytical disciplines 175, 176, 182, 192
Andrade, V. 109
Appleyard, D. 60, 113, 114, 179, 182, 185
Archigram 54
architecture 5, 15, 16, 24, 27, 45, 56, 106
armatures 35–7, 40, 50, 54, 67–8, 186, 203
Arrigadan, D. 188
assemblage(s) 15–16, 46, 59, 63, 125, 189, 196–7; cities as 31–3; coded 131
Augé, M. 48, 127, 154
augmented space 125, 127
Augoyard, J.-F. 102
Austin, J.L. 57
authentic walking 101–2
Ayuthaya, M.I. 169

Bacon, E.N. 95, 181
Bale, J. 105
ballet metaphor 24, 138, 145–6, 152, 153, 202
Bangkok, modes of transportation 163–4
Bangkok Sky Train (BTS) 116–17, 154, 162–70, 171–2
Banham, R. 114, 188
Barcelona second beltway 187
Bauman, Z. 27, 29, 87
Beck, U. 72

behaviour in public places 75–6
Beijing Ring Road 189
belonging 26, 29, 66, 125, 134
Bender, T. 34
Benjamin, W. 66–8
Birenbaum, A. 78
Bissell, D. 25
blasé attitude 71
body language 147
body signs 117–18, 120
body-work 81
Borja, J. 21, 30
Bouchet, D. 73
'bowling alone' phenomenon 28
Brenner, N. 23, 30
Buehler, R. 108
Burgess, E.W. 28
Buscher, M. 82

Calabrese, L.M. 55, 188
car driving 110–15, 185
car embodiment 111–13
car spaces 113–15
carbon-based mobility systems 39
Carmona, M. 180
cars 181–2
Casey, E.S. 29, 30, 96–7, 125
Castells, M. 19, 20, 21, 30, 32, 34
CeMore research centre 26
channel prototypes 49
Chicago School 28, 70
choreography 7, 48, 120, 145, 199
Christaller, W. 53
circulation, regimes of 101
circulation pattern 49
cities 19–20; as assemblages 31–3; flow in and between 20–3; as networks 30–5
civic meaning 186
civil inattention 75, 157

co-presence 11, 12, 131, 201
co-present mobile withs 82
code 131, 136, 198, 200
code/space 123, 125, 128–9, 131
coded assemblages 131
commercial discourses 79
Conley, J. 65
connectivity 19, 20; transnational 30; *see also* proximity–connectivity nexus
control 85, 86, 101, 127, 133
Convention of Paris (1909) 60
coordination in motion 96, 120, 199
Copenhagen Metro 154, 156–62, 170–1
Cosmobilities Network 26
Crang, M. 134
Cresswell, T. 26, 28, 30, 34, 39, 194
critical mobilities thinking 7–8, 40–2, 102, 176, 184, 189, 192, 193, 195, 202, 203
Critical Points of Contact (CPC) 32–3, 59, 181
Cullen, G. 45, 96
cultures of mobilities 90, 100–1, 198–9
cyberspace 85, 126
cycling 106–10; citizenship 109; as political statement 108, 109

Dahl, H. 35, 157
Dant, T. 111
'dark sides' of mobilities 41, 86, 90, 101, 127, 172, 189–91, 193, 195, 202, 203
Dear, M.J. 19
DeCerteau, M. 5, 102
decision points 59
DeLanda, M. 32, 156
Deleuze, G. 21, 28, 29, 59, 133
Denmark: cycling in 107, 108; road design 61–2; *see also* Copenhagen Metro
Dennis, K. 39, 189, 190
design of mobilities 175–93, 204
digital divide 129
digital ground 123, 128
disconnectivity 20
Dispostif 101
districts 51
Dodge, M. 123, 128–9, 131
Dovey, K. 30, 32, 125
dramaturgical metaphor 7, 74, 156
driving anger 90
Duchamp, M. 186
Duff, C. 99–100, 102
Durkheim, E. 38, 74

Easterling, K. 31–2
Eco, U. 56

economic division of labour 71
edges 51
Ek, R. 34
Elliott, A. 38, 94
embodied performances 14–15, 92–120, 199
emotional geographies 112
emotions/affects 52, 98–100, 111–13
enclaves 35–7, 133
enclosure 133
escorts 81
eurocentrism 26
everyday-life mobilities 25, 73–88, 89, 128, 197
everyware 131–2
experience economy 71
expert systems 72

face-to-face interactions 11, 74, 75, 93, 155
face work 75
Falling Down (film) 90
Farias, I. 31, 32, 34, 156
Featherstone, M. 111
feelings 99
Fisker, C.E. 12
flâneur 67
flight, lines of 21
flow(s) 20–3, 23–4, 33, 49, 68, 126, 127, 159, 160, 186, 198
Foster, N. 154
Foucault, M. 68, 101, 133
free running 104, 106
freeways/motorways 114–15, 183, 188
friction of distance 53
Friedman, J. 191
front stage/back stage 7, 47, 74, 105, 202
frontal meeting 147, 151
Fuller, G. 25, 57, 59
Fuller, R.B. 28, 29
fun 52
Furness, Z. 106–7
Futurists 185–6

Game, A. 68
Gänshirt, C. 177
gated communities 166
gatherings 13, 15
Gehl, J. 46, 102, 152, 179, 184
geosemiotics 55–6, 57–9, 63, 196
Gibson, J.J. 93, 94–5
Giddens, A. 13, 38, 72, 87
Girot, C. 68
global Me 29

Goffman, E. 8, 18, 45, 65, 66, 68–9, 73–83, 89–90, 96, 116, 130, 144, 155; civil inattention 75; dramaturgical metaphor 7, 74, 156; front stage/backstage concept 7, 47; on the self 87, 88, 93; on situational interactions 10, 11–12, 14, 15, 75–83, 138, 146, 156; notion of the team 82–3; withs 77, 78
Gordon, E. 11, 123, 128, 129–30
GPS (Global Positioning Systems) 85, 90, 124, 128
Graham, S. 23, 34, 123, 128, 134, 156
Grand Central Station, New York 47
Guattari, F. 21, 28, 29, 59
Gutierrez, L. 188

Hack, G. 8, 52–3, 185
Hajer, M. 19, 134
Hall, E.T. 46, 47, 48, 93–4, 102
Halprin, L. 92, 96, 103, 109, 114, 115, 145, 181, 182–3, 184
hand-in-hand mobile withs 81
Hård, M. 33
Harley, R. 57
Harvey, D. 22
Heidegger, M. 27, 97
Hertzian landscapes 126
heterotopias 133
Highway Code 117–18
Hilberseimer, L. 180
Hippocrates 56
hobos 28
Hoskins, J. 167
Houben, F. 55, 187
houses 33–4

icons, signs as 56
identity 29, 52, 66, 68, 69, 88, 103, 125, 134
Ihde, D. 97–8, 114
inclusion 4, 7
indexes, signs as 56, 57–8
individual as a unit 76–8, 80
information and communication technologies 10–11, 12, 62, 85–8, 123–37
infrastructural discourses 79
infrastructures 5, 16, 31–2, 54, 55, 63, 100–1; as art 185–6; positive valorisation of 186–7
Ingersoll, R. 55, 115, 185–6
instrumental mobilities 52, 53
intellectuality 71
Intelligent Traffic Systems (ITS) 12, 131, 136, 200

intentions, and signs/semiotic systems 56–7
interaction 95; *see also* social interaction
interchanges 183
Internet 87
interventionist disciplines 175, 176, 182, 192
Irigaray, L. 21
isolation 70

Jacobs, J. 54, 67, 145, 179, 184
Jacobsen, M.H. 69
Jenkins, R. 82
Jensen, O.B. 30–1, 32, 41, 52, 83–4, 100–1, 108, 132, 133
Jones III, J.P. 28, 68
Jones Lang LaSalle 165
Jones, P. 109
Jørgensen, K.G. 56
Jørgensen, K.M. 135
Jørgensen, U. 132, 156
jump-cut urbanism 185–6

Katz, J. 112–13, 114
Kaufmann, V. 24, 26
Kellerman, A. 66
Kempf, P. 3
Khaldûn, I. 26
kinaesthetic investments 112
Kingwall, M. 146
Kinopravda 185
Kitchin, R. 123, 128–9, 131
Knowles, C. 23, 24
Kolb, D. 27, 34–5
Koolhaas, R. 169
Kristiansen, S. 69

landmarks 51
landscape urbanism 184, 186–7
Landy, S. 166
Latham, A. 25, 32
Latour, B. 34, 76, 93, 105, 132, 155–6
Lawson, B. 46, 175, 179, 180
Le Corbusier 185
Lechner, F.J. 70
Lefebvre, H. 23, 25, 33–4, 97, 131
Levine, J. 78
Ling, R. 82
locales 13
location 86, 126
London 'Tube' 116, 154, 159, 160
loneliness 70
Los Angeles freeway system 188
Lynch, K. 8, 35, 45–6, 48–55, 93, 95, 114, 177, 178, 179, 180, 185, 186

McCormack, D.P. 32
McCullough, M. 98, 123, 126, 128, 134, 135
McFarlane, C. 32
machine powered mobility 40
machine-to-machine (M2M) communication 9
Mackenzie, A. 126
McLuhan, M. 97
Manovich, L. 125, 127
Marling, G. 168
Marvin, S. 23, 34, 123, 128, 156
Marx, K. 72, 175
mass transit *see* public transit spaces; public transport
Massey, D. 22–3, 30, 34, 126
Massumi, B. 92, 93, 99
materialities of mobilities 175–93
mCenter 26
meaning-production 56
mediated technologies 125–8
mega-regions 30
Mekvichai, B. 167, 168
melodic organisation 180
mental maps 50–2
Merleau-Ponty, M. 97, 98
Merrifield, D. 22
Merriman, P. 39, 114
metaphors 21, 74, 144–5
metaphor(s): ballet 24, 138, 145–6, 152, 153, 202; dramaturgical 74; river 24, 138, 145, 152–3, 202
methods of mobilities research 40
metro mobilities 154–72
metroscapes 116, 154–6, 172, 202
Meyrowitz, J. 12
migration 21
militarization of urbanism 128
Misa, T.J. 33
mobil.TUM 26
mobile biotopes 47–8, 62, 195
mobile body semiotics 117–18, 120, 199
mobile kinaesthetic 120, 199
mobile other 14, 84, 132, 146, 201
mobile phones 12, 82
mobile sensations 119–20, 199; and car driving 112–13, 114
mobile sense making 138, 151, 196
mobile situationism 10–13, 38
mobile subject types 100, 132–3
mobile withs 4, 77–8, 79–84, 89, 91, 138, 146, 151, 152, 154–5, 160, 161, 170, 197
mobilities capital 4
mobilities control 50

mobilities divides 129, 136, 199–200
mobilities potential thinking 184–7, 192–3, 202, 203
mobilities technology 49–50
mobilities turn 4, 19, 20–3, 38, 46, 176, 193, 202, 204; critics of 23–6
mobility action chains 12
mobility codes 131, 136, 198, 200
mobility cultures 90, 100–1, 198–9
mobility nodes 40, 51
modal choice 49
modal separation 49
Modernity 71, 72
Moles, K. 103
moments of encounter 21
money economy 71–2
Monö, R. 177
monotopia 30–1
montage 185
moral geography 48
Morelli, N. 32
Morley, D. 30
motility 4, 72
motion awareness 51
motorways/freeways 114–15, 183, 188
movement space 152, 180
muscular powered mobility modes 40

nation-state boundaries 30
Natter, W. 28, 68
nearness 73
negotiation in motion 4, 83–4, 96, 103, 138–53, 197, 201–2
neo-liberalism 24
net locality 123, 125, 128, 129–30
network city 21, 30
network society 30, 32
networked ecologies 31
networked self 84–8, 89, 91, 197
networked technologies 10–11, 12, 15, 41, 62, 82, 85–8, 123–37, 181, 199–201
networks 24, 33–5, 189
Nietzsche, F. 41
Niuwenhuis, C. 27
nodes 40, 51
nomadism 21, 26–30, 37
non-human mobility staging 9
non-place 28, 48, 127
non-proxemic interactions 11, 12, 130
non-representational theory 93
Nordberg-Schulz, C. 27
Norman, D. 177
Nytorv Square, Aalborg 138–44, 147–50, 152–3

objective life forces 72
off-grid living 129
Ohno, H. 188
Olesen, F. 113
online culture 86
orthogonal meeting 147, 151
Osmond, H. 46
other 68, 86; mobile 14, 84, 132, 146, 201

Pan-American Mobilities Network 26
parallel meeting 147, 151
Paris Metro 154, 159, 160
Park, R.E. 28
parkour 104, 106
paths 50, 51, 180
Patton, J.W. 68, 109
Pearl River Delta freeway 188
Peirce, C.S. 55, 56
Pels, D. 106
perception 93–8, 119; micro- and macro dimensions of 97
performativity 14–15, 197, 199; of signs 57
personal media technologies 135
personal space 116
Pesses, M.W. 108
Petersen, J. 109–10
phenomenology 27–8
Pinder, D. 67
placement 126
place(s) 33–5, 66, 68, 86, 125, 126; as moments of encounters 22; relational sense of 23, 34, 189; sedentary sense of 27, 34; spaces of 21
platforms for action 48
pleasure 52, 53
politics: cycling and 108, 109; of scale 23; of visibility 127, 129, 134, 135
Portefaix, V. 188
post-carbon future 189–91
Poster, M. 29
potential thinking 41, 184–7, 190, 191, 192–3, 195, 202, 203
power 86, 127, 133, 151, 172, 195, 201, 202
Price, C. 9, 54
proximity–connectivity nexus 130, 131, 136, 200
public domains 54, 55, 127, 134
public space 134
public transit spaces 138–53
public transport 73, 115–17
public/private distinction 7, 68
Pucher, J. 108

Putnam, R.D. 28

queues 78

Raban, J. 86–7
reciprocity 13
refugees 21
regimes of circulation 101
regulatory discourses 79
regulatory regimes 101
Reijndorp, A. 19, 134
relational geography 21, 30, 41, 126, 183, 203
relational theory 23, 34
remoteness 73
RFID (Radio Frequency Identification) 85, 125
rhythm analysis 25
Ribeiro, G. 166
Richardson, T. 30–1, 100, 132, 133
risk society 72
rituals 77
Ritzer, G. 70
river metaphor 24, 138, 145, 152–3, 202
road rage 90
road signs 60–2, 63
road systems 50, 53–4, 60–2, 179, 180; see also motorways/freeways
role play 7, 74
Room with a View, A project 187–8
routes 30
running 103–6, 146; free (parkour) 104, 106; instrumental and rationalised practice of 105; routing decisions 104–5

Sagarin, E. 78
sailor–landlubber binary 29
Sassen, S. 31
scale 32, 126; politics of 23
scenic highway 182–3
scenography 7, 48, 94
Schelling, T. 146
Schmitz, M. 102
Schusterman, R. 98
Scientific Management 101
Scollon, R. and Scollon, S. 55–6, 57–8, 59, 77, 79, 82, 90, 103
scripts 74
sedentary thought 26–30
seeming unawareness 146
segregated mobilities practices 172, 202
Seiler, C. 101, 114
self 86–7, 88; networked 84–8, 89, 91,

Index 227

197; and other relation 68; presentation of 93
semiotic aggregates 79
semiotics 55–62, 62–3, 117–18, 120, 196, 197
Sennett, R. 26–7
sensations *see* mobile sensations
sensescapes 94
sensual over-stimulation 71
sentient city 124, 125, 128, 137
serial vision 96
setting 15
Shane, D.G. 35, 37, 50, 177, 186
Shared Space project 84
Sheller, M. 17, 111, 112, 134
Shepard, M. 124, 125, 128
Shields, R. 20–1
shopping malls 47
signs 55–62, 62–3, 77, 196; airport 57; body 117–18, 120; as decision points 59; as icons 56; as indexes 56, 57–8; and intentions 56–7; performative capacity of 57; road 60–2, 63; as symbols 56
Silva, A.S. 11, 123, 128, 129–30
Simmel, G. 65, 66, 68–73, 86, 89–90, 123, 136
Simonsen, K. 24–5, 33
Simpson, D. 29
singles 78
the situated 126
situated mobilities 41–2, 201
situated technologies 86
situation 15, 130
Situationist movement 67
smooth/striate spaces 21
social exclusion 4, 7, 160, 172, 189, 195, 202
social integration 13
social interaction 14–15, 65–91, 125, 127, 138–9, 150, 151, 201
social media 87
social occasions 13, 15
social segregation 166, 168–9, 171–2
social space 180
sociofugal spaces 46, 47, 62, 152, 195
sociograms 132
sociopetal 46–7, 62, 152, 195; staying 152; transit 127; virtual/cyber 85, 126
sociopetal spaces 46–7, 62, 152, 195
socio-technical systems 34, 41, 63, 89, 125, 128, 132–3, 134–5, 155, 189, 196–7, 202
Sommer, R. 46, 116

space(s) 13–16, 21, 22, 23, 70; augmented 125, 127; car 113–15; movement 152, 180; personal 116; public 134; public transit 138–53; smooth/striate 21; social 180; sociofugal 46, 47, 62, 152, 195
spaces of flows 21
spaces of place 21
spatial determinism 70
speech act theory 57
speed 20, 37, 48, 59, 63, 97, 114, 115, 146, 151, 201
splintering urbanism 123, 128
sprawl 34
staging from above/below 3, 4, 5, 9, 55, 57, 62, 67, 79, 94, 100, 105, 119, 133, 195, 204
stasis 6, 20, 21, 23, 25, 27
staying space 152
stillness 25
strangers 73
street hierarchy 180
street-meeting 75–6
streets 54, 67–8, 178–9
stretched mobile interactions 14, 130
stretched mobile withs 82
subject position 101
subjective life forces 72
subjectivity 68, 119
subway systems: behaviour on 78–9; *see also* metroscapes
surveillance technologies 103, 137, 200
Suwanarit, A. 167
symbolic interactionism 74
symbols, signs as 56
system integration 13

Tapananont, N. 167, 169
teams 82–3
technograms 132
temporary congregations 4, 138, 151, 152, 155, 159, 170, 197, 201
terminals 54
Thiessen, M. 25
Thrift, N. 21, 22, 34, 93, 99, 102, 112, 133
time 165, 171
time–space 13
Tokyo Ring Line 188
tracking 133, 135, 137
trajectories 30
Transeuropean Transport Net 30
transgressive discourses 79
transit spaces 127
transnational connectivity 30
transportation, cost perception of 53

travel: as cost 53; as pleasure 52, 53
travel distance, management of 49
trust 72
Tuan, Y. 97

uncivilised inattention 90
United States, cycling in 107, 108
urban design 6, 45, 46–55, 175–93
urban morphology 49–50
Urry, J. 4–5, 20, 21, 23, 25, 39, 75, 94, 126, 128, 134, 194; on car driving 111, 112; and mobilities turn 24, 38; on post-car mobilities system 189, 190, 191; space, definition of 33
utilities 53–4
utopian thinking 191

Valderrama, A. 132, 156
Vanderbilt, T. 138, 146
Vannini, P. 5–6, 20, 23, 26, 194
Van't Hof, C. 128, 134
Varnelis, K. 31
vehicular units 77
Vertov, D. 185
Vienna Convention on Road Signs (1968) 60

Ville Radieuse, La 185
Virilio, P. 25, 28–9
virtual space 85, 126
visibility, politics of 127, 129, 134, 135
von Thünen, H. 53

Wagner, A. 60, 61
Waldheim, C. 55, 114, 186, 187
walking 101–3
Wall, A. 186–7
Wasiak, J. 128
the way 67
Weber, M. 72, 111
Whyte, W.H. 46, 65, 92, 175
will to connection 123, 136, 137, 200, 201
Willis, K.S. 123
Wissink, B. 166
Wolff, M. 78
Wood, D.M. 135

Yan, H. 189
YouTube 158

Zachary, G.P. 29